YOU
& YOUR
A.D.D.
CHILD

YOU & YOUR A.D.D. CHILD

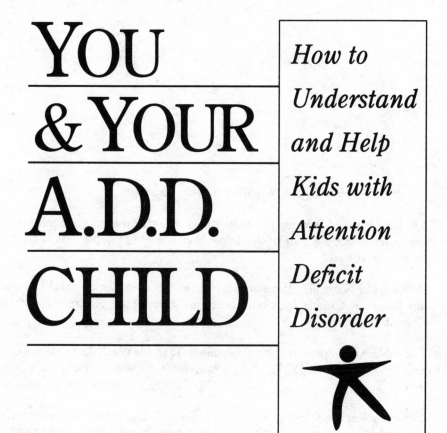

How to Understand and Help Kids with Attention Deficit Disorder

Paul Warren, M.D.
Jody Capehart, M.Ed.

with
Sandy Dengler

A JANET THOMA BOOK

THOMAS NELSON PUBLISHERS
Nashville • Atlanta • London • Vancouver

Published in Nashville, Tennessee, by Thomas Nelson, Inc., Publishers, and distributed in Canada by Word Communications, Ltd., Richmond, British Columbia.

The Bible version used in this publication is THE NEW KING JAMES VER-SION. Copyright © 1979, 1980, 1982, 1990 Thomas Nelson, Inc., Publishers.

Incidents, anecdotes, and case histories included in this volume are composites of actual cases. Names and other details have been changed to protect identities.

Library of Congress Cataloging-in-Publication Data

Warren, Paul, 1949–
    You & your A.D.D. child : how to understand and help kids with attention deficit disorder / Paul Warren, Jody Capehart.
      p. cm.
    ISBN 0-7852-7895-8
    1. Attention-deficit hyperactivity disorder—Popular works.
I. Capehart, Jody. II. Title.
RJ506.H9W37 1995
618.92′ 8589—dc20   95–8255
                                             CIP

Printed in the United States of America.

10 11 12 13 14 15 QBP 01 00 99 98 97

We want to dedicate this book to all the children who have taught us so much about Attention Deficit Disorder. We applaud the parents and teachers who are in there day after day dealing with these children. We wrote this book to show you that we understand the struggle, we support you, and we want to help you. This book is for you!

Contents

Acknowledgments

We wish to warmly acknowledge the support of our families and the challenge of Janet Thoma, vice president of Thomas Nelson Books. We also gratefully acknowledge the careful editorial support of Emily Kirkpatrick and Lisa Moyers. We wish to express our appreciation to Sandy Dengler who took our "academic information" and wove it into a warm narrative.

Jody wishes to express a special thanks to her stepson, Damon, who has been an invaluable resource for learning in the area of Attention Deficit Disorder.

IF IT AIN'T BROKE, FIX IT

*E*ITHER BETH MULRONEY was
a lousy, rotten mother or God was
out to get her. As she watched her seven-year-old son, Andrew, literally
come slamming out the glass school door, drop one of his two books,
neglect to pick it up, kick bark out of the planters onto the walkway,
stomp on the bark chips to see if they'd shatter, discover they didn't,
drop his pencil without noticing, then breaking into a run again and
slamming *(there was that word again)* into the side of the Mulroney
van, Beth decided: Probably both.

With a dramatic heave-ho, Andrew yanked the van door open and
scrambled inside.

Beth grabbed the door before he could close it; she caught it barely
in time. "Go back and get your pencil and book."

"Oh." Gazelle-like, Andrew bounded out of the van and ran back
up the walk, bumping into a little girl. He came bounding back with
the pencil.

"And the book, Andrew!"

"What book?"

But the graying, portly Mrs. Loring was bringing it down the walk
with the resigned air of a teacher who is seriously considering early
retirement. With a forced smile, she handed it to Beth.

With an equally forced smile Beth accepted it, greeted Mrs. Loring, and thanked her. Then she tossed the book in back and climbed into the driver's seat.

She twisted around as she snapped her seatbelt. "Andrew, your seatbelt."

"I'm opening the window."

Beth could see that. Andrew was on his knees on the backseat, trying to force the side window open. He certainly knew it didn't open. It had always stuck, even when the van was new.

"Andrew, that one doesn't open, remember?"

"I'm trying to get it open."

"Sit down!"

"I want the window open."

Beth's voice rose another ten decibels. "There are car-poolers behind us who can't leave until we do, and I won't leave until your seatbelt is snapped. Do it!"

"But I want the window open!"

In desperation, Beth pulled ahead, parked in a slot at the far end of the asphalt, and crawled into the back. Physically, she yanked Andrew away from the window, slammed him *(there was that word again)* into a seat, and belted him down. "You move before we get home, young man, and you're dead meat!"

He was out of his seatbelt and struggling with the window again before she had left the parking lot.

Andrew illustrates some of a group of signs evaluators use in determining whether attention deficit disorder, ADD, is present in an unruly or overly active child. In this book we will guide you through the maze of claims about what ADD is—and whether it even exists, as some would dispute—and what parents and teachers can do to bring a child with these signs through a successful childhood into a happy and successful adulthood. As any parent whose child exhibits these signs will attest, it sure isn't easy! But there are some excellent ways to guide such children effectively.

First, let us tell you a little about the authors of this book. Dr. Paul Warren, a behavioral pediatrician at the Minirth Meier New Life Clinic, has developed something of a specialty in working with such children. He knows well what can damage and what can help.

Some years ago, Jody Capehart established a private school where she became an expert in multisensory teaching methods and attention deficit disorder. This came about in part to help the many children in her school who displayed signs of ADD and in part to help her own stepson, who grew up with difficulties stemming from ADD. Her school still thrives in Dallas, and Mrs. Capehart now lectures and teaches widely, serves as the children's pastor in her church, and carves out time for some hands-on teaching in classrooms, her first love. She considers herself first and foremost an advocate of ADD and of children who are shortchanged by education and by life.

Each day Mrs. Capehart and Dr. Warren—along with many, many parents and teachers—deal routinely with children like Andrew. Let's look at the signs of ADD.

All children exhibit one or more of these ADD signs to some degree, and even a child who appears to be a "cut-and-dried" example of ADD in fact may be suffering from some other problem altogether. We will discuss those possible complications later.

With that caveat, weigh these observations against what you see in a child or children about whom you are concerned.

The Hallmarks of
Attention Deficit Disorder

Let's watch Andrew again. Notice he consistently overdoes things, slamming from here to there, moving dramatically, exaggerating and speeding up his movements. Andrew runs a lot, whether or not he has to. He is constantly in motion and doesn't seem to care whether he is, for instance, scattering bark mulch that ought not be scattered or dropping school supplies. If he bumped into a little girl it was probably her fault. He became fixated upon opening a window, not recalling that it didn't open, and he could not be deterred. He did not mind well, did not remember he had dropped his book, and did not notice the things most persons notice—such as dropping the pencil. His mom sent him back to retrieve two items; he remembered only half of her directive, returning with one.

And this was one of Andrew's good days.

Evaluators recognize a number of indicators that clue them in to the presence of ADD. No child shows every one of the signs, but usually a child with diagnosable ADD will display at least seven or eight of them.

Some Indicators of Attention Deficit Disorder

____ 1. The child can be looking right at you when you speak and still not hear you.

____ 2. The child does not follow instructions well and sometimes not at all, even though he or she may seem to understand them.

____ 3. The child gets bored *fast*. Routine tasks and rote drill cannot hold the child's attention for more than a few minutes.

____ 4. The child procrastinates dreadfully, especially when difficult projects, chores, or homework are the tasks at hand.

____ 5. The child's attention and enthusiasm bounce from thing to thing; repeatedly, the child starts projects eagerly only to abandon them, unfinished.

____ 6. The child displays amazing artistic skill and creativity, particularly in one-on-one interactions.

____ 7. The child's attention may become so focused upon something—Nintendo, for example, or action TV—that you can't tear the kid away.

____ 8. The child constantly lives in a sphere of noise; if the noise does not come from outside, the child creates it.

____ 9. The child loses things a lot, usually through carelessness or forgetfulness.

____ 10. The child *talks*. This does not mean sustained conversation. The child talks loudly and randomly, bouncing from subject to subject sometimes in midsentence.

____ 11. The child constantly irritates others by interrupting and butting in, paying no attention to others' sensibilities or needs, acting inappropriately (often highly so), wrongly responding to others' behavior, refusing to take turns in an orderly way. In other words, social skills are zilch.

____ 12. The child very often acts without thinking. He or she might run out into the street after a ball, turn and punch a kid without considering the consequences, blurt out answers before the question is completed, or do "dumb stuff" that can be just plain dangerous.

____ 13. The child is very easily distracted. The noise of a fan, pictures on the wall, peripheral movement such as another child sharpening a pencil, a bird, a dust mote—anything, and sometimes nothing—seizes the child's attention at the expense of the project at hand or schoolwork.

_____ 14. The child's mind wanders. Daydreaming, wool-gathering, being spacey, call it what you will, this predilection to wandering dominates the child's mental processes.

_____ 15. The child, like Andrew, moves constantly and forcefully, fidgeting, running, slamming around, failing to sit still for more than a few minutes at a time.

_____ 16. The child's moods swing like a pendulum and are largely unpredictable or inappropriately expressed. Anger is instantaneous and quite often overdone for the situation, joy is so grotesquely joyous as to be annoying, and so on.

_____ 17. The child needs constant attention and instant gratification. Attention *now!* A reward *now!* More attention *now!* A need or perceived need met *now! More* attention *now!* All the time.

_____ 18. The child shows great difficulty completing workbooks, math problems, and the like, as well as complex assignments and other linear-thinking tasks.

_____ 19. The child craves constant stimulation, but at the same time, he or she cannot handle stress at all. The child goes ballistic when overstimulated and yet starts caroming off the walls if external stimulation is withdrawn or is minimal.

_____ 20. The child's mind and surroundings are either chaotic and disorganized (the normal state for ADD kids) or, in older children at times, obsessively ordered.

Attention deficit disorder and hyperactivity—that is, excessive go-go-go-wild-and-crazy behavior—do not always exist hand in hand. The excessively active kid is constantly in your face and therefore cannot avoid being noticed. However, a nonhyperactive ADD child, and there are many, sits quietly in the seat, daydreaming life away, doing poorly at whatever tasks are given, largely unnoticed. "What a dull child," sniffs the teacher or parent, and lets it go at that. In the case of girls, the labels "spacey" or "airhead" are often substituted for "hyperactive."

These external observations arise from the things that are going on internally within the ADD child. It helps the observer of the child—the parent, teacher, Sunday school instructor, friend, and neighbor—to know what is happening internally and why it is happening that way. There are several characteristics highly typical of attention deficit disorder.

The Characteristics of ADD

Neither Mrs. Capehart nor Dr. Warren like calling attention deficit disorder a "disorder"; nor do they like talking about "diagnosing" it. The words "disorder" and "diagnosis" suggest that illness is involved—that something is broken. But that is not the case! ADD is nothing more than a description of one kind of neurological makeup and patterning—a person's hard wiring, if you will. It is, in the truest sense, a developmental difference.

That, then, is one of the characteristics: ADD is present to some degree right from the beginning.

ADD Is There at Birth. Although the ADD child was born with that kind of neurological wiring, the signs and symptoms may not become prominent until several years later, at about the time the child enters kindergarten.

Because the condition is neurological, born into the child, we know that these are some things ADD is *not:*

- ADD is not a result of poor parenting. Poor parenting may exacerbate the condition, making a child with difficulties encounter worse difficulties, but perfect parenting will not eliminate it.
- ADD is not a result of something parents did. Fetal alcohol syndrome, for example, exhibits some of ADD's signs but is not itself ADD. This book is not intended to address problems such as fetal alcohol disorders except to say that, so far as we can tell, use of drugs or alcohol apparently will not create ADD prenatally in a child.

The second internal characteristic stems from the fact that ADD is developmental in nature; it will change, usually for the better, with the child's maturity.

The Symptoms Will Abate. The signs we will describe below will, over time, improve measurably. True, it's a slow process, but they do get better. ADD kids mature at a slower pace than most children. We are finding, however, that the differences generated by ADD never fully disappear, even in adulthood.

Also, because ADD is developmental, ADD kids often seem immature for their age. Their central nervous systems seem slower to develop and mature than do most kids'. Eventually they will catch up—almost.

The characteristic that first drew interest to ADD is the problem these kids have paying attention.

ADD Kids Have Serious Trouble Paying Attention.   Here's what gives the condition its name. The kids can't pay attention. They can't concentrate. On the flip side, their attention may rivet on something so firmly it cannot be ripped away. Either extreme can prevent the child's success at school and at work. It may internalize as the child matures, but it never quite leaves.

ADD Kids Are Easily Distracted.   In other words, ADD kids attend to *every* distraction around them, therefore attending to *nothing* for very long. Someone said it's like a TV turned on without a channel selector, so all the channels are playing at once.

Another characteristic that usually does not disappear completely is impulsivity—acting without thinking.

ADD Kids Act Impulsively.   Every kid acts without thinking on occasion. Indeed, adults do that now and then. Sometimes our impulse saves the day; occasionally we can regret for a lifetime our momentary lapse of thought. The ADD child lives with impulsivity as a normal part of life. The ADD child has almost no experience with thinking through the possible consequences of an action.

The fourth characteristic does not occur in all ADD kids, but it's found in most of them; it is the characteristic some people think is synonymous with ADD: hyperactivity.

The ADD Kid Is Often Overly Active.   Most people in the field hesitate to use the word *hyperactive* because in a way, it's a demeaning or even derogatory term these days. Basically, it means that the large-motor muscles—the running, jumping, standing-up muscles—work overtime.

So do the fine-motor muscles, the ones that provide delicately coordinated movement. They manifest themselves as fidgeting, fiddling with toys or pencils, spinning a ruler on a pencil point—little annoying stuff. Fine-motor muscle activity is not a diagnostic characteristic of ADD, but it's present and noticeable in a lot of ADD kids.

Another telling characteristic is a general lack of a good social sense.

The ADD Child Lacks Social Skills. Getting along with people requires making a lot of choices. *Which words shall I use? Do I press a point or back off? What does this person need from me?* Social skills very often consist simply of keeping one's mouth shut. ADD kids don't make those kinds of choices and decisions well.

We will discuss later the way we think the brain handles the complex sorting and analyzing of social cues. Suffice it to say at the moment, the ADD child's frontal brain lobes don't do too well at this. The child acts and speaks inappropriately, cannot tell when he or she is irritating the wits out of other people, and cannot understand why those other people become angry or rejecting. The child interrupts, blurts the wrong things at the wrong times, and reacts angrily to harmless teasing.

Another characteristic is that ADD children cannot seem to keep their lives in order.

ADD Kids Are Poor at Organizing and Planning. Organization and planning, like social skills, are also frontal brain functions. Not only does this part of the brain plan and map out strategies, it coordinates the sequencing of behaviors. Generally speaking, it works in logical, linear progression.

For example, how do you perform long division? You *draw* a bracket around the number to be divided, then position the divisor. You *divide*. You *multiply* and position the answer exactly. Then you *subtract*. Now you *bring down* more numbers to divide. Again you divide, multiply, and subtract. Easy for an adult accustomed to that particular skill. Impossible and downright crazy for an ADD child. Not only can a child like Andrew not understand why a skill called *division* entails subtraction and multiplication, he cannot keep the sequence straight.

Sequencing is involved in just about everything associated with everyday life. It's not just major tasks like schoolwork or cleaning out the closet that require sequencing. So does any sort of organizing, handling coherent conversation with someone, answering a question, or determining how to solve a conflict. Every aspect of life requires planning and strategizing, organization and sequencing, and these are areas that just don't work well for ADD kids.

Related to that is cognitive processing in general.

Some ADD Children Struggle with Slow Cognitive Processing. Cognitive processing is, roughly speaking, figuring things out. The child is not dumb, but he or she may require more time to sift things through than most people do.

Signs and Symptoms
of
Attention Deficit Disorder

Not all ADD children will display all of these signs. However, most ADD children will possess most of them.

1. Disorder of attention
Poor ability to maintain focus on a subject or activity.

2. Distractibility
Anything—things happening around about the child or thoughts surfacing internally—can seize the child's attention.

3. Impulsivity
Acting without thinking.

4. Excessive motor activity, hyperactivity
Present in many ADD children but not all by any means.

5. Poor social skills
Consistently poor judgment in dealing with others.

6. Poor planning and organizational skills
Can't get his or her act together.

7. And in some: slow speed of cognitive processing
This is a fancy way of saying the child can't think quickly.

Adults often hit this same problem when they're tired or busy, suddenly realizing, *Wait a minute; I can do this* [a math function, perhaps] *in my sleep; why am I having trouble with it now?* Then maybe the harried adult has to add up the column of figures twice when earlier in the day he or she would have had the answer in a snap. The adult is not dumb. Just as true, the ADD child is not stupid, not in the least.

All these criteria, however, can be attributed to a couple of underlying characteristics.

The Root Causes of ADD

In essence, the ADD child is plagued with poor regulatory ability. Andrew could not easily regulate his impulses, his thoughts, his attention, his behavior, or his responses to his mom and to the world around him. His brain and body took over, in a sense, and went charging off on their own, beyond his control.

Poor Regulation

We cannot say simply that the child is inattentive; reality is far more than that. The child cannot regulate attention. Attention wanders when it should be fixed, and it fixates, as on an engrossing project or video game, when it should be more global. In other words, it is out of control in both directions—over-attentive and under-attentive. The child can't hit a happy medium.

If a given task, for example learning multiplication tables, is rote, boring, and repetitive, with no immediate payback in sight, the child quickly zones out. ADD is a disorder, then, of vigilance. Things don't hold and keep ADD kids' attention nearly as well as they do ordinary kids'. ADD kids never finish the routine task before skating on to other thoughts and projects. However, if the task is immediately gratifying (such as winning a video game level) or engrossing (the razzle-dazzle of frenetic TV programs, for example), attention may be so complete that other people cannot get through. You literally have to unplug the object of the child's attention in order to break in. The attention span is out of regulation in both directions.

Similarly, distractibility is under-regulated. The ADD child receives constant stimuli from all directions, as do we all. But he or she cannot pick and choose among them, subduing the unchosen and concentrating on the chosen. An ordinary child or adult zeros in on an object of attention and stays with it. The ADD child cannot.

Dr. Warren's office is distracting on purpose. Windows on two sides offer birds and clouds and traffic outside. Stacks of games and toys grace the shelves, interesting pictures fill the walls. A child's distractibility, if it is present, will show up quickly.

That is external distractibility, responses to stimuli coming in from the outside world. There is also internal distractibility, responses to the myriad thoughts swirling in our heads. Everyone thinks random thoughts all the time, thoughts that are brought to mind by external or internal stimuli. In essence, this is what the brain is getting paid to do. In well-regulated persons, most of those random thoughts never reach the conscious surface. If they do, we discard them because we're busy with something else.

In the poorly regulated ADD children, they pop in and out, uncontrolled, unstifled. These kids attend to every thought that comes to mind, literally. You can see it in their conversation if they are verbal. They may be talking about one subject and quickly change to another subject—whatever new thought has popped into their heads. It's really not bizarre thinking; it's simply distracted thinking.

Remember Goldie Hawn's shtick on the old *Laugh In* show when she would babble rapid-fire (usually to an endlessly enduring Dan Rowan) from topic to topic, never once finishing a sentence? That is an illustration of internal distraction to the extreme. Internal distractibility is probably present in younger children—preschoolers—but it is usually not obvious.

Frequently as distractible kids grow older, they manage to regulate external distractions with some success, but the internal distractions still present a problem. The surface sign is daydreaming and an inability to concentrate.

And finally, there's the Big Regulatory Problem: Impulsivity. Poor regulation of behavior. We think of four definitions when we want to put a handle on the abstract term *impulsivity*.

Impulsivity is acting without thinking on a consistent basis. This shows up especially in unstructured or stimulating circumstances, such as free-play time on a playground or in an open lunchroom. It's not that these kids don't know what to do or to avoid doing (kicking playmates, throwing peas, dumping a kid out of the swing, going up the sliding board). It's that they cannot mentally line up the appropriate rule with the behavior at hand in such a way that the rule governs the behavior. These kids make the same mistakes and disobey in the same way over and over and over because they cannot use what they know to regulate what they do.

ADD kids don't think through what will happen *if . . . If I turn around and talk in my seat. If that kid irritates me, so I punch him. If*

I yell something out. The consequences, totally unanticipated, seem to come as a surprise or an insult.

A second definition of impulsivity is, in technical terms, "reactive lability and intensity." That means, in plain language, that *these children's responses to situations around them are more intense than the situation warrants, more extreme than the responses most kids would make.* This overdoing-it brings both gifts and disasters. ADD kids cannot hold in or regulate emotion and feelings well. As a consequence you know what's going on immediately. That's the gift. But . . . when they get angry, they get *verrry* angry. *Flash! Fury!* Similarly, their sadness is utter and total misery, and their happiness is unbearable for others to tolerate. They rant louder, laugh louder, wail louder.

Girls with ADD may express an overly dramatic flair. Dr. Warren tells of a young lady who was deliciously dramatic at everything she did. Describing something discouraging that had just happened at school, she lay the back of her hand to her forehead and with a heavy sigh moaned, "Oh, Mother! I simply don't know what I'm going to do." She was born just about a hundred years too late for the Victorian era.

Boys, in contrast, tend to be ragers. All too often, the frustrated parents begin to back off on limits because they don't want another explosion, for explosion it is. Moreover, they are usually at a loss to handle such explosions when they occur.

Another definition of impulsivity is *a lack of regulation in persistence.* Persistence is indeed a virtue, to a point. But ADD kids carry it to the extreme, as they carry so many things to the extreme. Let us take as an example a child's desire to cruise the toy aisle at the grocery store. The child may have in mind getting a super-sized squirt gun, or the thought of "toy" may be diffuse and undirected. Once he or she gets the thought, the desire takes over, dominating the child's mind, unregulated.

The child expresses the wish even before Mom gets out of the car. Mom says "No. No toy today." They enter the store and the child makes a beeline for the toys. The kid just *has* to see the toys. That develops instantly into not just seeing but buying a toy.

Mom repeats, "No. We're not going to get toys."

But her child has blinders on. "Mah-ahm, pleeeze?! I'll pay you back. I have money for it. It's not very much. I only want one thing. Please? Just one. Just this once." And on and on and on. Eventually the child will either wear Mom down or explode into a temper outburst.

So focused do ADD children become that they will persevere in a desire well outside of reason. There may be not a chance in the world that the child can obtain that toy, but he or she cannot forget it. The obsession is too strong, too unregulated.

A fourth and final definition of impulsivity is *stimulus-seeking behavior*. These kids are stimulation junkies. They *must* find something to provide constant stimulation. The stimuli can be annoying or beneficial or harmless.

One mother told Dr. Warren, "My kid is addicted to play. He has to be doing something all the time." Not a terrible complaint.

Sit still and engage in a conversation? Sit in church without something to do? Dream on. If things even begin to get slow, these kids will make something happen. They'll start an argument, crumple the church bulletin, bug a kid nearby, kick the seat in front, braid the place-marker ribbons in the hymnal, make paper airplanes out of the song sheets or even the hymnal pages, and generally bounce around like a Kewpie doll on a rubber band.

This is why ADD kids seem to wear magnets that attract each other. They offer mutual stimulation. They will lump together in a class, overstimulate each other, and then get in trouble together.

Perhaps an adjunct of this (the jury's still out) is that many but not all ADD kids have a wicked obsession with sugar, which can provide a temporary buzz. It's not uncommon for parents to say they dare not keep anything with sugar in the house because their ADD kids compulsively seek it out and eat it.

Dr. Warren relates this case in point. When he first joined the clinic, he was the only one who saw many kids, and the waiting room was set up for adults. It offered free soft drinks, and a coffee maker with mounds of sugar packets nearby. The receptionists got pretty good at making an accurate preliminary diagnosis of ADD kids simply by observing who drank soft drink after soft drink and who ate, literally, mounds of sugar, one packet after the other.

Some researchers say that sugar increases activity, providing a burst of energy. Others can't find any correlation between sugar consumption and activity increase. Many parents swear to the reality of sugar jags. Others don't notice any. At any rate, these kids seem fascinated with eating sugar.

Another underlying hallmark of ADD is intensity.

Intensity

The behavior of ADD kids is not disturbed or abnormal. ADD kids do the normal things all kids do, but ADD kids do them so much more intensely. Ferociously. Exuberantly.

All kids are impulsive to a degree, talking when they shouldn't now and then, acting without thinking, but they can regulate their behavior to some extent. The degree of regulation, of course, depends greatly upon their age and level of maturity. ADD kids do the same things other kids do, but they tend to do them over and over and over and . . . well, you get the picture. Usually it is not the *quality* of their behavior but the sheer, overwhelming quantity of it.

And finally, variability marks the ADD child.

Variability

There are good days and bad days. ADD kids seem less affected by the problem on some days, dangling hope before the eyes of harried parents and teachers. Hard on the heels of respite, though, come bad days. Terrible days.

Unfortunately, adults expect steady, even progress with no backing up. They fail to grasp that's just not the way ADD works. They voice their defeated expectations in such admonitions as, "I know you can sit in your chair if you really want to because you did it two days ago." But that's not a realistic expectation. Two days ago was a good day. Today's not.

Similar Conditions and Problems

There is a catch to all this neat, orderly analysis: Nearly all the symptoms of ADD can occur in unrelated disorders and problems. This prevents ADD from being an easy condition to identify. Qualified professionals weigh not only the child's behavior but the climate at home, the school environment, and whether other members of the family exhibit similar signs of ADD. A medical workup rules out physiological sources for problems.

A depressed or anxious child, upset by family problems or turmoil in the home or neighborhood, can display many symptoms of ADD. A child whose neurological makeup is what we call "strongly global," or "strongly right-brain," may react with ADD-like signs to a school situation that does not embrace the child's particular learning style. (We'll examine this situation at length later, for it also adversely affects most ADD kids.)

Some physiological malfunctions can mimic ADD, including thyroid malfunctions and inner-ear problems. Mood disorders such as manic-depressive disorder can ape ADD. We are finding that Tourette's syndrome is a lot more common than people once thought. Besides motor tics, Tourette's can produce ADD-like signs in kids, such as distractibility, impulsivity, and inappropriate behaviors (making inappropriate noises or words, or speaking wrongly or out of turn, for example).

Similar symptoms may be present in disorders related to fetal health, such as fetal alcohol syndrome. Again, these problems and ADD are unrelated. They just look alike on the surface.

Identifying ADD, however, is certainly not a by-guess-and-by-golly sort of situation. There are solid criteria for determining whether ADD is present. They are found in the so-called "bible" of the American Psychiatric Association, titled *Diagnostic and Statistical Review Manual of Mental Disorders,* fourth edition *(DSM-IV).* In Appendix A we have outlined the *DSM-IV* designations related to ADD.

Even though it is considered "the bible" in the field of mental health, the droning precision of the reference book's descriptions does not prevent a swirl of controversy.

The Controversy Surrounding ADD

In the late 1980s, certain special interest groups launched a massive campaign to shape public opinion against the use of drugs in ADD management and even against recognition of the disorder itself. Through a relentless and clever public relations campaign, such as writing articles, appearing on talk radio and television, and bringing lawsuits, they turned parents, doctors, and educators against the conventional treatments of ADD. They even sued the American Psychiatric Association for fraud. Among their claims:

- The problem did not really exist. Mental health professionals, drug companies, teachers, and such were just trying to grow themselves a money tree.
- Up to a third of public school children were being medicated merely so teachers had an easier time maintaining discipline.
- The drugs used were being routinely abused.
- The use of these drugs opened the door to marked alcohol and other substance abuse later in the children's lives.

A large segment of the public bought these myths, never noticing that none of the claims was backed up with any kind of evidence. Figures were grossly bloated, claims made with no documentation, and no one hollered. For example, the percentage of children actually treated for ADD was at times one-tenth of the percentage these people claimed. Certain other lies were exposed, such as the one that schools pressured parents wholesale into drugging unruly children for the sake of convenience.

Fearful of being sued, doctors backed off the ADD issue and often refused altogether to prescribe drug therapy. Fortunately, the parents of ADD children—the people in the trenches—joined together in mutual support, forming organizations such as CHADD (Children and Adults with Attention Deficit Syndrome), to counteract this negative publicity with the facts.

From all the smoke and furor, a balanced viewpoint is emerging. The drugs in question have been around for a long time—in common use for three decades at least—and many longitudinal studies have been done. In this case *longitudinal* means people have examined the effects of the ADD therapy, drugs and other methods, through time. How did the children treated for ADD turn out in adulthood? The facts are:

- The drugs used in ADD management are not addictive in the doses prescribed. They are not widely abused.
- Abused or not, these drugs do not lead to substance abuse in later life. In fact, the opposite seems to pertain: Children treated for ADD appear less disposed toward drug and alcohol abuse than are untreated children, perhaps because treatment enabled the children to have a more successful childhood and less spotty education.
- Although certain criteria of the syndrome have changed as we have gotten better acquainted with it, there has never been any controversy or argument that the problem does not exist. Its causes still elude us, but the syndrome itself is well defined and universally accepted within the mental health and teaching professions. It is now accepted as a biological phenomenon rather than a psychological one—a function of unique physiology rather than emotions.

The late 1980s brouhaha is not the only source of controversy. ADD is possibly the most overdiagnosed and at the same time the most underdiagnosed problem in kids. Some people automatically say, "attention deficit disorder!" every time something's going wrong in a child's life. Others refuse to admit the condition exists at all and assign the symptoms to a variety of other causes. In the great middle ground are people who have never heard of it.

Another area of controversy is choice of treatment. Do you medicate a child who is not sick? If so, is that medication intended to help the child or to make the parents' and teachers' lives merely more convenient? How far should we go in homogenizing all kids to behave "properly"?

In this book we are not going to take sides. We will present the options parents have for treating ADD, one of which is drugs in conjunction with other resources. Drugs without other treatment is not a satisfactory option. The choice of which options to use will remain the parents'.

Remember, though, that while we can offer a wide range of diagnosis and treatment options, there is only one goal:

We must help each child find success socially, emotionally, academically, and spiritually in childhood and in adulthood.

Tell Beth Mulroney. There were many days when she despaired of seeing Andrew succeed with anything at all. Indeed, there were many days when she despaired of seeing him avoid prison.

It's not that she didn't try. "Andrew, I've told you a hundred times! Close the screen door!" And she did indeed tell him a hundred times. More. It's no exaggeration.

"Andrew, stop stalling! If you'd just sit down and apply yourself, you could have these subtraction problems finished in ten minutes!"

"Andrew, you must clean up your room before you can go out to play. And that is not anyone's version of clean! It's still a mess."

"No, you cannot." This answer more often than not precipitated temper explosions that greatly frightened Beth. If Andrew was this powerful and menacing and uncontrollable at seven, what was he going to be at fourteen?

These admonitions may sound very familiar to you, the reader. Perhaps your child or the child of a friend acts like that. *Why can't the kid shape up?* you wonder.

This book will explore the reasons ADD children possess a unique outlook on life, and it will help you learn how you can help them fit better into a society that does not understand or tolerate them well. By using that new knowledge, the adult working with an ADD child can change the child's future, literally.

ADD kids are greatly at risk for self-destructive, damaging behavior, and a lifetime of what could be called caustic misery. By changing tactics, the parent of an ADD child can alter that grim prognosis and give the child a greatly improved chance at happiness and productivity. By employing understanding and different methods, parents and teachers can change negative to positive in the child's life. We want to show you how to do it as well as lay out your options.

In Beth's case one option was medication for Andrew. However, when a school counselor raised the possibility of ADD and told Beth that medications sometimes helped, Beth adamantly refused to consider it. Andrew could just learn to behave, she said. She wasn't going to watch him become a slave to a drug. But this constant, relentless war in which Beth could see no progress was rapidly eroding her idealism. She had to do something.

"He's not broken, Mrs. Mulroney," the counselor assured her. "Just different."

No, Beth was not a lousy, rotten mother. She was an excellent mother. And God was certainly not out to get her. Still, Andrew's differentness was driving Beth to distraction.

The counselor's point is well taken. The ADD child is not broken. Knowing that, here's how we might go about fixing it.

EVALUATING ADD

2

G*UNTHER STEINFELDER*
kept his life in comfortable order.
His days marched in lockstep through the years, just the way he wanted
it. True, there were a few speed bumps along this productive tramp
through time. His son William was one of the most enduring of them.
William had always been a strong-willed, angry, defiant child. He deliberately forgot instructions whenever it was convenient to do so and
neglected to perform the simplest tasks, such as taking out the trash.
The quality of his schoolwork was inexcusable. Absolutely inexcusable.

Gunther had to admit he himself possessed something of a temper.
He understood where William would get his quick trigger and aggressiveness. A certain degree of controlled aggressiveness was a credit to
one's makeup. All the best leaders possessed it. But Gunther's anger was
always a justified anger and always, always controlled. William's fury
exploded unpredictably, for no reason. That could not be condoned.

Today Gunther, his wife, Ellen, and William sat in Dr. Warren's
office, seething. The two younger children, Hannah and John, had been
left with a sitter because Gunther didn't want them any more involved
in this current ugliness than they had to be. He had just described his
life with William, his problems raising the boy, and the most recent
crisis that had propelled him into this office.

"It's a mess," he concluded.

"It would seem so." From his leather chair, Dr. Warren looked at William in the wingback across the room. Sullen, the gangly, blond sixteen-year-old fidgeted as he studied details of the carpet.

Gunther and Ellen sat on the sofa, about two feet of space between them. Ellen, a slim, pretty, brown-haired woman, perched with her legs crossed. Her elevated foot bobbed rhythmically. She seemed sad.

Gunther had been blond once, obviously, but his hair had darkened and was beginning to gray. So far he had lost none of the robustness of youth. He was a bull of a man, extremely imposing.

Because of that difference in body build—Gunther the bear and William the scrawny stripling—Dr. Warren was surprised about the story the Steinfelders told. Apparently, one of the numerous shouting matches between father and son had deteriorated into an actual knock-down-drag-out fistfight. Gunther threw the first punch, a slap across the cheek for disrespect. William exploded with a well-placed knee and a fist in Gunther's face that put the big man down. While William stood in startled disbelief—his only big mistake, pugilistically speaking—Daddy gathered himself up well enough to lunge at William from the ground, pull him down, and strike him twice, open-handed. Mom dragged him off the boy, then had to throw herself across William to keep him from renewing the fight.

Now Dr. Warren understood the reason for the bandage across Gunther's broken nose and the mouse under each of William's eyes.

Impulsively, William bounded up out of the wingback and crossed to the window. He glared down at Collins Boulevard, his hands stuffed into his pockets.

Gunther opened his mouth to yell at the boy, but Dr. Warren quickly raised a hand, a let-him-be gesture.

Gunther scowled at his son's back. "I insisted on military school. Ellen says that if William goes to military school, she will leave me. It's the only time she's ever opposed me that way—ever refused to go along with what I know is best. The only time. Her unexpected stand has made me pause. I probably shouldn't say it this way, Dr. Warren, but you are the compromise. I agreed to see what you have to say."

"You and William never came to blows before?"

"Never. Close. But no. I am not an abuser, Doctor."

Dr. Warren nodded. He was often the compromise, the next-to-last resort before a parent took drastic measures. "Why did you let it get that far?"

Gunther sounded weary. "I was so sick to death of his constant defiance. He will *not* direct his anger toward his parents! He will *not*."

"William? He outweighs you two to one. Why did you do it?"

The boy turned to look at him. "I don't know. I was mad, I guess." He shrugged. "I don't know."

"That's not an adequate answer," Gunther snarled.

Dr. Warren engaged in a bit of peacemaking. "I would suspect he's telling the truth. He probably doesn't know."

Then he turned to the father again. "Mr. Steinfelder, our first step in evaluating a child is to do a complete medical workup and rule out physiological causes for behavior difficulties."

The Initial Evaluation

Gunther frowned. "You mean a tumor or something?"

"That possibility is remote, but it's a possibility," Dr. Warren answered. "There are other possibilities of a physical or chemical imbalance, so we always start with a medical workup."

Physical Evaluation

"Rarely do we find something, and frankly, I don't expect to find anything," Dr. Warren continued. "That kind of cause is extremely rare, but it happens; there's a variety of possibilities. Inner-ear problems, perhaps. Some evaluators look for possible thyroid imbalance. It's a matter of covering the bases. Also, we know that certain physical variations often accompany certain disorders. While they're not diagnostic— that is, they don't point a finger to a specific disorder—they corroborate a diagnosis made by other means. We also do an evaluation to screen for psychological problems."

Further Evaluation

"He's not nuts," said William's father, "just defiant."

"Nuts? Not at all. I agree. The psychological series seeks out conditions that produce the kind of symptoms you've described: inability to maintain attention or to remember and follow directives, anger and defiance, distractibility. We look for family problems. They often cause behavioral problems. In order to do that, we take a careful and extensive history, paying special attention to emotional and health issues."

Because a number of other situations can give rise to the surface symptoms of ADD, evaluators must tread very carefully here. Depressed children, for example, frequently experience poor concentration and mood lability—that is, their moods bounce up and down excessively.

Anxious kids may be quite distractible, with poor concentration, poor organization, and moodiness.

Dr. Warren went on. "We look at physiological and psychological milestones—what the child should be doing or achieving at a particular age. And—"

"Like a driver's license?" Gunther frowned.

"The driver's license is a biggie. It's the closest thing our culture has to a rite of passage."

"It's also what we fight most about. I insist he's not ready to drive responsibly, and he insists he has the right to drive. I tell him it's not a right; it's a privilege. We go round and round on this."

Mrs. Steinfelder's brow puckered. "But what about little children who aren't even close to a driver's license? They all can't be William's age. What about John and Hannah?"

Diagnosis in young children is extremely difficult before the age of six or seven. The normal behavior of a three- or four-year-old is one of constant go-go-go anyway. They have little social sense yet because they have had little social contact from which to learn. They aren't good at sequencing because, again, they haven't had time to polish the skill. They're too busy blotting up their brand-new world to spend much time analyzing how to deal with it.

On rare occasion, a child as early as two and a half will show signs of hyperactivity and ADD. That child will be virtually unmanageable every waking moment. Such children, let us emphasize, are very, very rare. Almost always, we're looking at kindergarten or school age before ADD becomes a possible issue.

"In small children, we look at inability to cooperate with a well-attached adult caregiver. From what you and your husband have said about your other two children, there doesn't seem to be a problem there." Dr. Warren continued, "In assessing an older child like William, most of all we spend time with the child. Talking. Somewhere in the process I also like to do a neurological exam."

William looked worried. "What kind of neurological thing?"

Neurological Evaluation

Dr. Warren waved a hand casually. "Oh, to check reflexes, gross motor coordination. An expanded neurological check looks for what you might call neurologic soft signs. Mild abnormalities in fine tuning that are not diagnostic of any particular condition but correlate highly with several problems, attention deficit disorder among them."

"That's it!" William's mom exclaimed. "That's what William's counselor said! She said she thinks William has attention whatever disorder."

"And I," Gunther fumed, "think that's just an excuse for disobedience."

William asked warily, "What kind of neurological stuff? Shots or something?"

"Not at all." Dr. Warren demonstrated as he spoke. "I'll ask you to hold your hands out like this, hold them still." He did not say aloud that he would look for motion and fidgeting. ADD kids cannot keep their hands still. He also neglected to mention that he might ask him to stick his tongue out. The tongue of an ADD child tends to keep moving, posturing itself (wiggles a lot).

He continued, "I check the ability of the eye to track by asking you to follow the green tip end of my pen here without moving your head. I might ask you to use your thumb like this to count off on your fingers, touching the thumb like this to each fingertip in turn. Kids ten and under can't do it well. If a child over ten has trouble, it suggests delayed development. Or I might ask you to balance on one leg."

William burst into a grin. "You know what that is? That's a drunk test. Cop pulls you over and gives you a drunk test, like for drunk driving. He asks you to do that stuff."

Dr. Warren smiled and nodded. "Fine neurological control is the first thing to go in a person under the influence."

Dr. Warren did not elaborate on several other points such as: It is essential that the evaluator simply spend time with the child. Even a person well trained to observe distractibility may see little evidence of it on an initial visit. Dr. Warren and Mrs. Capehart bump into that constantly. Also, ADD children will be more cautious about their behavior with a male counselor or evaluator, letting it all hang out quicker and more freely with a female. We aren't sure whether that's a fear factor of some sort, or simply the reflection of some differing expectation.

Frequently, Dr. Warren claims, the child may not show much to an evaluator on a first visit. As a rule, ADD kids do better in new situations; they're better able to regulate their attention. Not only is the new environment stimulating—right up their alley—but the session is generally one on one, and that individualized attention is far less distracting than a group session.

"I saw this one boy three or four times," Dr. Warren claims, "and it was hard to see any distractibility at first. Now it's terrible."

This phenomenon may be the source of the myth that doctors prescribe drugs for active children simply to please harried teachers. The parent sends an overactive child to the doctor for evaluation. In that new and interesting one-on-one situation, especially with a male doctor, the symptoms don't show up. The doctor sees nothing out of the ordinary and claims the child is fine. The teacher and parents, aghast, roar, "How could you say that?" They see this child's worst side, essentially a different child altogether. They see excessive activity in the daily routine when the child is most distracted. The doctor may end up prescribing medicine based upon the accumulative observations of all these people who know the child well, even though he himself did not observe the problem.

Along with psychological considerations, we study the child's personality.

Personality Evaluation

We look at a number of aspects of the child's personality. One of them is entitlement. Entitlement is a fancy two-dollar substitute for the fifty-cent term "spoiled rotten." The entitled kid grows up knowing the meaning of life, which is: Life is there to meet his or her every narcissistic want and need. Other people are destined to serve him. This kind of attitude can drum up a very good imitation of actual attention deficit.

There are many measures and classifications of personality. Several psychologists have developed different ways to look at personality classifications. The purpose of all these personality classifications is simply to put together "suites," or groupings, of signs and symptoms that define a certain kind of person. That definition then helps us deal with the person effectively, for no two personality types react to the same parenting and teaching methods in the same ways. We will deal with them in detail when we discuss the educational needs of the ADD child. We mention them here to remind you that they also play a part in the initial evaluation.

The strong-willed kid may simply have to learn not to be a control freak. The child who was never trained to respect authority or think of others is going to have to learn some new tricks for getting along.

Some children can appear to be airheads because they're forgetful of what they consider inconsequentials—that's anything not directly involved in interpersonal relationships, such as whether the room is cleaned up. Another type is an ardent perfectionist who might get stuck emotionally or feel overwhelmed by a whole, huge project supposedly requiring perfection. This person sees the big picture so clearly he or she cannot pick it apart into sequential tasks and therefore cannot get started. This spinning of wheels appears as the procrastination so prevalent in ADD children. Quirks of personality and temperament, then, may be diagnosed as ADD even though they are altogether different.

Although we'll examine personality types later, note that here, as the initial evaluation is made, we take them into consideration as possible sources of symptoms. Later on, when we look at them more closely, we will use them to help ADD children improve control of themselves.

Psychological Testing

Contrary to what a lot of parents think and hope, formal testing will not make a specific diagnosis of attention deficit disorder in a child. Formal tests may well provide important clues that ADD is present. Their primary purpose, however, is to identify the emotional problems, learning disorders, and memory problems the child may have. Some of them exist concurrently with ADD itself. Some mimic ADD. Some are simply there and should be addressed. This testing is done by an educational diagnostician (a person trained to administer and analyze such tests) or a psychologist.

Behavior Rating Scales

Andrew, remember, did a lot of *slamming* and had trouble remembering things. How do you quantify that—mark it down and score it on a piece of paper? Various people have tried, with some amazing success. There are now several different behavior rating scales that have become standard tools of the trade. They can often help confirm a diagnosis of ADD.

Generally speaking, these scales ask the adults who know the child best—parents, teachers, caretakers—to give a numerical rating to the child's behavior in terms of attention span, distractibility, activity level, and various social skills. Again, while these ratings are very helpful, they do not in and of themselves offer a diagnosis. They indicate and support; they cast nothing in cement.

Finally, we evaluate the child's school situation, and for that we often call in help.

Using Other Sources As Evaluators

Outside sources can be of immense help when school difficulties are part of a child's suite of problems. The parents, the teachers, and certain qualified school counselors can offer invaluable insights. We never hesitate to use them.

Evaluation of Learning Style and Possible Problems

Here is where a professional educator, such as Jody Capehart, steps in where psychiatrists and angels fear to tread. Learning style is such an immensely important part of the ADD child's world that we will devote a full chapter to it later. Suffice it for now to say that learning style is one of the things we evaluate early on in clients such as William Steinfelder.

Sometimes the root cause of problems is actual learning difficulties. Children with learning difficulties may often seem to have ADD; in reality, it's some other neurological wiring difference altogether.

"Mrs. Steinfelder," Dr. Warren asked, "what did William's school counselor say about the possibility of attention deficit disorder?"

"Just that it might be his problem and we ought to get it checked. She's just a counselor. She's not qualified to diagnose something like that, is she?"

"School psychologists and counselors as well as psychiatrists and psychologists all evaluate for ADD. They have a number of different tests available for the purpose. We all work together."

She nodded absently, lost in thought for a moment. "They sent a test home for me to fill out. Two or three pages, and you had to put numbers in boxes. There were all these sentences to describe his behavior. It was too confusing. I had to give up on it. But apparently his teachers filled one out, too, and they used that."

"So what," asked Gunther, "do you do about it if you decide he has this attention deficit disorder?"

"That's an excellent question and one not easily answered. First we have to determine whether the symptoms are severe or mild and what other conditions are present as well. ADD kids rarely are dealing with ADD alone. There are almost always complicating factors."

"Such as . . . ?"

"All the other things we've just been talking about—depression, anxiety, and such."

But Mrs. Steinfelder was thinking about other things, frowning at William. "How would *you* know what a roadside drunk test is like?"

The picture is not nearly as simple as we are making it appear. Problems can pile upon problems. Difficulties cannot always be classified as either-or but perhaps also as this-*and*-that.

Evaluation of the Extent of Problems

Here is a big, big kink in the plowline. All the situations we discussed above that may *resemble* ADD on the surface may also be present in the ADD child. The child with learning difficulties may also have ADD to an extent, but the learning difficulty remains the primary problem. Depression and anxiety often happen to the ADD child. Spoiled children may also be ADD kids.

Even when the ADD is treated, perhaps even neutralized, these other problems remain. In fact, the parent or teacher may believe that treatment of ADD *caused* the other problem, not realizing it had been there all the time, cloaked behind the ADD.

The big question remained, of course: What, if anything, ought to be done about William's difficulties? Could they be eased, and if so, how? Who would be involved in helping him? Would drugs be of benefit? All these decisions would be made not by evaluators or counselors but by the parents. Professionals could offer suggestions and provide information. The final choice remained the parents'.

In other words, Gunther was going to have to sort through a lot of material alien to his understanding before launching out on a course of action.

Determining a Course of Action

Gunther Steinfelder did not believe in the mystical hocus-pocus of psychology. He certainly did not consider it a science. Science you can weigh and measure. Science gets you to the moon. Psychology is guesswork elevated to doctoral status. He listened with considerable skepticism to all this about evaluation. What it sounded like most to him was a source of money for a vast array of evaluators.

Except teachers. Teachers did not receive nearly enough money for what they did, especially these days. He was all for competent teachers. And although he did not trust psychologists, psychiatrists, and their ilk any farther than he could finance a major-league franchise, he did trust certain teachers at William's school. When they told him something, he generally believed them.

Therefore he made an appointment that same day with William's homeroom teacher, Jana Carella, and met her after school the next afternoon. He sat down across from her desk in one of those student desk-chairs. She brought her own chair around beside her desk, the better to talk without that barrier. She looked weary to Gunther, but then teachers always looked weary at the end of a school day.

"Tell me," he asked, "what purpose does it serve to treat attention deficit disorder? And how does one go about it?"

The first point to remember is that no one is to blame.

Recognize There Is No Blame

She leaned back, laced her fingers behind her head, and studied the ceiling a couple of moments. Gunther admired that about her; she provided considered decisions. "First, your first question. There's considerable controversy about details, but the general rule is to help the child regulate attention, impulsivity, and distractibility better. You know what causes ADD, don't you?"

"No."

She smiled. "Neither do we. Research offers a whole lot of hints but no facts. We do know it's biological. ADD kids are wired inside differently from ordinary people, but not distressingly so. I mean, it's not a serious wiring problem. ADD is certainly not a psychological or psychiatric disorder. *However!* If it's not treated, the child is at very high risk for psychological and developmental problems. In fact, most ADD kids end up with psychological problems. That's as good a reason why as any, right there."

"I don't understand." This was all psychobabble to Gunther. "How can a physical thing cause psychological problems?"

"The same way a child whose growth is stunted usually suffers from feelings of inadequacy or becomes aggressive or defensive to make up for his or her small stature. Or the same way a person who is disfigured builds up emotional defenses. People's brains do interesting things to compensate for physical differences."

Gunther thought about his five-foot-six college roommate years ago. The man was called "the bantie rooster" because of his attitude toward the world. And Napoleon Bonaparte . . .

"Besides," Mrs. Carella continued, "here's a kid who's always being yelled at and told he's lazy and bad. It isn't long at all before he believes it. He tries so hard to be the person the world seems to think he ought to be, but he's just not wired to do it. All reprimands and no successes take their toll. Eventually, he becomes hostile and angry, frustrated by a world he can't handle or understand. A world that won't accept him."

She was telling the Steinfelder story! "Yes!" Gunther burst out. "But if he would only apply himself. If he would only listen!"

"Exactly!" Mrs. Carella grew animated. "But he physically cannot apply himself—any more than he could pick up a Lincoln Continental by the back bumper. He physically *cannot.* And yet the world expects him to lift luxury cars every day in school and at home."

"Our other son, John, has no problem picking up luxury cars, as you say."

"He's wired differently. He has a built-in mental forklift. The world—the school system especially—is geared to kids with forklifts, and most kids have them. The ones who don't are usually not accommodated. Your William is one of those."

There. She'd said the name. William. Of course she knew Gunther came to talk about William, but he had been hoping to keep this conversation on a technical level without bringing in personalities and people.

He studied the creases in his slacks. "What kind of wiring? How bad is it?"

"We're not sure. That's why I say we don't know the causes exactly. The brains of ADD kids metabolize differently—more slowly—than do most people's, and ADD kids generally have trouble with functions handled by the frontal lobe of the brain. One of these is what you might call social sharpness. They can't read social cues; that is, they can't monitor or use nonverbal social cues. They don't know when to butt in or butt out; they don't immediately perceive that someone is irritated with them or why. They have no grasp of social cause and effect."

That was William, all right!

She went on. "There are certain other frontal-lobe specialties that ADD kids have a hard time with. Emotional volatility. Overreacting and going off half-cocked. Impuls—"

"Yes! Anger!"

"—and anger management."

Gunther was rapidly developing a new respect for this ADD. He looked at Mrs. Carella. "You did not ask me about the bandage on my nose."

She smiled. "I was trying to be polite. Actually, I already know. Your son John had it spread all over the school before nine this morning. Social services got wind and called at noon. I talked to them and explained you'd made an appointment with me, and that you and William went to a psychiatrist yesterday. So the situation was being handled by professionals. It should keep them off your back for a while."

"Social services . . ."

"They get very edgy about bruises on kids' faces. They'll pull a battered child out of the home in a heartbeat. I think I've convinced them that's not the case here." She dropped her elbows to the arms of her chair and laced her fingers across her middle. "Anyway, to continue . . . There's an interesting speculation as to why ADD seems to occur more often in boys. Boys in utero—before they're born—are producing testosterone, and testosterone alters fetal brain development in certain ways. ADD is one of the possible ways."

"I heard something about that once. That boys are brain-damaged."

"Brain-damaged!" She made a face. "No, that's not true. The word *different* does not mean *damaged*. Also, ADD shows up in families so much that we're sure there's a solid genetic link, that the differences in wiring are genetically caused."

"You mean like eye color and male pattern baldness?"

"Exactly," she continued. "Even as we speak, researchers are trying to identify the genetic component."

Gunther grunted. He was growing increasingly sensitive to male-bashing. Mrs. Carella seemed to be taking pains to refrain. "You don't see this kind of behavior in girls, though. This anger."

"We do. Increasingly so. But not as much. ADD frequently produces different symptoms in girls. A girl with ADD may appear spacey—an airhead, if you will. She can't handle math or detailed forms. She's histrionic, overly emotional at times. The butt of all those dumb-blonde jokes sounds kind of like an ADD girl."

That was Ellen! She was describing his Ellen!

"And it is often inherited. Often." She pressed home her point by jabbing her chair arm with a finger. "So you see, it's not anyone's fault. There is no blame to lay at anyone's door. It's not the parents' fault and certainly not the child's. Before parents can really dig in and help their child, they have to recognize there is no blame. No fault. That way, parents and child can work together as a team. That's what it's going to take. A team. Now. About your other question—what to do about it."

"Yes. How do you change the wiring?"

The second point forces upon us the fact that you can't change the wiring. You can, however, deal with it in other ways.

Accept That It Cannot Be Changed, But It Can Be Dealt With

"You don't change the wiring—you can't," Mrs. Carella said. "You compensate . . . in several ways."

Gunther sighed heavily. "I was hoping for a simple answer."

"Simple answer? Mr. Steinfelder, don't be greedy. Just be grateful there *is* an answer."

The Goals of Dealing with ADD

The goal, remember, is to help the child succeed socially, academically, behaviorally, and spiritually. The goal is not to transform the child into what all the other kids seem to be or what the parents or teachers seem to think the child ought to be.

We try to meet the goal in three ways. The easiest way, and it is amazingly effective, is to alter the child's environment. Sometimes simple changes achieve success. Sometimes the changes are more elaborate or difficult, as when we must alter the way the child is educated. The second way is to alter our way of thinking about the child and to encourage the child's own knowledge that he or she is not damaged goods. This change of attitude allays some of the emotional damage ADD can cause.

The third and most controversial means of achieving the goal involves medication. Medication is never used alone as a cure, so to speak. Its only value is in helping the child settle down long enough and concentrate well enough that he or she can learn to handle the peculiarities of ADD. As long as the child is unable to focus well enough to learn the self, that child cannot master life well. The medication is chosen carefully to increase the child's attention span, decrease distractibility and impulsivity. There are indeed medications that do that and only that. They are almost always a temporary measure, tools to achieve greater aims and not ends in themselves.

We will not get into the pro-medication, anti-medication fight. Our purpose will be to define the problems these extraordinary kids face and then define options, only one of which is medication. In short, this is not a book that tells what you should do but rather what you can do.

What to do and how much to do it always remains the decision of the informed parent. We reiterate that ADD wiring in some people is a part of God's creation as is every other variation on personality and ability. It simply requires a different approach. Let us look at the different approaches in turn, starting with the most controversial one, medication.

Despite the fact that it is the last resort for people dealing with ADD or possible ADD, medication is the method that always comes up first in conversation and parental concern. The fearful parent may ask, "Must my child take medicine?" or in desperation plead, "Please give the kid something!"

So let us deal with this thorny issue first.

USING
MEDICATION
AS A TREATMENT
OPTION

3

I'M SCARED SPITLESS." Beth Mulroney looked just plain terrified. She sat on the edge of her chair in Jody Capehart's office as if the whole place were going to explode. Actually, the place looked like it had already exploded in a glorious cacophony of silk flowers and stuffed bears, country baskets and charming toys. Books—many, many books—jammed the shelves. But you got the feeling that in this carefully controlled warm environment of coordinated blues and old rose, Jody Capehart could find any little item on any shelf in the place.

Mrs. Capehart, an effervescent blonde whose slowest gear is third, settled into her own chair. "What scares you?"

Beth flirted briefly with offering an answer she thought Mrs. Capehart would want to hear and took the bold plunge of speaking the truth. "I'm afraid you'll tell me everything that's wrong with the way I've raised Andrew. My parenting skills. And I'm afraid you're going to tell me to dope him up." There. She had said it. She felt naked. Vulnerable.

"Drugs."

"I've heard it happens."

Mrs. Capehart grinned. "It certainly does, in a sense, but never is a child doped up. It's funny, though. When a kid who's always been wildly overactive finally gets his life under control, he thinks he's a zombie. He's never been ordinary before. He's not used to not bouncing off the walls. But no, they're never doped in the sense you're using. And as for your skills as a parent, I'm amazed Andrew is doing as well as he is. You've worked wonders with him."

Beth wasn't going to say anything, but she hated when a person tried to flatter her with empty praise.

But Mrs. Capehart was rolling right along, locomotive-strong. "Here, let me show you. This is the series of evaluation tests you participated in. Here are your scores on the parents' version. And here are Mrs. Loring's. See?"

"Frankly, no." It had taken Beth three days to fill in all the items and write comments. She wasn't very articulate anyway, and Andrew's behavior raised really intense feelings. Now she studied the totals at the bottom, the final scores. Hers and the school counselor's and Mrs. Loring's were remarkably similar. They all went up and down the graph at the same time.

"This shows several very good things." Mrs. Capehart pointed here and there. "For one, you're very well attuned to your son. You're sensitive to how he approaches life. You'd be amazed how many parents are not well keyed into their children. Also, he seems to have a minimum of emotional problems. A good many overly active children, the kids that have difficulty settling down in school and can't learn well, carry quite a load of additional problems, anger in particular. Andrew does not appear excessively angry and frustrated, and that's your good coaching. Your patience."

"He can fly into a rage like you wouldn't believe."

"Sure! ADD kids are volatile. That's not the same thing exactly. When we talk about anger in this context, we're talking more about an underlying base of anger, you might say. Anger unresolved."

Beth felt suddenly overwhelmed, in over her head. This woman was talking about a lot of issues psychologists and other head shrinkers talk about. Beth didn't know anything about that sort of thing.

All she knew was that her ex-husband had said so many times, as he watched Andrew or looked at the boy's report cards, "It used to be like that when I was a kid too. The whole world was out to get me. Still is." Ralph was gone from her life now. He had walked out one day, and Beth couldn't even remember the pretext anymore. He just walked out. Took his jet ski, his mountain bike, and his boat, and left. He called now and then, and often he promised to send support. It never showed up. He never remembered Andrew's birthday. He was a little better about remembering Christmas.

Big deal.

And now she was facing head shrinkers and other professionals alone, with no backup. She wanted so much to just melt into a puddle and cry her eyes out.

Psychological Considerations

A number of considerations come into play once ADD is reasonably believed to be present and drugs are posed as an option. Four questions in particular must be answered, and all are psychological rather than physiological in nature.

1. What is our motive in treating this child?
2. Success being the goal, how do we define that success? What exactly are we out to achieve?
3. How can the child achieve success best?
4. What do we tell the child?

First, What Is the Motive?

- Beth Mulroney answered, "To get Andrew to straighten up. I'm at the end of my rope. I don't know what else to do, and he's getting worse, not better."
- Gunther Steinfelder answered, "To make William accept his responsibilities as an adult. I can't turn him loose on the world this way."
- Peter and Viveca, the parents of twelve-year-old Amy Eglund, answered: "To get Amy to think. She's so vulnerable." They did not say the word *airhead* aloud, but that's what they meant. Peter and Viveca often just seemed to sit there blinking, not sure what to do with their spacey, histrionic girl who didn't seem to have a single saving thought in her head.

When her schoolmates confided to her that people can get worms in their heads just like cabbage does, she let them carefully check her scalp for entry holes. The ridicule that followed devastated her. She flunked math. She read her textbooks sporadically and then not well. Not only could she not memorize dates to save her life, she couldn't remember how to look them up. She loved movies and TV shows but couldn't describe the plotlines once they were over. Her biggest concern in life was owning and wearing the correct shoes. At one point, "correct shoes" were army boots big and clunky enough to dip sheep in.

Throughout her first six years of school Amy was labeled as a pretty but very dim girl who would be lucky to keep an entry-level job in a fast-food joint. She was twelve when her mom read a magazine article describing Amy to a T and laying the condition at the door of ADD. Virtually working blind, Viveca and Peter read everything they could about ADD. They were on the road to getting Amy the help she needed to succeed in life.

Their motive—to get Amy to think—was as good as any.

Frankly, a more common motive—"make the child conform"—is almost never a useful goal. God programmed variety into the human race for important reasons, certainly many more reasons than we have been able to ferret out. The child who is forced to conform to a rigid standard of obedience or performance for which he or she is not programmed faces a lifetime of misery and frustration.

We say "almost." When the child is antisocial—dare we say sociopathic or nearly so?—closer conformation to ethical standards is certainly a worthy goal. Most parents do not face that sort of situation. Most simply want the child to shut up and obey and quit being so annoying.

That was Beth Mulroney's primary concern for Andrew. She wanted the lad to shape up, conform. While we say it's not the best of motives, in her case we do not in any way condemn it. Beth had an extraordinarily difficult row to hoe, raising an ADD child on her own, and many, many parents are in just that position. In those cases where a child is identified as ADD, very frequently we find that a parent, most usually the father, is ADD also. The mother finds herself having to deal in the child with the very traits that estranged her and the child's father, living the frustration and heartache all over again. Beth was one of those people. She needed some sort of respite from the constant, wearying, fruitless burden of trying to keep Andrew from driving the world crazy.

We led Beth through a three-step process as she worked on this business of underlying motivation. First she acknowledged her motives. Then we discussed what Andrew needed. She came to understand that any changes made in Andrew's best interests profited her as well, for as he showed improvement and little successes in life, her burden eased. Moreover, as she and Andrew both experienced positive feedback from the world and from each other, both their lives would sweeten. She had not truly realized until we discussed it that she and Andrew were a team with a mutual goal of bringing Andrew up through childhood into a clean and productive adulthood.

In summary, the best motives, the only really effective ones, are those in which the child's needs to develop and grow come first. Please take a moment to consider what's motivating your wish to cause changes in your child:

- First, we beg you to examine your motives closely. If you could change your difficult child, what changes would you make? There's no need to list all the many changes you would wish. Just the most prominent.
- Next, consider at length: Are those changes beneficial to the child primarily or to you primarily? Certainly the child will benefit from improved obedience. If nothing else, the kid will learn how to get along in the army. But whose convenience would best be served by the dreamed-of changes?
- If treatment would work any sort of changes you wished, discount your own wants and needs for the moment and think about what changes you would most want *that would give your child lasting happiness.*
- Finally, what positive attributes does your child's present situation provide him or her? What do you think ADD is giving your child that will help him or her through life? Are you willing to preserve those positives? And by the way, just what is success?

Second, How Do We Define Exactly What We Hope to Achieve?

Again, every parent has his or her own answer. May we suggest a fourfold definition for success? Success in the child's life is earning a level of respect among his or her peers that is about equal to what his or her companions achieve. The child is not perfect. Not even superior. He or she simply has respect.

Success is learning enough academically to make it in today's world. Success is developing sufficient skill in obeying rules and sequencing actions to hold down a good job. Here "good job" does not necessarily mean "high-paying prestige position." A good job is a legal line of work the person does well and enjoys. Trash collection is just as good a job as university professor, and just as necessary—perhaps more so. Our civilization would certainly suffer greatly without professors, but at least it could continue to exist. Without trash collectors? Well, that's another story.

Success is coming to know and enjoy God on a personal basis.

Every child, ADD or not, holds the potential for success to some degree. No doubt you've so often heard the adage "God doesn't make junk" that it's trite now. Keep in mind that God doesn't make any perfect people either. Not a one. Every human being plays the hand dealt him or her, and it's never a royal flush.

Third, How Can the Child Best Achieve Success?

Beth Mulroney, Gunther and Ellen Steinfelder, and Peter and Viveca Eglund each had a different problem because each had a unique child to work with. In fact, Gunther and Ellen, for example, were not working with the same child because Gunther related to William much differently than Ellen did. Ellen instinctively understood William pretty well; she shared many of his qualities. Gunther, almost the total opposite of William in most regards, found himself constantly at loggerheads. Ellen could not successfully employ the same methods Gunther used; she simply did not think that way. And vice versa. Neither Peter nor Viveca could empathize with their Amy. Both felt at sea.

The answer then to the question "How to achieve success?" is, "Tailor a plan of action to your child's uniqueness and to your own uniqueness." We will look at that in detail as we go.

Let us assume for the moment that one of these sets of parents has examined the option of medication and decided to try it. How we approach the child with this decision will govern the child's self-image and attempts to succeed for years to come.

Fourth, What Do We Tell the Child?

Says Dr. Warren, "This scenario happens constantly. I'll ask a child in counsel, 'Why are you here?'

"And he—he or she, let's call it a he this time—will say, 'Because I'm dumb' or 'lazy' or 'bad.' It's often something highly self-deprecating.

"Then I'll reply, 'I understand that you're here because things aren't always going well at school or home. You have trouble making good choices.' Then I'll go on to explain, 'There are reasons these things are happening. There are always reasons. And it's not that you're dumb. Not at all.' Then I'll show him some of our test results and say, 'See? I can show you you're a pretty bright kid. The reason you're here is so we can help you have less trouble.'"

Never does a counselor say or even imply, "Oh, you poor thing; you're going to be an emotional cripple."

Explains Mrs. Capehart, "We try to teach them just the opposite. We say, 'There are things you can do to make life easier and better, and that's what you and your parents are going to work on. I'll help. I can't do it for you. You and your folks will do it. But I'll help.'"

Dr. Warren continues, "If medication is an option the parents have decided to try, we tell the child, 'One of the things we're going to do is a trial of certain kinds of medicine. The stuff won't change what you think or the way you think, but it may help you think more easily. Its only purpose will be to help you grab better control of the choices you make. And at the same time we'll teach you how to do that without medication.'"

We emphasize that. The medicine won't do it. The medication never *ever* does it. Learning to overcome will do it.

If medication is advisable into junior high, during that difficult time of separation and individuation the early teen experiences, the child may rebel, perhaps to the point of refusing to take the medicine. By having to take medicine, the child often feels singled out or different at a time when children strive to look like each other while remaining apart from the adult world. The rebellion is actually an expected, even necessary, part of growing up.

When it occurs, we attempt to prevent the matter of medication from becoming an issue between parent and child. From the start we try to keep medication a matter of discussion between the child and the doctor. Although the parents made the original decision (and in fact either maintain or alter that decision throughout the child's life, but always in the background), when the child voices objections to the parents, they need only tell him or her, "Well, if you feel strongly about it, discuss it with Dr. So-and-So." Enough issues arise between parents and kids during this difficult time without adding another topic to the pile.

What does medication actually do? We've been using these drugs long enough now to know that there are many things they can't do. They won't turn normal kids into zombies. They can't work miracles. They can't cure.

The Role of Medication in Treatment

"So why use it?" Beth's question was a legitimate one.

Mrs. Capehart popped open a notebook. Mrs. Capehart is well known for her constantly busy notebook. She never leaves home without it. "I draw a circle on a blank sheet of paper, like this. This is a lake. This little circle I'm drawing in the middle of the big one is an island. Now, how is the child going to get from shore here out to the island?"

"Is this a trick question?"

Mrs. Capehart laughed. "How would Andrew answer it? He's extremely creative and clever, you know."

"I know. I just wish he were creative and clever in constructive ways." Beth studied the picture. "Depending on the size and the depth of the lake, I suppose you could wade out or take a boat. Maybe a helicopter.

If it's Andrew trying to get out there, forget swimming. He's just plain reckless around water. I'm afraid for his safety, but he's not coordinated enough to swim well."

"Helicopter's too expensive. No boat. Too deep to wade."

Beth frowned. "This *is* a trick question!"

"No it's not." Mrs. Capehart sat back. "The ADD child is like a person trying to get from the lakeshore to the island. The child sees wealthy people fly over to it, but that's out of the question for the child. There go boat-owners over. So the child drags a log down to the shore and stretches out on it and paddles over, like a raft. It's not as good as a boat, but it gets him there."

"This is a parable, I take it. Like Jesus told."

Mrs. Capehart giggled. "Hardly as wise as Jesus, but yes. It's a parable. The wealthy people are all those super-intelligent types who seem to have the world by the ear. The boat-owners are average people who have the kind of abilities that get them ahead in the world: good academics, good coordination, good lots of things. And then there's the ADD kid. The log is the medication we've been discussing. It's not as good as a boat, but it will get him there. Maybe by the time he approaches the island he'll be old enough to have gained the coordination to swim the rest of the way. The log is a tool. Nothing more. In essence, it's your last resort when nothing else will take you where you want to go."

"What's the first one?"

"A variety of modifications in Andrew's environment—his surroundings, that is—and the way he is being taught in school and at home. Adjustments we can make in attitude. But those things will work only if he has enough focus to be able to stay on task and learn. Not just learn schoolwork, although that's extremely important. Learn about life. How to accomplish tasks around the house. How to get along. It's all learning."

"You're saying the medication prepares him so that this other stuff we do can get through to him."

Mrs. Capehart sat back, triumphant. "That's it exactly! Medication is plowing the field. Then we plant and cultivate and reap the harvest. But the seeds won't grow and the harvest won't come if the soil hasn't been tilled to receive the seed. And once the crop is growing, you don't need the plow."

Beth sat back in her chair (a remarkably comfortable chair) and chewed on her knuckles. She noticed Mrs. Capehart noticing her nervous habit and quickly stopped. She folded her hands together tightly in her lap. "This is frightening. I'm committing my son to medicine when he's not sick."

"Not sick, no. But in need of help nonetheless. We'll try other things first, a variety of things. If they don't bring improvement, and if you agree, then we can try getting him to slow down and pay better attention through the use of medication. It's the last thing to try, not the first."

"What kind of medicine?"

"Another good question! There's quite a variety for use in different situations. I suggest you have your doctor describe and explain them to you."

Available Medications

Let's survey the drugs commonly used for children with ADD and ADHD (the ADD designation when hyperactivity is a major factor). We will examine the drug, its advantages and disadvantages, and its possible side effects as they would appear in a child like Andrew. In fact, let's use seven-year-old hyperactive Andrew as the model.

The drugs can be grouped into several categories—traditional stimulants, tricyclic antidepressants, and miscellaneous others.

Traditional Stimulants

The word *neurotransmitter* refers to a fascinating dance between certain chemicals and the tip ends of thread-like nerves in the human body. As the chemicals appear, change, and disappear, a fleeting message is sent from nerve tip to nerve tip. We believe that in ordinary people, stimulants increase the efficiency of certain neurotransmitter functions; to explain inexactly, the nerves fire more dependably.

But in ADD kids, the neurotransmitters apparently do not fire as efficiently. Because their neurotransmitters aren't working well, the kids have more trouble regulating the brain processes that we see on the outside as attention, impulsive actions, and distraction. Organizing and processing take a lot of well-controlled thought and analysis. The neurotransmitters may work better at some times than at others; Andrew had his good days.

Stimulants, we believe, make the ADD child's neurotransmitters fire more dependably and efficiently by increasing their ability to fire when they're supposed to. Moreover they especially affect functions such as regulation and control (areas, you will remember, where ADD kids have a rough time).

Ritalin (methylphenidate)

The calming effect of stimulants upon some overly active kids was accidentally discovered more than a generation ago. It is an amphetamine-like compound, as is its companion medicine, Dexedrine. It is not true that Ritalin can be used as a diagnostic tool in assessing ADD, that if a child's behavior improves while taking Ritalin then ADD is definitely present. In very small dosages, Ritalin can improve just about anyone's attention and regulatory control.

Advantages of Ritalin. Ritalin provides a significant increase in attention span and a noticeable decrease in distractibility and impulsivity. In other words, Andrew would be better able to regulate those functions instead of living always at the extremes. When his mom strapped him into his seatbelt that day, for example, and told him not to mess with the stuck window, he would have been able to shake his attention loose from the window and move it on to other things. He would also have been able to sit still more easily during the ride home.

Another advantage of Ritalin is that it is specific to the areas of regulation ADD kids have trouble with.

Still another is that the effects of Ritalin, as well as most of the other drugs we'll discuss, are not greatly influenced by body weight. The size of the child does not necessarily govern the drug's effects. Many children grow rapidly, and not having to constantly adjust for changing size is definitely an advantage.

A fourth advantage is that it acts quickly. Within half an hour of taking the medicine, a child will show the effects of it. When it wears off, three or four hours later, there is no residual effect. This on-or-off quality helps parents and doctors immensely in assessing Ritalin's value for a particular child. Because of it, they can give the medicine an effective trial in a brief period of time. If it's going to work, you know right now. If it isn't, you know that also. You can adjust the dosage quickly if adjustment seems appropriate. Also, by taking the child off periodically, you can see immediately whether he or she is getting along pretty well without it.

Disadvantages of Ritalin. The immediacy of Ritalin is also its biggest disadvantage. Once it wears off, usually in three to four hours, it is gone. The child is finished with the medicine but not the school day. There is now a sustained-release form of the drug that lasts seven to eight hours.

Side Effects. Ritalin may cause a decrease in appetite. Beth would probably say, "I wouldn't call that a clear disadvantage. Do you realize how much food Andrew puts away? *Between* meals!" The effect is usually mild, and may even go away after a couple of weeks. Like the other attributes of Ritalin, it exists only while the medicine is producing its effects. As soon as the drug wears off, appetite returns to normal. To minimize the problem if it exists, parents usually provide the medicine after breakfast. Lunch may be affected, but by suppertime the child's appetite is normal.

The story that Ritalin stunts growth is overblown. It is true that in a small percentage of kids high growth may be slowed. If that occurs, the doctor will probably want to consider other forms of medication. However, if the child is indeed falling off his or her high growth curve, dropping the medication restores the full rate of growth immediately.

Other side effects may include stomachaches and mild but annoying headaches. Rarely, irritability and depression occur. If the child turns cranky while on medication, stop the drug or change kinds.

More common than any of those side effects is rebound. As the medication wears off, the child becomes increasingly moody and cranky, hard to get along with. The presence of rebound is an indication to stop the medication or adjust dosage times.

Many parents have worried that prolonged use of Ritalin can lead to drug abuse or dependency. There's no indication over the years that in the dosages used for ADD, Ritalin or these other drugs become addictive. They have been abused on occasion, certainly. So has airplane glue. But normal use at appropriate dosages in no way constitutes abuse. We are confident of the nonaddictive nature of these drugs because a child can stop and start medication at any time without trouble.

Moreover, this axiom is worth repeating: Starting children on ADD drug treatments does not make them dependent upon drugs. The children at highest risk for alcohol and drug abuse may be those who go untreated. ADD kids are not happy in our society. Deliberately or instinctively, they will self-medicate with whatever they can find to ease the unhappiness.

Dexedrine (dextroamphetamine)

If Ritalin is one hand, Dexedrine is the other. Dexedrine and Ritalin produce similar effects, but each works differently. For that reason, one might work in one child whereas the next child will respond best to the other.

Advantages of Dexedrine.　　Dexedrine is available as different salts. In nonchemical language, that means that various forms of the drug release at different times. It still shares Ritalin's gift of immediacy, and like Ritalin it possesses no residual effects. Once the child's body has metabolized it, it's gone.

Disadvantages and Side Effects of Dexedrine.　　Dexedrine's disadvantages and side effects are pretty much the same as Ritalin's.

Adderall

Fairly new to the market, Adderall is a combination of several forms of Dexedrine. By releasing at different times, Adderall allows one dose to provide longer-acting effects. Adderall may be indicated for the child who needs a stimulant medication but for one reason or another cannot tolerate Ritalin. This drug's advantages, disadvantages, and side effects approximate those of Ritalin and Dexedrine.

Cylert (pemoline)

Cylert is a stimulant-like medicine, but it's not a true stimulant. It was first produced in order to get away from the nuisance of constantly administering multiple doses of Ritalin. One dose lasts about twenty-four hours.

Advantages of Cylert.　　Like the stimulants above, Cylert decreases impulsivity and distractibility and increases the attention span. The obvious advantage is that it is long acting. For the greatly overactive child whose medication ought not be limited to school hours, Cylert can be a blessing.

Disadvantages of Cylert.　　Cylert not only works longer, it takes longer before it begins to work. Were Andrew to go on Cylert, Beth would not see the first indications that the boy was on medication for three or perhaps four weeks. Cylert therefore lacks the flexibility of Ritalin and Dexedrine. Once you start it, you normally do not stop it. You stick with it, at least for a while.

Side Effects of Cylert.　　Were Andrew to suffer insomnia, Beth would take that as a sign to stop the medication. Very rarely, anemia and liver problems crop up. However rare they might be, we routinely screen for them with blood tests (a complete blood count and blood chemistry tests) during the drug regimen. They are reversible if caught early.

Tricyclic Antidepressants

Tofranil (imipramine) and Related Drugs.   Elavil (amitriptyline), Norpramin (desipramine), Pamelor (nortryptiline)—a whole family of generic and brand-name drugs act similarly on ADD kids. Antidepressants are effective in many ADD children. They apparently do their work in a similar fashion to stimulants, improving the effectiveness of the neurotransmitters.

Were Andrew to begin an antidepressant regimen, he would take a dose once or twice daily, depending upon the medication and the dosage. Frequently, tricyclics are used in combination with Ritalin or other stimulants in an effort to help the child stabilize wildly unregulated moods.

Advantages of Tricyclics.   These medications help kids who cannot tolerate stimulants or fail to respond to stimulants. For example, were Andrew to display symptoms of Tourette's syndrome—nervous tics, sudden utterances, moans, or outbursts—the stimulant medicines would probably make the tics worse.

These can be helpful in the child who is depressed, whether or not the depression is directly linked to ADD, as well as in the older child and adolescent who develops mood swings or irritability. In teens especially, raging hormones may force you to look to new medications because of the mood swings common in adolescents.

Disadvantages of Tricyclics.   Like Cylert, the antidepressants must be taken daily and require several weeks before they become effective. This makes dosage adjustments slow and tedious, a problem that is multiplied by the fact that kids grow and change so rapidly. Results, whether positive or negative, would not be immediate. Andrew would have to keep with it over a period of time.

Side Effects of Tricyclics.   One side effect is drowsiness, and it's not always easy for parents to see a child like picture-slamming, razzamatazz Andrew nodding off in the middle of the day. As much as Beth dreamed of that on occasion, she didn't want it to occur. It's a possible side effect of antidepressant use. Other side effects include a dry mouth, constipation, and (rarely) cardiac arrhythmias.

This latter problem, heart irregularities, is an important thing to monitor. The drug will directly affect the conduction system of any person's heart but usually to a very, very modest extent—barely detectable. The dosage range is usually safe, and any heart irregularity is so slight it doesn't show. Still, it's very important to administer an electrocardiogram both before and during treatment. Fortunately, the ADD child, insatiably curious about new and arcane wonders, will probably participate eagerly in EKGs, not to mention the lavish attention paid.

Other Medications

Catapres (clonidine).   This is a blood pressure medication very occasionally administered to ADD kids. When used safely and appropriately, with tiny dosages administered several times during the day or in a slow-release patch on the child's back, it does not affect blood pressure. It's primarily effective for hyperactivity and impulsivity, but it doesn't do as much as other drugs to increase attention span or decrease distractibility.

The most common possible side effect is drowsiness.

Others.   Some other medications are tried in specialized or unusual situations. Major tranquilizers such as Mellaril, Haldol, and Thorazine are reserved for very special and rare occasions. Other medications are being tried as well, particularly in limited uses, but their clinical effectiveness has not been established.

Caffeine, probably one of mankind's commonest stimulants, ends up in ADD kids a lot. For many kids with ADD, caffeine acts as a true stimulant, increasing activity. For others, it helps reduce excessive activity and fidgeting. We don't know why.

We do know that ADD kids will self-medicate on coffee. Older kids in particular will stumble across it as an answer, usually responding below conscious level. They become coffee addicts, but they don't know why.

Antihistamines such as Benadryl may produce a *paradoxical response* in ADD kids. That fancy medical term means that although most kids and adults zonk out when taking antihistamines (remember that warning on the label about operating heavy machinery?), ADD kids go hyper, becoming nervous and agitated. It is wise to consult a doctor if you think your child should use those over-the-counter medicines.

In fact, these kids simply do not respond to many drugs the way ordinary people do. Dosages of every medicine the child takes, whether specifically to influence ADD or not, should be monitored by a doctor. He or she will work to establish the optimal dosage as well as the drug of choice.

How Dosage Is Determined

The fear tickling Beth Mulroney's heart hadn't settled a bit despite her long chats with Jody Capehart. A lengthy session with the pediatrician also had failed to quell it. She sat now on a park bench while Andrew scrambled up through the monkey bars in the big sand area. She took the bottle of pills out of her purse and looked at it again.

Mrs. Capehart and the doctor had both warned her, "This is not a cure-all." She desperately hoped it would cure all Andrew's problems.

They had warned her also, "You'll have to monitor carefully." Deep down inside, a large part of her wanted to forget the *carefully*. She wanted to really lay this stuff on her son thickly and flatten out Andrew's exasperating energy and volatility. She was so very tired of living with a buzz saw.

But that other part of her, her guilt, kept mumbling, "You're a lousy, rotten mother. You're letting Andrew's behavior, the discipline and shaping that you ought to be doing yourself, come out of a bottle instead. If you were halfway adequate in this job, you could teach him to walk without this crutch. You lazy, lousy, rotten mother!"

Over on the monkey bars, Andrew shrieked an angry epithet at a fellow monkey-gymnast, a girl slightly smaller than he. Beth gasped; where would a seven-year-old learn that word? Here came the girl, running, screaming, and crying, claiming Andrew had hit her. Beth didn't doubt that he had; he was still flailing. She bolted to her feet and ran across the grass to the sandpit. She grabbed her out-of-control son, gave him a swat on the hip pockets—not his first by any means—and dragged him back toward the bench.

She couldn't wait to start that medication!

Medications such as the Ritalin regimen Beth would begin with Andrew the next morning are always, always, administered under the close supervision of a physician. But the parent, of course, must also know what he or she can expect and then watch for those effects.

If the parent has decided to try medication as a tool, we start with a limited trial of a substance like Dexedrine or Ritalin, something which seems to work well on most kids. We watch closely for side effects. Close communication between parents, teachers, and doctors is necessary to monitor its effectiveness. Teamwork. The bottom line, always and ever, is, "How is the kid doing with this?"

The dosage has to be optimal, or the child will not do well. Too high a dosage sends both behavior and the child's learning ability—learning efficiency curve, in the jargon—into a tailspin. In other words, you can easily have too much of a good thing. Unmonitored, the wrong dosage, in particular too high a dosage, can make the child's situation worse. The evaluation here must come from parents and teachers. We can't do it clinically.

Beth would watch Andrew's behavior both on and off the medicine, and watch his grades. She would watch his level of interest and attention span at home after school. She and his teacher would then put their heads together to assess Andrew's progress, not just from one six-week grading period to the next, but weekly or more often. Particularly, she would watch for increased irritability, as well as a zombie-like state some kids slip into. Such signs would indicate that the doctor should either decrease the dosage or try a different drug altogether.

Bear in mind that a child's complaint that he or she feels like a zombie does not equate with the child's actually becoming lethargic and spaced-out. When kids are brought into normal, balanced control of their activity and learning, they often feel like zombies compared to the hyperkinetic, overly stimulating life they used to lead. Monitor behavior, not feelings.

Beth and Andrew worked on the drug treatment for six months. During that time they worked on a number of other aspects of Andrew's life, aspects to which we will devote whole chapters. The drug helped him buckle down. He did the work himself. The doctor soon had Andrew on a dosage that dramatically improved his ability to deal with schoolwork and chores at home. For the first time in years, Beth saw hope. Did it ever look good!

But how long should Andrew take his medicine? What if he outgrew the need for it and nobody noticed? An important part of drug therapy is to program in gaps of time in which the drug is not used—drug vacations, if you will.

Oh how Beth dreaded those drug vacations!

Drug Vacations

Back in the old days, the short-term therapeutic drugs were administered in such a way that they affected only the child's school day. Ten years ago, Andrew would have received his Ritalin in the morning and bounced off the walls all the way home from school (perhaps missing, for all practical purposes, his last hour of school instruction). He would then drive his siblings and parents nuts and fight going to bed at a decent hour (ADD kids with hyperactivity simply don't want to stop long enough to sleep, and given the opportunity, they'll just keep going). On weekends and vacations, he would not receive medicine. Good luck driving to Niagara Falls with a hyper kid in the backseat!

The unspoken theory was, we suppose, "School is for learning. Home is for play." It's false, of course. Children learn every minute they're awake. Indeed, they learn more at home in the long run because that's where the firmest relationship attachments lie, and kids learn the most about life and love and coping with the world through their relationships.

No, ADD is not a problem in school only; it affects all behavior. In all behavior lurk important lessons. As a general rule, then, we currently look not at an arbitrary schedule of medication but at the end goal: The child must experience success. That's the first priority.

The higher goal is the child's welfare (and not, incidentally, the parent's convenience. Yes, the parents may well end up driving to Niagara Falls with a hyper kid in the backseat, if that's the way the long-range plan works out). We now know enough about the medications involved that we can safely and with confidence suggest that medication is okay whenever the child needs help with self-control.

The higher goal then is not to arbitrarily limit or administer medication but to use it to give the child enough self-control to see success in his life.

Drug vacations, perhaps mini ones, remain a need, however. They serve two purposes: to assess how the drug is working and to decide when the child has matured sufficiently that the drug may be discontinued.

Most children learn to regulate their own behavior by the age of twelve or so. Some benefit from medication on into their teens. In a few cases, neurological functions—the wiring—never matures to the point where the person can safely and comfortably navigate through the shoals of life. Those few people may profit by taking medicines into adulthood. In their case, of course, the choice to use or not use medication becomes the adult's.

But the primary use of drug vacations is to assess the child's progress. By taking Andrew off his Ritalin now and then, Beth and Andrew's teachers and doctor can see how he's handling himself unaided. Does he have a pretty good handle on his emotions, attention, and behavior? And remember, the medication is not being used alone; Andrew is also receiving many other means of help.

Andrew's progress will be monitored closely, of course. If success seems to be sliding out of reach, if schoolwork is going downhill, if hard-won relationships are deteriorating, the medicine will either be curtailed, changed, or otherwise adjusted.

In short, Beth's fears that she was dooming Andrew to a lifetime of medication were unfounded. The treatment of ADD is nothing like the treatment of, for instance, hypertension. People with high blood pressure take blood pressure medicine, year in and year out, and that's all there is to it. Not so with ADD. The dosages are frequently adjusted, the goals assessed, and other treatments stepped up or abandoned or modified, all in a carefully orchestrated symphony to progress.

Beth found that no one in Andrew's circle of concerned adults was drug-happy, using a quick fix to solve the surface aspects of an annoying problem. The drug, however, provided a necessary tool. Andrew could never have done so well without it. However, his drug regimen was not the source of his successes at school and home. It was merely grease for the skids.

These days, people do not often attend a boat launching, so "grease for the skids" may not generate a quick image in your mind. A boat launching used to be quite a social occasion, with well-dressed society folk gathering to watch a brand-new sailing vessel, her paint still smelling fresh, slide down the runners into the water. Built on dry land just above the high-water line, the new ship rests on skids that look a little like temporary railroad tracks running between the ship and the water. When at last the vessel is ready to float, she is shoved down the skids into the water. To achieve this, the skids are liberally slathered in heavy grease, reducing friction.

In the best time-honored tradition, a man or woman intimately associated with the new vessel steps up to the bow (or steps out onto a platform constructed for the occasion) and flings a bottle of champagne at the ship's prow. Ideally, the bottle breaks on the first swing, conferring luck for the life of the ship. With plenty of help from winches, the ship inches backward toward the water. She slides faster, ever faster. The friction can be so great that as the ship enters the water toward the end of her slide the grease may even catch fire. By the time her stern hits water, raising a massive splash and wave, her momentum is sufficient to keep the water resistance from stopping her midway. It's majestic and awesome, and none of it would happen that smoothly without the grease.

Greasing the skids. That's what medication does for the ADD child.

But grease isn't the only thing that launches the ship. The vessel would not have moved at all without the winches—another means to the same end. Medication is not by any means the major alternative. Let us look at several others. In particular, let's examine in detail one of the easiest to implement, a tool that is amazingly effective. You can help an ADD child modify his or her behavior and learning simply by modifying his or her surroundings.

USING ENVIRONMENT AS A TREATMENT OPTION

*P*ARENTS ALL OVER Dallas were having fits.

Over in Mesquite, this little minidrama was playing out as Gunther Steinfelder confronted his sixteen-year-old William:

Gunther Steinfelder: "You're supposed to be doing your homework, not carrying your book around the house at a fast walk."

William Steinfelder, a personal tapeplayer on his belt and earphones on his head: "I *am* doing my homework. Social studies. See?" He waved his open textbook in the air.

Gunther suddenly reached out, pulled the earphones off, and pressed one to his own ear. "This is loud enough to reach the moon. What is this hideous music?"

William: "Oh come on, Dad! You know what rap is."

Gunther confiscated the tapeplayer: "No wonder your grades are so terrible. You can't listen to that junk and wander all over the house and get anything done. Go to your room, sit down, and get busy!"

Meanwhile, in Irving Beth Mulroney was lecturing Andrew at the dinner table.

Beth: "Andrew, now this is enough. Quit fooling around and finish your dinner! Sit up straight there!"

Andrew reluctantly shifted from kneeling in his chair to sitting in it. He picked up his bread and mashed it upside down on his peas.

Beth: "Stop it! Eat. Take a bite. Right now. I have to take a client out in half an hour, and I want you done by the time I leave."

Andrew picked up a chunk of potato with his fingers and popped it into his mouth. He simultaneously chewed on it and began a lengthy description of a video game he saw being played today.

Beth, her voice rising: "Andrew, you know better than to talk like that with your mouth full. Will you just eat, please?"

And while all this was going on, up north in Allen Peter Eglund was scowling at his twelve-year-old Amy. Her backside was in the easy chair by the television set, but that was the only part of her anatomy anywhere near where it ought to be in the chair. Her legs, crossed, ran up the chair back. Her shoulders rested out on the hassock in front of the chair, and her head dropped down the far side of it. She had a phone scrunched to one ear, the television blaring in the other, and a pile of papers on her chest. She was grunting into the phone and staring at one of the papers.

Peter: "What are you doing?"

Amy, looking at him from upside down: "Math."

Peter: "You don't have a pencil."

Amy: "I don't need one. I'm not working the problems yet. Jennifer's telling me how to do them." To the phone she said, "No, just Dad. You should see the look on his face." Pause. "No, I don't know why. Maybe something at work got to him. He's so hard to understand sometimes."

The situations? These three kids were all in their comfort zones. The problem? None of the parents were.

Comfort Zones

Generally speaking, and there are many exceptions to the rule, a child seeks the kind of environment that best promotes thinking.

"Hogwash!" roared Gunther.

"Get outta here!" fumed Beth.

"I can't believe that," sighed Peter. "Do you realize how loud the TV was? *Math?*"

Incredulity aside, the wise parent simply watches and listens to the child awhile, assessing what attracts, how the child manipulates his or her surroundings, what kind of living situation the child seems to gravitate toward, given a choice. This, broadly speaking, is the child's comfort zone.

You see, every child has his or her own unique approach to both learning in school and blotting up the world. Later on, as we look at the ADD child in school, we will examine the way different children think and how their personalities shape what they prefer. But regardless of the kind of personality or learning style your child may have, that kid will do better in surroundings that are comfortable for him or her.

That concept seems simple enough, but there's a catch: In a great majority of cases, the parents are not of the same makeup as the children. Certainly a lot of teachers are not. And the parents (and teachers as well, but that's another subject) inflict their own comfort zones upon the children, making several consecutive false assumptions. The parents' thinking follows a line something like this:

1. There is a best way to learn.
2. I learned best by adjusting my surroundings in such-and-so way.
3. Therefore to learn best my child must adjust his or her surroundings similarly to what worked for me.

That line of thinking simply does not hold true. It's a myth.

The Myth of the Correct Learning Environment

Gunther had spent his whole high school career sitting up straight at a desk, furiously taking notes. At home he kept his desk in order so that he could find exactly what he wanted instantly. He put reference books on a shelf above the lamp and maintained a hanging-file system for notes and handouts.

That was the way it *ought* to be done.

In high school, Beth Mulroney had preferred spreading her homework out on the living room floor so she could see it all at once, then working through it. But the living room had no overhead light fixture, so her mom, explaining that she'd ruin her eyes, wouldn't let her do that. Beth was not allowed to spread her work out on her bed, either—there's no good posture support in that position, and you don't want to hunch over so much or your bones will start growing that way. Her parents had insisted she sit at the table and straight-back chair in the kitchen with lots of light.

That was the way it *ought* to be done.

Peter Eglund abhorred excessive noise. He disliked bustle. His favorite place was down by his little orchard (only four trees, but in spring, they were glorious!), sitting in the Adirondack chair there, surrounded by the whisper of leaves and the occasional hum of an insect, reading a book. Try as he would, he could not get Amy to spend any more than five minutes at a time there. That frustrated him. She'd do so much better if only she would study in the peace and quiet of nature.

That was the way it *ought* to be done.

These examples are not far-fetched. Rare indeed are the parent and child who see eye to eye on comfort zones. Keep in mind that there is no ugliness here in parents' motivations. We are not bad-mouthing the parents by any stretch of the imagination. We do point out, however, that very, very few parents realize that their children's environmental needs may differ markedly from their own and that what worked for the parents may not work at all for the children. This applies in spades for ADD kids and their parents.

For example, when Gunther insisted that William go sit down, Gunther was severely damaging William's ability to learn. It's the last thing in the world Gunther would want to do. Here's how to keep that sort of thing from happening. First, determine what your child's best learning environment actually is.

The Reality of the Correct Learning Environment

Let's analyze the comfort zone of a child about whom you are concerned; in the process we will analyze yours as well. First let's consider the raw material for our analysis. Think for the moment about your child. Does he or she . . .

____ 1. Gravitate toward noise and make noise?

____ 2. Use the telephone excessively (in your opinion)? Is he or she a chatterbox, and could talk a monkey deaf?

When the child arrives home from school:

____ 3. Do all the lights in the house get flicked on immediately?

____ 4. Does the child head straight for the fridge?

____ 5. Do the books, homework, jacket, and lunchbox all land on a pile by the door or on the child's bed or elsewhere?

____ 6. Does the child complain about the temperature or start fiddling with the thermostat?

____ 7. How many nanoseconds elapse between the time the child enters the door and the television set comes on?

Now let's look at your preferences.

___ 8. Was the TV already on when the child came home?

___ 9. If you have a letter or report to write in a hurry (this is at home rather than at work), where do you go to do it? A desk? The kitchen? The sofa? The patio? Your bed?

___ 10. When you're reading for pleasure, do you tend to sprawl out on a bed or recliner, or do you sit up straight on the sofa or a straight chair?

___ 11. Which do you prefer for keeping contact with close friends and relatives, the phone or mail?

___ 12. On the average, how long can you sit in church before you start to get restless?

Now think for a moment about what you were taught. What was the counsel of your parents about the best place to get work done, the best place to study, the best place to relax? Can you remember if their counsel ran counter to your own behavior and preferences, or did they barely or never mention it because you were already doing it the way they wanted it done?

Beth Mulroney's childhood preferences were somewhat the same as what her Andrew's would turn out to be. However, Beth had had it drummed into her by well-meaning parents that those preferences were not the best preferences. Like so many, she would eventually forget what her own comfort zone was and, when she herself became a parent, adopt the one her parents had preached. For all she knew, her momma might have originally preferred spreading work out on the floor also but had been discouraged from doing so.

Your opinions may similarly be colored by what you were taught was "the right way." You must be alert to that possibility.

Based on research conducted by Dr. Rita and Kenneth Dunn, we will look primarily at five things that can be altered in most homes: sound, light, temperature, general busyness (distractions), and arrangement.

Analyzing Your Comfort Zone

What is your real comfort zone, not the one you were taught but the one you lean toward naturally? To start, look at question 8. Do you prefer some background noise or music in your home? Stop and think about background or white noise. It's not always music or talk shows and commercials.

A friend of Dr. Warren's claimed that she much preferred a silent house. He visited one day and in the space of an hour heard the cuckoo clock chime and cuckoo four times; in addition to that, he heard three different windup clocks ticking away here and there—one that bonged on the hour—as well as the family's loquacious parakeet, who chattered away during all but about five minutes of Dr. Warren's visit. He also noticed that the refrigerator snored. In short, this woman's background noise was not TV, radio, or player, but rather clocks, a bird, and the refrigerator.

Some people become downright defensive when the topic of white noise comes up. They always have been taught that you turn off the TV or radio if you're not listening. Besides, everyone knows noise is distracting, right?

In summary, what background sound level do you prefer, deep down inside?

Now think back to the questionnaire. Question 12 reflects one of the best tests of attention span for adults—church.

If you visit the ruined church at Tumacacori National Monument in southern Arizona, you can step into a quiet, cavernous sanctuary that once served Indians in the area. It's one of Padre Eusebio Kino's chain of missions extending from Mexico to the California coast. Dirt floor. No pews, no chairs, no benches, except for the priest's use. The worshipers stood, sat, or knelt in the dirt.

Today, we prefer padded pews. Many churches follow the worship precept "kneel to pray, stand to praise, and sit for instruction." Many others sit the whole time, even for the songs. Physical limitations aside—some people simply cannot stand for protracted lengths of time—most people benefit from moving a little. Most ADD people, children especially, benefit from moving a whole lot.

The service at Tumacacori two hundred years ago would be right up the alley for an ADD child, even for an ADD adult. It would drive a person like Gunther nuts. How would it strike you? Do you wish your church service allowed more movement—standing up, sitting down, perhaps walking to the altar for Communion rather than accepting the elements while seated? Or do you prefer it the way it is?

In summary, do you pay attention better when you're moving around or sitting still?

How about question 11? The person who prefers words, speaking, and hearing—approaching the world in auditory ways—will gravitate toward the phone for keeping in contact with friends and family members. The visually oriented person will prefer letters or E-mail. Which are you?

Let's say you have to think fast and well, as question 9 indicates. No time to follow Momma's teaching of old or to do what you wish your kids would do. Where in your home are you likely to end up to write a letter or report? Keep that scenario in mind for later.

Finally, question 10, answered honestly, reflects your real preferences and therefore comes as close to your comfort zone as you're likely to get. Casual reading does not carry the burden of propriety that "important" work does. Where do you end up when you let it all hang out?

Keeping all this tucked in the back of your mind, now analyze your child.

Analyzing Your Child's Comfort Zone

Gunther would answer the first six questions of our quiz with "yes" and on the seventh say "less than one." Then he might add in undertone, "Disgusting!" But then again he might backpedal a bit. "The one about the lights, question 3. No, William doesn't turn on all the lights. That's John. William just forgets to turn them off."

The first six questions are designed to get you thinking about your child's natural preferences for light level, noise level, distraction level, even temperature level. Rather than just rotely looking at each question, use them to build a composite picture of what you think your child's comfort level is. We remind you that it is easy to simply project your own preferences onto your child. Avoid that!

Does your child prefer some surrounding noise or seem indifferent to it? Does he or she prefer sitting up to sprawling or vice versa? Like it warmer, cooler, or the same as the usual house temperature? Move a lot, move about a "normal" amount, or seem sluggish?

When William roamed as he read his textbook, he was in his comfort zone. The antithesis of comfort to him was sitting in the kind of chair his dad used. Amy did not just prefer her music and sprawl; she *needed* them to function well. But her dad absolutely could not see that because her surroundings were nowhere near his comfort zone. See how it works?

Now compare your child's sphere of comfort with your own. Is your child primarily auditory (in love with the phone, the TV, noise) or visual (in love with books and, again, TV)? Do you and your child share this preference?

Keep in mind that there is also a matter of degree. Most people will find profound differences within their preferences—a little noise is all right but not rap at eighty decibels, or vice versa.

Now we're going to build an environment for the child to work in. Since you know about your own preferences, you are armed against the trap of insinuating your preferences into the child's world. This will be your child's comfort zone—*not* yours! Proceed with extreme caution in this regard.

Building a Good Environment for Your ADD Child

A caveat: ADD kids differ within their group as much as any other groups of kids differ, but ADD kids tend to have certain preferences. We repeat: *They tend to.* Your ADD child may differ completely from what we'll be talking about below. We'll be describing the majority ADD child, not necessarily your ADD child. If it does not fit well, do not impose upon your child an environment that other ADD kids might prefer. First and foremost, you must listen and observe. Listen and observe. Listen and observe!

Sound is one of the easiest elements to manipulate.

Sound

William Steinfelder liked his rap music cranked up so high his hair vibrated. Amy Eglund didn't need a violent number of decibels (her father, being a silence lover, tended to overestimate loudness), but she did like noise. If it didn't surround her, she created it. Andrew made noise at every opportunity.

Most ADD kids need and prefer surrounding noise. They work better with noise around them. But there is noise and there is distraction. Most ADD kids don't mind being distracted, particularly when they are being distracted away from boring, odious tasks—chores or schoolwork, for example. Song lyrics are distracting if a child is trying to read text. Lyrics are somewhat less distracting if the task at hand is sums or something physical, like cutting out pictures for a poster.

TV sound is usually distracting because it is designed specifically to hold one's attention. Its sole purpose is to distract a person away from anything else and bring his or her attention to the TV set. Radio commercials are distracting for much the same reason. A nice alternative, if your child likes radio, is to allow a stretch and some movement during most commercials. Let the commercials be the break signal, especially if it's an FM station (fewer interruptions, by and large).

Gunther, on the advice of Jana Carella, decided to allow William some noise. It grated Gunther's soul to give in on that point, but anything was worth a try. (Well, almost anything.) Gunther encouraged William to try out different kinds of music that did not have words for use when studying text. Upon Jana's ardent counsel, Gunther let rap during math remain an option.

William didn't like any suggestion Gunther put forth. Then they found a quirky old Philadelphia Symphony recording of snatches of classical pieces done to a strong rock beat. William died laughing. How corny! How dumb! How quaint! Ha-ha-ha-ha-ha!

William must have listened to that record constantly for a solid month.

Another environmental factor that is easily manipulated is light.

Light

The quality and quantity of light are amazingly important in an ADD child's world. As a general rule, ADD kids prefer indirect, subdued light, but one certainly doesn't need ADD in order to appreciate soft lighting. In her youth Beth Mulroney had spread her work out on the living room floor not just because she liked to see it all at once but because the light was diffuse. She didn't know it then. She didn't know it now, in fact, until she and Jody Capehart got to talking in detail about Beth's comfort zone.

Forget about the admonitions most sources make to "provide the student with a strong light over the left shoulder." The ADD student won't do well with it. Rather, try lights in the corner, or use a gooseneck lamp aimed at the wall. In any case, assiduously avoid overhead fluorescents. They often contribute to increased overactivity and deteriorating behavior.

Temperature is not nearly as easy to alter.

Temperature

ADD kids are particularly sensitive to temperature. If your child comes home complaining that the house is too warm or too cold, the appropriate response is not, "Nonsense. It's just right." It's just right for you, perhaps, but the child's needs differ. If possible, allow the child an area where he or she can have it as warm or as cool as he or she wishes. Adjusting the whole house to the child's preference is generally not practical. More importantly, the child must learn to coexist with everyone else.

A household cannot always limit distractions, either.

General Busyness (Distractions)

A major factor in the lives of ADD kids that particularly intrigues Jody Capehart is hypersensory acuity. *Acuity* means sharpness, and *hypersensory* means overly sensitive. In essence, kids, ADD kids especially, take in too much information through their senses. Sight, hearing, touch, taste, smell—it all works overtime, loading them with too many sensations and things to notice. Then it all scrambles, all receives nearly equal attention, all bombards the child's thoughts. That overload occurs pretty easily.

ADD kids need a certain degree of hypersensory acuity. They work best, as we shall see, when they're learning (especially in school) through more than one sense; the kinesthetic mode, we call it. Somehow, the parent has to strike a balance between overloading the child and underloading, so to speak. Unfortunately, there's no real way to explain it, let alone do it. Manipulating the surroundings, the environment, is the only way to come close to balancing the child's world, however.

One rule of thumb—and the first step of any course of action—is to watch the child closely. What seems to distract him or her the easiest? What does not seem to jump in front of the child's attention as quickly?

After observation, the second rule of thumb is to create an environment that minimizes distractions without looking sterile or institutional. We're talking about a lot of experimentation here, trial and error until child and parents together figure out what kind of surroundings are needed to help keep the child's focus from flitting. It's hard to do.

Some things to look upon with suspicion are:

- Posters, especially big sports posters, and pictures
- Bright prints in curtains and spreads
- Moving things—fish in a goldfish bowl, lava lamps, toys or mobiles that move on the slightest breeze
- Windows, particularly if they open onto a scene with movement, such as a street, a park, a tree frequented by birds
- Mirrors, especially large ones
- People or animals in the room or nearby where they can be seen or heard. For example, a hamster can be terribly distracting rattling around in its cage rearranging its bedding and its stores of seed, for it both moves and makes random noise. If John is shooting

baskets against the front of the garage while William is trying to study—hearing the incessant thuds of the dribbled ball and the thunks of the ball hitting the backboard and garage wall—William isn't going to get a thing done.

A particularly busy house, such as one decorated elaborately in the Victorian style, is probably not an easy environment for a distractible ADD kid. This is not to say that Mom and Dad ought to redo the house. Not at all. It does suggest, though, that perhaps the child can have a place—an intact room if possible—that does not offer so much to trigger hypersensory acuity.

Viveca Eglund would wrinkle her nose at that. Her home is done faithfully in 1885 Victorian. Beaded curtains, tasseled lamps, lush Oriental rugs, even the picture molding a foot below the high ceiling—the place swims in detail. Viveca's kitchen stove is electric burner units mounted inside a rebuilt Queen Range wood stove; even the biscuit warmer on the stovepipe looks real. People who visit gasp in wonder and suggest an eight-page spread in *House Beautiful*.

As they began to work with Amy's possible ADD, the Eglunds observed that she spent most of her time in the den. Fully paneled, the basement room served as a storm cellar (Peter Eglund believed in being prepared) and was the only place in the house not done in mid-Victorian. Here sat the TV set, the easy chair, and the hassock—Amy's natural habitat. So the Eglunds further simplified the den's decor, removing a number of large pictures from the wall, and painted it a gentle pastel.

Amy's bedroom with its canopy four-poster bed became more a showplace than a living space. She hardly went there anymore, preferring to sleep on a daybed in the den. Her mother was happy; she could put Amy's bedroom in order and leave its door open, converting it from a cluttered eyesore into one more showpiece room. They just never invited anyone down to the basement.

If only improving the child's environment meant nothing more than simplifying it, but it's not that simple. There's still the matter of background noise, conducive lighting, and controlled distractions. Remember that the child works best with some background commotion. Amy liked her TV, William needed his rap, Andrew worked with anything at all.

We generally recommend against allowing television as a distraction. Television programs are very carefully crafted to catch and hold attention, with extremely rapid changes of camera shots and scenes, compelling set design, and lots of motion and laughter. The ADD child is, excuse the expression, a perfect sucker for that kind of attention-grabber.

Peter allowed TV mostly because it was already so much a part of Amy's life. Beth decided to cut Andrew off cold turkey. Gunther didn't like the TV blaring while William tried to do homework or chores but was only minimally successful in curtailing it. Each parent-child team must work out tailored TV rules of their own. But do work them out.

Removing and minimizing distractions extends not just to decor but to the spatial arrangement of furniture and open areas.

Arrangement

Halfway through his second year of grade school, Andrew Mulroney got his own office. Mom had her office at the realty business, and now Andrew had his. The casual observer probably wouldn't recognize it as an office; a stranger might call it a cubicle, or even a cubbyhole.

Based upon pictures and diagrams in books Jody Capehart provided, Beth created a tiny "room" with light pastel walls. It was roughly cubed, six feet high (two feet lower than her ceiling) by six wide by six deep. It was walled on three sides and tucked into the corner of the living room. With the help of a neighbor who was handy with tools, she built one shelflike desk that just fit Andrew when he sat in a chair. On the opposite cubicle wall she built a shelflike desk that just fit Andrew when he was not sitting; it was a desk he could stand at.

For his birthday, Andrew received a boom box with separating speakers. The handyman cut just the right-sized holes in the cubicle wall to fit the speakers so he could enjoy built-in stereo sound. This was fancy stuff! Under the higher of the two desks, Beth installed a file drawer in which to put school supplies, handy but out of sight.

Andrew always had a great deal of trouble sitting still. With his cubicle he could now sit at his desk or stand up at his desk. Many times in the months that followed, Beth would see him standing at his desk, finishing his math problems, his feet shuffling and fidgeting beneath him.

Most of all, this was exclusively Andrew's space. He rated his own office. He was special!

Beth Mulroney had built that cubicle for Andrew in part so he could work more effectively, but also so she could keep an eye on him. She dared not do otherwise, even for a second. The cubicle was perfect; there he'd be, out in the living room in easy view, oblivious to the fact that he was being monitored. He had found his comfort zone.

Similarly, Amy Eglund took to the basement room like a rhino to a wallow. This was a place of her own that did not look like something off an 1885 postcard. She always felt like she ought to be wearing a bustle dress when she was upstairs. But down here there were no windows, no frills, no people bustling around. She felt secure and cozy; she had found her comfort zone.

Gunther and his William had a little more trouble adjusting. All right, let's say a lot more trouble.

On his third visit to Dr. Warren, Gunther grumbled, "I never thought I'd be doing something like this, a child's exercise." He perched in a chair in Dr. Warren's office, working at the little desk Dr. Warren hardly ever sits at ("I need it to hold the phone," he is fond of explaining), drawing the layout of the Steinfelder home. He studied his diagram a few moments, erased a line and moved it over, then handed it to Dr. Warren.

Moments later, sprawled out on the floor with a beanbag lap desk, William turned in his diagram of the house.

Dr. Warren held the drawings next to each other for a moment and then lay them aside. "You are here today, Mr. Steinfelder—incidentally, sir, I invite you to sit in the wingback. It's much more comfortable—in order to put together a plan for altering William's home environment."

Gunther crossed to the wingback and settled in. "And that grates on me. I should think William could adapt to the home he has, not the reverse."

"He has adapted to it—or at least he has tried to. I'm not going to ask you and Mrs. Steinfelder to turn your home upside down. But right now it is exclusively yours, and yours alone. Yet five diverse people live there."

"And a dog," William added, grinning.

"He isn't allowed in the house." Gunther looked sullen.

"And a dog." Dr. Warren continued. "You want William's room to meet your expectations, not his. You insist his presence in the rest of the house meet your expectations, not his. Do you see what I'm getting at? If we would adjust William's environment to better suit his learning needs, he should have an area, perhaps just a small area, that meets *his* expectations."

Gunther nodded. "If William's room met his expectations, it would be full of detritus armpit high. He's a slob about keeping his room in order."

"So?"

Gunther stared.

Dr. Warren met the stare casually. "It is William's room. Can he not live as he wishes in it?"

"*Yessss!*" William punched a jubilant fist skyward.

"Disaster. It would be disaster."

"To you who has a clear concept of what *your* comfort zone is. Not to William." Dr. Warren sat forward. "Mrs. Carella, with whom you've spoken—and that's excellent, Mr. Steinfelder! I applaud you for seeking wise counsel—explained the results of her tests."

"Yes, but—" Gunther stopped. No more *yes buts*. They did no good anyway. "She thinks that William's differences can be exploited. Do you?"

"Absolutely." And he drove home his point. "Based on what we now know about William, let's alter his study methods, his micro-environment—which is to say let's give him a place he can truly call his own without being criticized, meals and food perhaps somewhat, his schedule, and your expectations for him. Let's work on altering those things to suit his needs. He's nearly an adult. In a few years he'll be on his own. In those few years you can help him learn how to meet the world on its terms and succeed, how to get along."

"He's certainly not to that point yet." Gunther sat back deeper in the wingback. He could tell this was going to be a long, long session. "Incidentally, why the diagrams of the house?"

"Curiosity, in part—not to tell me more about the home but about the two of you." Dr. Warren picked up Gunther's drawing. "You have a gift for precision. I am going to assume from the proportions I see here that your diagram is very nearly accurate. It looks right. But notice you had to move this wall. You drew William's room too big at first and had to change it. William's room looms very large in your life. Either you enjoy that room or it's a thorn in your side."

Gunther chuckled. "Guess which."

"Now William's drawing here is quite good. Notice that it's very similar to yours in proportion. You have an excellent eye, William, and I see you spend a lot of time in the attached garage. It's your favorite place. Your garage sketch is bigger than your father's and far more detailed."

William's eyes widened.

"Now that you mention it, if you need him he's usually out there fiddling around." Gunther sounded like a person who had never noticed that before.

Dr. Warren lay the pictures aside. "Let me hazard a guess. The garage is plain inside, fairly austere, extremely neat and orderly with everything in its place."

"The opposite of his room. Curious."

"Not really so unexpected. He cannot by nature organize well. Right-brained ADD kids lack organizational skills. But he appreciates organization. Only by having everything perfectly organized can he find what he wants—a tool, for instance. More than most people, ADD kids and adults have short-term memory problems. They cannot remember where they just put, say, a hammer. Unless they put it in its place, they can't find it again easily. Also, the garage offers fewer distractions if he wants to think. And it's the home of automobiles. I am going to hazard another guess—William loves cars."

"He does." Gunther nodded. "But he's too immature to drive. Too scatterbrained."

William opened his mouth, glanced at Dr. Warren, and closed it again. He and the doctor had discussed this very thing, this painful topic.

"May I suggest a covenant, Mr. Steinfelder. In two years, William will have a better level of maturity, and he will have learned some excellent coping skills if we are diligent with the adjustments we'll talk about. How about: He agrees to wait until at least his eighteenth birthday before applying for a learner's permit, and you agree to let him have a car now to work on. A fixer-upper. It needn't be licensed or insured since it will sit in your garage for two years."

William's grin spread out wide enough to accommodate a Ford bumper.

"I would rather he receive the car as a reward for shaping up."

"The learner's permit would be a satisfactory reward. The car would be an encouragement, and your son needs encouragement, Mr. Steinfelder. He's received almost none his whole life."

That's when Gunther's thought processes more or less skidded to a halt. No encouragement? Why, Gunther spent his whole fatherhood encouraging William to do better!

Hardly! He harangued. Prodded. Yelled. Insisted. Forced. Threatened. Criticized. Coerced.

But encouraged? No.

It was all Gunther could do to keep from weeping.

Mental Adjustments the Parent Must Make

Making massive shifts in permissions and thinking is hard on the parent. The parent already believed he or she was doing the best thing. Now that best thing is being tossed aside in favor of some other best thing the adult does not trust.

Gunther could not believe he was giving William permission to keep his room as he pleased. In his opinion it was nothing but an open door to wrack and ruin! Even less could he believe he would buy William a junker. However, as much as his spirit rebelled against such nonsense, his common sense told him that these professionals knew what they were talking about. They had described the problem exactly, predicted how William (and Gunther as well!) behaved in various situations, and seemed to have some answers. Gunther needed, more than anything else in the world, some answers.

Now, fresh from his visit to Dr. Warren's office, Gunther stood in the middle of William's room and looked around. It was in what Gunther would call a medium state of arrested decay. He had seen it worse; he'd seen it better.

William started pointing with the air of a tycoon building a new shopping mall. "I want to get rid of that desk lamp. In fact, I'd like to get rid of the desk. I don't—"

Gunther stared aghast. "Where would you do your homework?" Silly question. Not once had Gunther ever seen William use the desk to study. "And where would you put your computer?"

"Here. Mom showed me this." William grabbed a slick sale flyer off his unmade bed. "Modular units. They're on sale here, see? You stack them, arrange 'em any way you want. Bins and cubbyholes and look, this thing right here, it's perfect for the console and monitor and I'd have the keyboard in my lap, of course. I like these big boxes here, sort of like apple cartons. And this right here, this unit, would be perfect to stash my winter boots and stuff. All in one place. A whole wall full of these units to put stuff in."

"'All in one place' sounds like organization. You expect to get organized?"

William paused. "Well, yeah, I guess, sort of."

Against his better judgment, Gunther allowed William to move the desk, the chair, and the lamp into his little brother John's room. They bought a wall full of modular storage units—the sale price took a tiny bit of the sting out of it. On Dr. Warren's advice, William took down his Indy 500 posters. "Dr. Warren's right," William claimed. "They're sure easy to look at—too easy." He put sixty-watt bulbs in the overhead fixture and set up a gooseneck floor lamp from the garage so that it shone on a blank wall in the corner.

William's mom had taken off his closet doors so he couldn't just toss everything on the floor inside it. The closet was supposed to remain available for casual inspection, as it were. Now the doors went back on to lessen the distraction of the closet contents.

Crowed William as he looked about his revitalized room, "Man, this is living!"

His father didn't have the heart to say aloud, "If you're an anarchist."

What changes, specifically, work for most ADD children? William employed most of them—reducing distractibility, creating comfort, improving organization, and making lists and possessions accessible.

Reducing Distractibility.   More or less subconsciously, William strove to reduce distractions without making his room a sterile box. In the months ahead, a few car posters would go back up. His mom would make white curtains to mask the contents of the open cubbyholes in his wall units. Add, subtract, arrange until it seems right.

A rule of thumb might be: *"Does this grab my attention when it shouldn't?"*

William recognized that about his posters. Incidentally, he kept one wall blank, the wall with the light. When he needed to think, he faced in that direction, his back to the few remaining posters.

Often something as simple as moving a desk or chair so it faces away from a window can make a big difference. If your ADD child can have a place that is his or hers alone, put your heads together to decide how to arrange it. The child may offer some amazing insights. Listen. Advise. Allow.

Dr. Warren casually suggested limiting Nintendo time. As William thought about that, he agreed. Once he got cooking on a game, he couldn't quit. So he got rid of the Nintendo completely—foisted it off on his little sister—and set up his PC in a lower cubbyhole so he could stretch out on the floor with the keyboard. Which raises another point:

Create Comfort.   Another good rule of thumb might be: *"Does this irritate?"* The desk and lamp bothered William without his actually noticing simply because they represented a way of working that was alien to him. He improved the comfort level by removing the irritant.

Here's an important third consideration: *"Is it physically comfortable?"*

William didn't like the straight chair. He loved sprawling on his bed with its super-soft mattress. He did most of his homework on the floor and found in a thrift shop one of those beanbag lap desks for use when he was propped up on his bed.

Finally, assess the child's environment and ask yourself: *"Can it be organized?"*

Make Organization Easy.   William recognized better than anyone that when his room was the way he thought he liked it—in upheaval— he couldn't find a solitary thing. He'd call Mom in and they'd search together—until Dad put the kibosh on that. Said Dad, "He must figure out how to get his own life in order. You won't be here for him forever, Ellen."

Where does a guy turn when his mom turns away? To his girlfriend, of course. With his latest flame Mel (Amelia, in her school records), he sat down with a pencil and paper. "Okay," Mel said, "how do you clean up your room? What do you do first?"

William took the pencil and started a list. "Step by step, right? My little brother's ADD. Mom has to make these breakdown lists for him to do his chores. Okay. First you get everything off the floor and put it on your bed."

"The keyboard's attached."

"When you come to it, stick it on the shelf. Everything else goes on the bed." He wrote it down.

"Now pick up something off the bed. A shirt. Socks. Whatever. Put it away. Pick up something else up. Put it away. Understand?"

Mel took the pencil and paper from him and did the writing for a while. "Got a hamper?" she asked.

"No. Do I need one? Look. I don't want to get domestic; I just want to clean up my room."

She sighed. "You need a hamper so you don't have to leave the room, or you'll get distracted and end up doing something else. I know about these things, Will. Get a hamper."

"Okay, okay." He craned his neck to see her writing. Pretty writing, evenly spaced. "That's all you have to do?"

"Any dirty dishes and old food and stuff, put it on a pile and when everything else is put away, take the pile out to the kitchen."

"What makes you think I have dirty dishes and food?"

She looked at him.

"Okay, once in a while. So is *that* all I have to do?"

"Nope. Now you vacuum."

"Mom does that."

"You gonna call her to come vacuum for you when you're living in Anchorage or someplace?"

"I'll hire an Eskimo."

"You'll do it yourself. Then you dust. Start at one side of the room and work your way all the way around the walls to where you started." She paused. "Do you do windows?"

"Now wait a minute! Let's not get carried away."

"That's about it, then."

Because William's room was almost all open floor space, his list served him well. He had few complications to distract him, except perhaps for the keyboard. He taped the list to the back of his door and used it every week for two years. The list outlasted the romance by eighteen months.

Make Lists and Possessions Accessible.   Putting his list on the door served William well by sticking it right under his nose where he could be reminded. He ended up with a couple of other breakdown lists also before too long. And Mel's point about the hamper is well taken. If William had to leave the room with his dirty clothes, he could easily forget what he was supposed to be doing. Besides, the hamper, sitting beside the door, provided him a specific, convenient place to put dirty clothes. If he were to develop any sort of organization, he would need specific convenient places for everything.

Andrew Mulroney got into lists in a big way also. However, he received colored, metallic star stickers when he completed his lists. Because Beth's two-bedroom apartment was so cramped, the place always looked cluttered. She had to put Andrew's lists on the bathroom door because he had a shoe bag hanging on his. Their single bathroom was the one place, other than the kitchen, where he was sure to encounter his lists, and they had to be right under his nose.

She made sure he had a list with his chores broken down into increments. Following Mrs. Capehart's advice, she provided him with boxes for clothes and toys—places that were easy to access and easy to toss things into. This greatly facilitated cleanup and made things easier for him to find too.

He also had a list for when he got up in the morning, starting with "Get out of bed." Earning a star for that first essential step gave his day a good start. As Andrew got older, his room would take on more of his character and less of his mom's until the day came, as he reached twelve or so, when his room would be his own and the lists would have left the bathroom and come to live with him.

This environmental approach is helpful not just for ADD children but for children with Tourette's syndrome and for some other disorders, such as manic depression. This book does not address those conditions in detail, other than to mention that ADD kids may also have a propensity for these other problems. We bring up the point simply to illustrate in one more way how much difference altering surroundings can make.

As Beth, Gunther, and Peter all came to terms with their children's uniqueness, they found themselves running into numerous articles, books, and papers on additional ways to reduce the effects of ADD without the use of drugs. Some, of course, are excellent; some useless. Let us look next at some of these methods.

OTHER TREATMENT OPTIONS

*P*EOPLE ROUTINELY PAY to receive advice. Beth Mulroney noted ruefully that there are times when some advisers ought to have to pay dearly for the privilege of dispensing advice. Maybe it would cut some of the hooey. She sat amid a gaggle of mothers in her PTA group and listened with a manufactured smile as storms of suggestions raged around her ears.

"Attention deficit, eh? Now my Lennie," insisted Mrs. Plummer, "climbs the walls if he gets sugar. A real sugar high almost instantly! Never ever give the child sugar, and he'll be cured."

"Maybe, but don't forget wheat. My Sandra," Cara chimed in, "is allergic to wheat products. She just goes hyper if she gets wheat products. I'd keep your son off wheat if I were you, Beth. Rice cakes—give him rice cakes."

Another mother cut in: "Bleh! Rice cakes taste like overcooked cardboard. I'd worry more about tomatoes if I were you. Do you realize what raw tomatoes do to a child?"

Another said, "Fresh vegetables are never the villain. It's all the additives. You have to prepare strictly fresh vegetables and meats, or you get all these additives. I always cook from scratch. Fresh vegetables. Not even frozen ones. Some of the frozen ones have sulfites, you know."

"Sulfites? It's a bunch of malarkey that they're bad for you. Molasses. I swear by blackstrap molasses. Besides, the best molasses contains sulfur, and there's nothing better than sulfur for cleaning out a sluggish system."

Andrew's system was anything but sluggish. Beth left the meeting with the clear impression that everything you eat is going to both cure and destroy you. But what if there was a grain of truth in what the mothers suggested? Was Beth, and especially Andrew, missing out on something big here?

Food requires careful consideration.

Adjusting the Menu

Some years ago, the Feingold Diet and a few others came to prominence as corrective measures for dealing with ADD. The proponents of these measures claimed that food additives, the chemicals in tomatoes, certain food colors, and a few other things were the cause of ADD in children.

As we've watched Feingold graduates, so to speak—the kids who were treated through diet—mature down through the years, we've not often been able to see many significant differences. In other words, it appears that special diets do not work for the vast majority of children upon whom they are tried, particularly in the long term.

However. On a few children who adhere to them, genuine and dramatic improvement accrues. There are indeed children who do better with diet management, and there are a few who do remarkably better, even as there are a great number who do not.

Allergies?

Children who show through careful testing that they are allergic to certain food substances, chemicals, or combinations may, because of the allergy, behave similarly to kids with ADD. This similarity has led to several different lines of research and treatment aimed at reducing the child's contact with those foods and other substances.

An allergy is not just sneezing and sniffling. It can also evidence itself as nervousness, excessive activity, rashes and itching, crankiness and irritability, and other indications. Tests are not foolproof, but they can be extremely helpful in discovering the kinds of things the child may be reacting to adversely. Sometimes an allergy is discovered more by guess and by golly than by scientific testing. Keep in mind that if you suspect that your child is being adversely affected by a food—let's say wheat, as in the case Beth's friend Cara noted—the child must remain totally off that food for at least two weeks before any kind of significant difference will begin to emerge. Food allergies are slow to show and slow to go.

One of the biggest food suspects, with no connection to allergy as such, is sugar.

Too Much Sugar?

Most children do better if their sugar intake is limited, and this is certainly true of ADD kids. Sugar does several things when it enters the system. As the sugar molecules pass through membranes into the blood, the pancreas is excited into producing insulin, the enzyme responsible for metabolizing sugar. That means it turns sugar from one chemical (all foods, you know, are nothing more than chemicals) into other chemicals plus energy.

Hit the system with a walloping dose of sugar and you get a walloping dose of insulin—in some persons, too much insulin. Normally, the blood carries a certain level of sugar around to feed cells that need it. An overabundance of insulin can metabolize too much sugar—the incoming sugar plus the sugars that are supposed to remain available in the blood. As the blood-sugar level dives, the body produces a hormone, adrenaline, as a reaction.

Adrenaline that is present when it isn't needed can cause excessive activity, anger, fear, excitement, impulsivity, and aggressiveness. Sound familiar?

Apparently, then, a sugar jag occurs in some kids as a secondary reaction to sugar intake and does not influence at all the other kids—the ones whose insulin balance can handle it.

Incidentally, there is almost no difference metabolically between refined sugar, raw sugar, turbinado, honey, molasses, other such sweeteners, and even certain artificial sweeteners. The kind of sugar may have nutrients and other added chemicals, but sugars are sugars. Sucrose is sucrose; on food labels "corn syrup" is still sugar. They all pass through the membranes into the bloodstream, and all trigger insulin (yes, even certain artificial sweeteners that mimic some sugar properties).

So we cannot say out of hand, "Diets don't matter." Normally they do not matter very much. But then there's that special case, the child whose problems can be ameliorated through a change of diet. Food management helps all kids, though, in other ways.

Better Regulation of Intake?

When Andrew gets home from school, his Ritalin has worn off and he's hungry. Says Gunther of William, "Every time his elbow bends, his mouth flies open." Arriving home, Amy slams the backdoor and opens the fridge door all in one sweeping motion. Amy at twelve is entering her hungry stage and William at sixteen is starting to taper off (but not so you could notice from the grocery bill).

A teenaged boy coming up through puberty will burn four thousand calories daily. Amy will burn twenty-five hundred to three thousand. The overactive ADD kid burns calories to the max, so it is wise to provide those calories rather than assume, "The kid is eating too much! He/she will be fat as a hog in ten years if we don't cut him/her back now!" That's faulty reasoning. Snacks freely offered are usually appropriate for ADD kids, who burn energy in prodigious quantities. We recommend against candy and soft drinks as snacks. Whether or not Mrs. Plummer is right in her assessment, kids just don't need lots of sugar, even if their systems seem to handle it just fine.

Adequate nutrition helps the child control ADD by providing enough of the nutrients essential for good cell replacement. Incidentally, a low-fat diet in a child without a weight problem is not advisable. We are not recommending an excess of fat and cholesterol, but remember that fats are a major energy source, and kids this age burn energy by the barrel. Fats are also important nutrients in nerve activity and metabolism. Depriving a young child of sufficient fats can actually reduce intelligence.

The child who is short on energy is not going to do well with chores and homework. Even an ordinary child in whom ADD is not a factor does not do well when he or she is tired or hungry. Weariness and hunger, including temporary just-before-dinner hunger, bother the ADD child even more.

Food management includes getting the food into the child. With some overly active ADD kids, sitting still long enough to eat a meal can be a chore—perhaps even impossible. We recommend letting the child come to the table after everyone else is seated, barely in time to join in the blessing. The child can then load a plate, start the meal, and finish it in the kitchen standing at the counter. It's amazing how much better some kids eat when allowed that simple adjustment of schedule and habit.

In fact, may we suggest letting ADD kids, in particular the overly active ones, eat more or less on demand. Within reason, they seem to know when their body needs fuel. Minimizing sweets and soft drinks also minimizes the tendency to eat sugary stuff for its own sake rather than for need.

Related to food management is possible allergy management, particularly because many allergies are food related. There are those who lean heavily toward allergies as a source of ADD or ADD-like problems, and others who discount it. Proceed with caution.

Food management is not by any means the only alternative. Some would say that Christians have been robbed of one of the alternatives popular at the moment, biofeedback. Essentially it helps calm the child by teaching the child to calm himself or herself.

Adjusting the Calm

For Noah, God set His sign in the sky, a rainbow. He declared it a token of His promise. Once upon a time, Christians were proud of God-given rainbows. And then persons of New Age persuasion adopted the rainbow into their own symbolism and now Christians, aghast, refuse to have anything to do with prismatic arches. Yes, we've been robbed (just like we've been robbed of some other thing. Once upon a time, for instance, *gay* meant "cheery." Try using it that way now).

Oriental religions and New Agers did much the same thing to the fine, old Christian practice of meditation. Christians by and large don't even pronounce the word anymore, seeing it as something that Far Eastern gurus do while looking at their navels. Contemplative orders in the church sort of keep mum about what they do. That's so sad. Meditation used to be a mainstay of piety.

It is also, in a larger sense, the mainstay of biofeedback. Most brain activity other than energy metabolism, oxygen use, and other chemical maintenance functions, is electrical in nature. While it thinks, the brain produces several kinds of waves detectable with the appropriate electronic sensors. Two of these, theta and beta waves, figure strongly in ADD. Beta waves are faster in that their periodicity is shorter; theta waves are slower. Brain waves in ADD kids are a different mix of beta and theta than are the waves of most people.

In the modern version of biofeedback being used to help ADD kids, a computer screen shows the child the patterns the brain is producing. The child then performs controlling methods to alter the pattern and bring calm. This "quieting response" the child learns does two good things. It quiets the excessive or aggressive activity. Just as importantly, it also teaches the child that a person *can* achieve control. The ADD child, who needs immediate gratification, sees right there on the monitor that he or she can make a difference.

Biofeedback, particularly feedback that is electronically augmented, requires a professional teacher. It can't be done from a book.

Says Dr. Warren, "There is growing research on biofeedback, but the computer-aided system being used on kids hasn't been around long enough to see how it works in the long run. There is certainly no reason not to try it. It is not satanic or New Age or anything of that sort. It is a tool. Of what value, we don't yet really know."

Neither do we know precisely what ADD is or whether rather it is a suite of confusingly different neurological phenomena. Most approaches, including drugs, treat the symptoms rather than the underlying cause because so little is known about underlying causes. Some persons are working with what could be a key to the basic wiring, vision and hearing. Researchers have noted that hearing, vision, and inner-ear problems are some of the wiring differences found in ADD kids and they're tackling the problem from that end, by adjusting intake from the primary senses.

Adjusting the Senses

Since babyhood, Andrew had been plagued with ear infections. From "Don't worry. He'll outgrow it," to "We could insert a plastic tube, but he's borderline; it probably wouldn't do much good," various pediatricians casually analyzed Andrew's problem. Beth, on the other hand, had to live with it.

Inner-ear problems are not just a nuisance. Many believe that all central nervous system functions tie either directly or indirectly to the inner ear. Often ADD children and other kids with learning problems have lots of inner-ear infections. Their balance, which is governed by the inner ear, may be off. Rather than "Yes, they're present" or "No, they're not," inner-ear symptoms span a broad spectrum from slight to extreme.

The most extreme end of the spectrum expresses itself as autism. The autistic child takes in so much auditory information, even to hearing blood roaring through the veins, that he or she hears what we either disregard or fail to detect at all. Moreover, these kids cannot focus on some sounds to the exclusion of others—exactly the same regulatory problem ADD kids face but to a much heavier degree. Autistics don't make eye contact, trying unconsciously to block out the visual in an attempt to balance the overwhelming auditory sensations. They tend to gravitate toward anything offering white noise. ADD kids usually function better on white noise.

Some feel that treating the inner ear and helping it improve balance and regulation can alleviate ADD.

The middle ear, the part that hears, also plays a role. As any parent of an ADD kid will tell you, listening is not hearing. The kid hears fine; he or she doesn't listen. Hearing is simply picking up sound. Listening is focusing on one sound and dismissing others which may even be louder or more persistent.

There are certain training methods available from specialists in hearing and listening that use sound itself to help children learn to focus their listening. In essence, these methods teach the ear to focus, to control. They also incorporate the motor skills and balance handled by the inner ear, for the whole system works in concert.

As some children are learning to focus with their ears, others are learning to better control their eyes. Another line of research and treatment involves visual patterning and scanning. Many times, an ADD child does not see the world, literally, the way most people do (this is true also of certain other learning disorders). There are measurable differences in the wiring itself—the neurological makeup. We might even call this visual focus "listening with the eyes."

Essentially, the treatment consists of analyzing the child's brain waves as they are affected by vision—what the child's brain scan looks like compared to what most others' would if looking at the same things. Then the child is fitted with glasses that correct not the external image but what the brain "sees." The neurological focus. As conventional glasses correct the eyes' lenses, so these send modified images to improve the patterns in the brain.

This is cutting-edge stuff without a lot of corroborating evidence as yet that it works well and consistently in the long run. Time will tell.

The problem, of course, is that we can make observations all day, but we still don't know what is really going on here. We detect that blood flow to the frontal lobe differs in ADD kids, but is that cause or effect? Listening patterns differ. Visual patterns differ. The inner ear doesn't do the same things other people's do. Which is influencing what and to what degree?

We are probably on the verge of major breakthroughs. Until then we can do much in addition to altering the child's environment, proceeding with new ideas in treatment and possibly resorting to drug intervention. For we have discovered a great deal about how different people think and learn, and ADD kids are profiting greatly from this knowledge.

Let's look now at learning styles, at how our brains handle input, and how that can help an ADD child (maybe you too!).

LEARNING
STYLE
AND
HEMISPHERICITY

*H*ERE'S AN EXPERIMENT for
you. Step into an open doorway
between indoors and outdoors. Close your eyes. No peeking! Now
keep track of what's happening in both worlds. What traffic, motor
and pedestrian, is passing? Who's walking down the hall behind you?
Anyone cooking? Is someone's car spewing exhaust and in need of a
tune-up? Any animals nearby? Do the buses use diesel or propane? Is
it warmer or cooler outside than in? Any breeze? What time of day as
measured by the angle of the sun (you must *feel* this without opening
your eyes)? Maybe it's raining. If clouds hide the sun, what other nonvi-
sual cues to direction are available?

Those of you who are blind will find the exercise no challenge at
all. You do this routinely. Sighted persons, though, usually depend
almost exclusively upon sight, using hearing as a secondary backup and
paying hardly any attention to touch and smell as dependable information sources. Closing the eyes gives visually oriented persons a small
taste of a world they do not normally pay much attention to.

If you stand on a street corner in downtown Tacoma, Washington,
the pedestrian signals will chirp and cuckoo at you. Not birds on the
signals but the signals themselves. Blind pedestrians can hear the signals
they cannot see and cross the street safely. One direction is a chirp, the

other a cuckoo, so you can cross to the correct signal. Society makes all sorts of adjustments to help the blind, and gladly so. But society is not nearly so accommodating to people who are visually impaired in other than physical ways.

Visually impaired people whose eyes work just fine? Yes. Now you're talking about some ADD kids. And people who are visually oriented don't even know this other world exists. It has to do with differences in learning styles. Here's the way this conundrum operates.

The Differences in Learning Styles

Let's go back to the two circles Jody Capehart drew for Beth Mulroney, the outer one the shore of a lake and the inner one an island. Wealthy people choppered over from shore to island. Who knows? Perhaps particularly adventurous ones could parachute in. Others boated. They might have had rowboats, yachts, sailing vessels, canoes, or a camouflage-color, square-prowed, duck hunter's boat. Despite the variety of conveyances, only two styles pertained—you flew or you floated. You couldn't walk.

. . . Unless you were a pearl diver. Breathing apparatus, weighted belt, and lead boots to keep you on the bottom—you could cross that way—trudging across the bottom of the lake.

Let's apply it to a child's learning style. Remember that we're not just talking about school. A child learns constantly, every waking hour. This is how he or she takes in the world.

For about 40 percent of us, our learning style is visual. Let's equate those people with the boaters. They look at pictures and at printed words. They scan graphs. The information enters their minds quickly and comfortably, and their brains process it. There may be a variety of conveyances, but they're all afloat. All visual.

Then there are the auditory learners who gather information primarily through hearing and speaking. Their eyes serve as backup. Let's say these are the folks who arrive by air; after all, there are fewer of them and sounds are airborne, so it fits. The auditory learner depends more upon the lecture than upon the textbook. He or she talks about it instead of reading about it. The auditory learner picks up spoken instructions quickly and well.

Ah, but then there are the pearl divers. Step by step they slog across the goopy lake bed. They feel the tug of currents and the clinging grasp of the mud. They see things no one else can, though the view might be murky. They experience a close, enclosing world all their own. And eventually, they *will* get there.

These are learners who are wired in such a way that they depend primarily upon touch and taste and feel. Their learning style is not primarily visual. Sometimes not even primarily auditory. We call them tactile learners. Hands-on learners. These are the kids who have to touch everything, who love to manipulate the physical world, whose hands are as important to the intake of information as are their eyes. The pearl divers might also be kinesthetic learners, very similar in style to the tactile folks.

People who fly and people who float simply do not understand the pearl divers. To them, learning is auditory or visual. Period. Sometimes the pearl divers wish they could fly or float, but they do well with what they have and are generally affable. The only real problem is that no one else accommodates their special needs. Few even realize the pearl divers are down there.

And that sometimes includes teachers.

Here again is a generalization with many exceptions: By and large, ADD kids will be auditory and/or tactile/kinesthetic learners. The visual learners are a minority. Also generally speaking, *if* an ADD kid's learning style is accommodated and served, the ADD child will prove to be just as bright as anyone else despite a miserable showing in school and an appearance of being dull-witted at home. They are pearl divers, and to the world floating or flying up above, they don't look so good. But they're actually doing splendidly in their own way.

All this fits in, you'll recall, with the tack some researchers are taking involving children's ability to listen and to focus visually. Let's review the primary kinds of learning styles. As you did with comfort zones, analyze your child's learning style but also analyze your own. It is very important to do so for this reason: Most teachers, and that certainly includes parents in the home, assume their own learning style is the only good way to learn, and they tend to impose it upon the children. If the child learns in a different style, friction and failure result. So it behooves the parent to understand how he or she ticks so as to avoid imposing his or her particular style upon the child.

What Are Your Preferences?

Let's explore your own preferences. First, answer these questions from your own viewpoint. Then go down through them again and respond from what you know to be your child's viewpoint, as if your child were answering. If your child is old enough—seven or older, perhaps—do it together. Make certain it is the child's actual view and not your own! It's so, *so easy,* to project one's own preferences upon another. If your response is "all of the above," go with your first impulse.

1. My favorite part of the newspaper is:
   ____ a. Comics.
   ____ b. Crossword puzzle.
   ____ c. Major front-page news and Op-Ed.
   ____ d. I don't read the paper much.
2. I'm in a modern science museum. I gravitate toward:
   ____ a. The kids' section with hands-on fun experiments.
   ____ b. Charts and graphs. They make all the info quick to grasp.
   ____ c. Models and taxidermy mounts, especially dioramas.
   ____ d. Those displays where you push a button and the appropriate light lights up on a panel, or colored water swirls to show tidal rip, or something like that.
   ____ e. Those mini-video presentations here and there.
3. The cuckoo clock in the hall stops. No ticks, no cuckoos. There is no repair shop in the area that can help. So I:
   ____ a. Find a library book or pamphlet on clock repair.
   ____ b. Take it apart. What's to lose? It isn't running.
   ____ c. Get on the phone to a guy in Kansas who can talk me through the repair.
   ____ d. Wish I could find an exploded drawing to work from.
   ____ e. Fiddle with it, hanging extra weights on the chain and stuff, hoping to get it running again.
4. I'm lost and afoot in a strange city. Pretending I cannot simply call a taxi to deliver me to my destination and the bus system isn't an option, how might I orient myself and find my way?
   ____ a. Walk a couple blocks to learn how the street signs orient you, and try to guess my location from the street numbers.
   ____ b. Ask people the way until I get where I want to go.
   ____ c. Buy a map at the corner newsstand, sit down, and find where I am and where I want to be. *Voila!*
5. I just moved to a new state, and I have to take the driver's license exam, including the road test. If I could prepare for it any way I wanted, my favorite way would be to:
   ____ a. Read the state driver's manual through.
   ____ b. Have someone explain the rules and tell me the info.
   ____ c. Just go take the test and if I pass, fine. If I don't, I know what it will be next time.

_____ d. Sort of walk through the test beforehand, perhaps even sitting in the car and going through the required motions.

What's Your Style?

Here's where we analyze the responses.

There are as many styles of learning as there are people on the earth, but the styles tend to lump together into three or four major modality categories as we've discussed, albeit with many, many variations. (Modality means the way in which one goes about doing something, in this case, learning.) We will focus on the modality aspect of the learning style spectrum for simplicity's sake. There are other strata of information and understanding about the subject. For those who would like a more in-depth look, we have listed some resources at the end of the book.

For simplicity, we will combine two somewhat different learning styles, tactile and kinesthetic, because, although they differ, they approach life from somewhat the same ways.

Visual

So many people are primarily visual in their approach to the world that they get pretty chauvinistic about it, not accepting that there are quite a few folks who don't function like that. Gunther Steinfelder and Peter Eglund were excellent examples.

Visual learners usually read well and don't mind taking the bulk of their information from the written word. They often love crossword puzzles. They take in the whole picture when they read comics and appreciate the skilled, subtle artwork in strips like *Calvin and Hobbes, Cathy,* and of course, *Prince Valiant.*

Visual folk will check the b answer in question 1 and maybe answer e in question 2, a and d in 3, c in 4, and a in 5. Print media are their friends.

These, then, are some of the hallmarks of visual learners:

The Written Word. They use the printed page with comfort and skill. They take notes well, write things down, use charts, graphs, and maps easily, and like worksheets such as the IRS provides in its tax instruction manual. They do well with complex tests such as psychological evaluations, working quickly and thoughtfully.

Surroundings.   They generally prefer a quiet environment—Peter so enjoyed his chair out in the orchard—and they appreciate orderly surroundings, particularly around a workstation.

If Gunther had his way, William would turn off that infernal music, sit quietly at his desk, and thereby become an A student.

Auditory

Auditory folk are going to prefer whatever comes through the ears to what they get from their eyes. They'll answer e in question 2 and then depend on the audio portion of the presentation, using the pictures for backup. If it's a silent video they'll probably wander off to something else.

They'll get on the phone, choose response c in 3, ask folks for directions (answer b in question 4), and yearn for someone to explain things to them (answer b in question 5).

The Written Word.   Auditory learners prefer to read aloud and may move their lips when they read silently; they are literally listening to the written word, converting it into the heard word. They prefer taped books to print books, enjoy being read to, and don't like workbook drills. The IRS instruction manual is gibberish. (Actually that's not such a good example; many visual folk would say the same thing.)

Here's something not even the auditory learners themselves may realize: in order to complete what we might call a learning loop—the transfer of information from one source into the learner—many auditory learners have to verbalize what they are learning. They have to say it aloud, repeat it back, maybe even interrupt.

Gunther would snort at that. "If William would just be quiet long enough to hear the explanation, he'd get it."

Not true. When William was verbalizing, he was learning.

In the 1840s and 1850s at a school for the blind in New York (this was way back when Brooklyn was a hick town, incidentally), teachers used a splendid method for reaching auditory learners. Their blind students were auditory by necessity whether or not they started out that way or not. The teacher would recite the lesson aloud. The children would repeat the recitation. They thus completed the learning loop, you see, though no one thought of it that way at the time. Reciting the lessons back was the key. The next day the children would repeat the recitations of the preceding day and then go on to new material.

Auditory folk just love panels, debates, and oral storytelling. Verbal interaction is their idea of heaven.

Surroundings. Disorder doesn't often bother auditory persons. Messes, even chaos, don't interfere with hearing something new. They generally work better with background noise or music, and they remember things better when they are set to music.

Tactile/Kinesthetic

Ah, the pearl divers.

The tactile learner and the kinesthetic learner share a need to lay their hands on anything being learned. They differ in that the kinesthetic learner is into whole body movement and gross motor coordination more than the tactile person is. Tactile and kinesthetic people probably don't read the paper much. They love these modern museums with the hands-on stuff, even if they can't exactly touch them, and they will likely choose response c as well as a and d in question 2. Tactile folk will take the clock apart or try to get it to run by fooling around with it (answers b and e in question 3). The kinesthetics will choose answer a in question 4 and d in question 5 while the tactiles will like response c in question 5.

The Written Word. Print media are okay as a supplement, but tactile/kinesthetic people have trouble getting the bulk of their information that way. Since nearly all of school is geared to the printed word, it comes as no surprise that these folks look pretty dumb in class. No one notices that they are brilliant mechanically—mechanical genius is not well recognized in our society.

The visual learner may understandably get upset when the tactile/kinesthetic auto mechanic starts tearing Visual's brakes apart without consulting the shop manual. Not to worry. The mechanic will do an excellent job, working virtually on instinct to disassemble and reassemble the brakes into perfect working order. Old Visual couldn't begin to do that and simply can't imagine Tactile doing it without written help.

Surroundings. Kinesthetics do terribly under fluorescent lights. No one knows why, though there are plenty of theories. They are certain that an orderly workbench is a sign of a sick mind.

The tactile/kinesthetic doodles, bends things, doubles back the magazine or comic book he or she is reading, pulls a notice off the bulletin board to read it. The tactile/kinesthetic person is constantly touching and bumping the environment, interacting with surroundings physically.

Most tactile/kinesthetic folk are right-brained. In fact, most ADD kids are right-brained. What does that mean? Just as most people are left- or right-handed, with a smattering of ambidextrous persons, most folks prefer one hemisphere of the brain over the other. This makes a profound difference in the way ADD kids in particular relate to their world.

Hemisphericity

If you were to dissect a human brain, not an appetizing prospect, you might begin by removing the top half of the skull by cutting horizontally at about the eyebrow line and lifting the "lid." Dissect away the membranes covering the actual brain. You'd see immediately that not only is the brain not a formless blob, it's two halves, divided vertically down the middle, front to back. The left half, like half of a walnut, is pretty much its own thing, and the right half is also independent.

As you probed deeper, you'd find that the two halves are connected at their bottom (more or less behind the eyes) by a tough, hard wad called the corpus callosum. You might notice that the cerebrum, the main part of the brain—the big, obvious part—is actually separate from a smaller, less convoluted brain part in the back of the head, the cerebellum. Those two parts are separate from an inner core part, the medulla (it's hard to find from where you're looking). The whole thing then, by means of the medulla, connects into the spinal cord.

Cerebrum, cerebellum, and medulla each have different tasks to perform in serving your body. Each processes different incoming data and makes different body functions work.

Moreover, different portions of each part have special jobs to do. In the cerebrum, where the conscious thinking goes on, a lot of data are stored and accessed. This storage is compartmentalized, and the compartments are tapped into when needed. The frontal lobes do much different work than do the parietal regions by the ear or the occipital areas in the very rear. Also, the right side does certain things, and the left side does other things. Sometimes both sides work on a problem together, but they do not duplicate each other's work.

And here's where hemisphericity comes in. Some people depend primarily upon the left side of their brain (not consciously, certainly; it's the wiring) for dealing with the world, and others depend upon the right. That means that because the two halves do not operate identically, while a person tapping into the left side of the brain will approach life and thought in one way, the person tapping into the right half will approach it in another.

How About You?

Most people gravitate toward their hemisphere preference, especially when learning new material. So picture what you would do if you just sort of acted in the following situations without thinking about it. Which response comes more naturally?

1. You come home from town, walk in the front door with a handful of mail, and
   ____ a. Sit in the wingback chair or at the table to read the mail.
   ____ b. Flop down in the sofa or easy chair, all asprawl, to read the mail.
2. At the doctor's office, you are given a two-page list of questions to answer. The fine-print questionnaire asks about your medical history.
   ____ a. You start at the top and go down to the end, finishing in a couple minutes.
   ____ b. You feel totally overwhelmed.
3. It's income tax time, and you don't have an accountant. You figure if you devote one day, all day, you can finish it. You'd better; it's April 14! You set up your workplace—
   ____ a. At a desk with plenty of light, pencil and scratch paper at hand, the phone unplugged, the receipts in one pile, the W-2 and dividend/interest forms in another, the instruction book before you, and a cup of coffee in easy reach. You're gonna nail this sucker!
   ____ b. On the floor, maybe, or on the bed—that's a nice broad surface—with reduced light, Kitaro on the CD player or maybe something with more beat to it, and your shoebox full of receipts and stuff. Wait; gotta get a pencil. You'd better not turn on the TV, although that's what you'd rather have playing now. You can do random figuring on the backs of these envelopes. You're all set up, and still you feel overwhelmed.
4. A guy in your office bounces a Nerf ball against the wall over and over and over while he talks on the phone. Your attitude:
   ____ a. The guy can't be getting anything serious done!
   ____ b. That doesn't look like too bad an idea, actually.
5. You have to figure how to get frantic Aunt Edna's cat down from a thirty-foot tree beside her garage. Climbing is out; the cat is up where the branches are too thin to support you. Assuring Aunt Edna that you never see cat skeletons in trees does no

good. The fire department doesn't rescue cats anymore. The Humane Society put you on hold.

_____ a. You figure if it went up, it can come down, and you try to entice it with liver bits and tuna. You might get a kid to climb up there, but then you'd be liable.

_____ b. You borrow your cousin's old butterfly net, climb a ladder to the garage roof, straddle the ridge as close to the tree as possible, extend the net way out under the cat, and shake the limb vigorously. The cat jumps, and you've got it.

The people relating more comfortably to the first responses are left-brainers. Right-brainers will lean more toward the b answers. Not many people score five out of five, but what was your majority choice? Let's see what that means.

Left Brain, or Linear Thinkers

To see a linear thinker, simply check out Gunther Steinfelder. There's Mr. Linear in the flesh. Orderly, logical, sequential (if we do A and B, C will result), straight-arrow. He likes to analyze. If you were to pick apart the way he analyzes, you would see that he identifies parts and patterns, then pieces together a whole. This makes left-brainers handy with math and physical sciences. Linear thinkers understand and appreciate rules. The Pharisees were great linear folk.

Linear thinking extends comfortably into the past and the future. The linear thinker can predict from the past what is likely happening in the present and from there predict what may happen in the future. Again, this process is linear, A, B, C. If you were worried about sending a kid up the tree and thus being liable for the child's injuries if he or she fell, you were projecting the past and present into a model of a possible future. That's pure left brain.

For learning, whether formal or informal, the left-brainer prefers bright direct light, quiet, and sitting properly at a desk or table. There the left-brainer can stay alert as well as spread out the work before him or her. This person prefers elegant, formal design and is probably conservative in preferences related to art and literary expression.

Right Brain, or Global Thinkers

William Steinfelder, bless his heart, is a strongly global thinker, though he didn't realize it. While his linear-thinking dad suspects William doesn't think at all, nothing could be further from the truth.

William can see the whole picture, but he doesn't line it up into a linear sequence. In fact, his brain really doesn't work in sequences at all. One and one could be two—or eleven. Both answers work. William will see the unusual answer that escapes his dad because William is not locked into sequencing. This is what makes right-brainers such creative people.

If you analyze the right-brainer's thinking style, he or she looks at the whole picture, then breaks it down into patterns and breaks the patterns into parts—just the reverse of the left-brainer. The right-brainer will probably prefer decor, art, and lighting featuring informal design. Many right-brainers are liberal or progressive in their attitude toward the world.

Linear thinkers met global thinkers in the old Carlisle Indian school in Pennsylvania with interesting results. The object of the Carlisle school was to turn "savage" Indian children into "respectable" and "proper" civilized people. It was one of the most horrific, uncivilized ideas the U.S. government ever came up with. For some years starting in the 1880s, Indian children from all over the West were uprooted from their homes and shipped off to boarding school.

One of the civilizing influences supposedly was sport. The boys were taught football and sent out to play against other area schools of like size (football great Jim Thorpe was a Carlisle grad). One bright afternoon, the opposing team clearly saw the ball snapped to the Carlisle quarterback. Then it disappeared. The opponents stood around puzzled. Moments later, the Carlisle carrier crossed under the goalposts, pulled the flattened ball out from under his jersey, and declared a touchdown. The rules required only that the team carry the ball into the end zone. When the left-brainers made the rules, they didn't say anything about whether the ball had to be inflated.

The global right-brainer will come up with the winning idea to save the day; the analytic left-brainer will probably throw a fit because of the violence done to those precious rules.

Many years ago, the government tried to find out why some navy pilots could fly through a storm and get where they ought to be while other pilots, identically equipped, would lose their bearings. Dr. Herman Witkin discovered that those pilots who were field dependent—that's another way of saying global—had to have their environment exactly the way they needed it in order to stay on track. The analytical (linear) persons, not dependent on their surroundings, could stay on course regardless of the environment. They were field independent.

Applying that concept to ADD kids, we've learned that they will not do well, will not stay on track, if their environment isn't the way they need it to be. We did not say "prefer." This time we said "need."

Global folk like to sprawl across the bed, the floor, the recliner to read or work. A teenaged girl we know does her best reading stretched out on her belly across her horse's back, head-toward-tail, her book open on the broad, flat rump. She reads and her horse, Major, grazes. Global people prefer soft, indirect light and background or white noise.

ADD and Hemisphericity

Not all ADD children are right-brained, but most are. Again we have a generalization, not a rule. The reverse is also true. Some right-brainers are ADD people, but most are not. In this discussion, we must be careful to keep those distinctions in mind, remembering that when we speak of "most ADD kids" as being this or that, it's not to be construed as "all ADD kids" or even "the vast majority." Also, we must keep in mind that all of us function from both hemispheres of the brain. Many of us are simply more comfortable functioning from one or the other, especially when under stress and/or when learning new material.

So the average child with ADD is probably right-brained, but there are ten million variants. Jody Capehart talks knowledgeably about kids who have what might be called an "island of linear thinking" in an otherwise global mind-set. For example, Mrs. Capehart's own son, Damon, is a whiz at physics, which is pure left-brain stuff. It came as a surprise to her when she asked him what he thought he might want to be and he announced, "a physicist." Damon is strongly global, strongly ADD. *No way,* she thought to herself.

So Jody whipped out some other diagnostic tests (educators always have a full quiver of these arrows to shoot). Her stepson tested out as "analytic sequential" on the Gregorc Style Delineator and as "analytic" or field independent on the Group Embedded Figures Test. This young man with all the right-brain signs has some left-brain islands of interest and gifting, and solid, sustaining ones at that. The human brain is fascinatingly complex, each of us created unique. God obviously abhors pigeonholes.

Jody still stands in awe of Damon's prodigious abilities. "This is a child who can't get to first base on some of the simpler tasks of life," she muses, "getting into college on the strength of his calculus and physics."

Damon approaches his left-brain specialty in right-brain ways. He studies kinesthetically, for he works better walking around, awash in background sound and soft light. He paces the floor with his textbook and tape recorder, taping the main points of what he is reading into an audio medium. Then he studies by listening to the tape. Typical of right-brainers, he cannot read and take notes with ease; he needs that auditory step in between.

He illustrates the key to helping an ADD child become comfortable in the world and function well—work with the child's unique style rather than fight it.

Now let's summarize.

Putting It All Together

Gunther was back in Jana Carella's office. He sat in the chair facing her desk, his legs asprawl, his shoulders sagging.

"You look tired," she commented, "maybe even sad."

"Sad. Yes, I think I am." Gunther paused a few moments, sorting through words the way a diamond buyer sorts through uncut gems. "I think . . ." He stopped and started over. He was not accustomed to baring his soul before the world. "I think I am dreadfully disappointed in my William."

"How so?"

"I have worked this out in my mind, and I think I am on the right track. You see, I so desperately want William to be as I am—able to think clearly, to seize a situation. And he isn't. He can't. I want him to have the qualities to succeed, as I have succeeded, and he does not. I have finally made peace with the fact that he is totally different from me, and it makes me extremely sad."

She pondered this a few moments. "You are a remarkably insightful man. You've been thinking about this quite a bit."

"I have."

She nodded. "Mr. Steinfelder. The tortoise and the hare. Who won?"

"The tortoise, of course, but that—"

"But that wasn't according to logic. Right. Still, the bottom line is, the tortoise won. Tortoises *can* win. So can hares."

"It is a story. Not fact."

"But it reflects reality." She sat forward. "You're familiar with hemisphericity—right brain versus left brain."

He nodded gravely. "That is what set me thinking about the chasm between us."

"Good. I'm not even going to venture to speculate whether the tortoise is left or right. The fact is, if you take into account the two major components of every person's approach to the world—hemisphericity plus learning style; audio, visual, tactile, or kinesthetic learning styles—and work within those two parameters, nearly everyone can succeed."

"Fine words." Gunther grimaced. He stopped in midthought, staring, because she was glaring at him.

"Mr. Steinfelder!" Her withering tone of voice told him he was in for a tongue-lashing. "You succeeded because you, as a linear thinker, built a good environment around yourself and capitalized on your learning style. You need quiet and all that kind of thing, right? So you insist upon them when you're working."

"Well, of course, I—"

"You know your strengths. You are a visual learner, so you work that way. Tick off everything you know about learning style and hemisphericity, right down the line, and you make sure that you provide yourself with the appropriate elements, the perfect surroundings. When you've given yourself every advantage like that, you can't help but be successful!"

"Yes, but . . ." There he was, saying *yes but* again.

"*But!* If you really want your son to be successful, if you will just get off this 'poor me' road you're on, you will do with him exactly as you did for yourself. Take—"

"It doesn't work! That odious music! And he won't sit. He won't study! He won't—"

Her voice, hard as ice, cut his off. "Please do not interrupt." It dropped twenty decibels. "Do with him exactly as you've done for yourself. That is, discover his natural learning style and cater to it, just as you cater to yours. Identify his hemisphericity, his unique needs, and capitalize upon them just as you did for yourself. Don't try to press him into your mold; press him into *his* mold. Then jump back because, Mr. Steinfelder, he is going to fly!"

The vast majority of kids, ADD or not, bloom vigorously if you free up their environment and adjust their world to what they need. And just how do you do that?

A child's habitat in our society is the schoolroom. For more than half the waking day, you'll find him or her there. But the child's natural habitat is the home, where his closest relationships lie. Home and school must work together to make his whole life a success. Let's talk about making the most of those habitats.

ATTITUDE AND ENCOURAGEMENT AT HOME

7

"To bed, to bed," says Sleepyhead,
"Tarry awhile," says Slow.
"Put on the pan," says Greedy Nan,
"We'll sup before we go."

*T*HAT OLD ENGLISH nursery rhyme has survived the centuries in fine fettle because it so clearly reflects the great truth about human beings—not one of us is like any other. Our differences strongly govern our preferences, our needs, our choice of a mate, and even our concept of God.

We might call some of those differences personality types.

Personality Types

Leave it to the linear thinkers, though, to attempt to qualify and label the differences. How they love their rules and pigeonholes! The human personality, however, is too diverse and too variant to qualify, let alone quantify.

Today there are a number of different systems that try to identify basic personality types, also called temperaments. From the perspective of the parent or teacher of an ADD child, the purpose in identifying these types is to better understand the child and therefore help him or her better succeed in life by working with him or her instead of being at cross-purposes. When looking at the whole picture of the child, then, we will consider the big three factors in how the child sees the world—hemisphericity, learning style, and temperament, or basic personality. All three profoundly influence the child's attitude and therefore influence our attitude toward the child. All three play a major, *major* role in education.

Rather than wade through all the details of these many and various analytical systems, which would be a whole book in itself, let's condense several different systems into a simplified method of looking at four basic personality types—fun-oriented, controlling, peaceful, and perfectionistic. Because we're not using any one particular method, the nuances and fine detail of any of these available systems will be lost. Indeed, we are generalizing dangerously, for people will not fit clearly and comfortably into one category to the exclusion of others. Also, keep in mind that there are degrees; a person may be strongly of one temperament or only mildly so.

Our goal here, though, is not to get bogged down in the delights (if you're linear) of analysis, but to help the child. Besides, because personalities are so diverse, people can exhibit tendencies in more than one category no matter how finely detailed the system of analysis. Let's look then at four kids we will name by their basic personality: Fun-Lover, Controller, Peaceable, and Perfectionist. Incidentally, there are no significant gender differences. Equal numbers of boys and girls display these indicators. We'll assign "he" and "she" arbitrarily.

Fun-Lover

In the Disney cartoon version of the *Jungle Book,* Baloo the bear was an example of laid-back enthusiasm on the hoof—or paw. Fun-loving and spontaneous, old Baloo felt perfectly comfortable at center stage; he talked a lot, genuinely liked others, let you know exactly how he felt at the moment, and was just plain appealing. Baloo, like most bears, was an opportunistic feeder, meaning he exploited whatever came his way and didn't sweat the small stuff. On the flip side, Baloo the Fun-Lover may be forgetful (albeit extremely apologetic for forgetting) and strongly lacking in discipline.

Fun-Lover will wear the T-shirt that reads, "Life is too short to not party." Popular Fun-Lover loves a good time, laughs a lot, and mixes extremely well with people. If Fun-Lover did not enjoy a learning experience, that experience would be considered pretty much of a waste, for the fun rather than the learning per se would be the primary interest. Fun-Lover can sell lawn mowers to Eskimos and plead a court case like nobody's business. Fun-Lover can turn a disaster into a funny episode.

How different is Controller.

Controller

Ever read any of Forster's classic Admiral Horatio Hornblower tales? The admiral was dyed-in-the-wool Controller. He took authority and control the way most people take a drink of water. He met challenges eagerly, was active, competitive, outgoing, and goal oriented. Once he set his mind to do something, he was going to do it. Period.

Any problems? You bet. When it comes to actually getting along with others, which is Fun-Lover's forte, Controller is insensitive, impatient, and dominating. He can't say "I'm sorry," to save him. Controller gets in your face without a second thought, a tendency that makes him difficult to discipline; besides, he's sure he knows better than the discipliner. And poor old Horatio didn't have a humorous bone in his body. He missed so much of what Fun-Lover holds dear—cheer and a good time—and never knew what he was missing. Loyal as Hornblower's crew might be, they probably would have preferred a quieter, more peaceful leader.

Peaceable

Easy does it, live and let live—Peaceable isn't going to win many pitched battles, being somewhat indecisive and lacking the necessary desire for leadership to fight hard, but she just might win the war. The patient peacemaker, Peaceable observes people, then uses wit and a relaxed, steady persistence (call it stubbornness) to gain the day. Peaceable can get your goat by making fun at your expense. Shy and introverted, Peaceable tends to keep her feelings to herself; you never quite know what she's thinking. Peaceable is so relaxed and low key, so quiet and apparently reconciled to life, that you don't realize how much she dislikes being pushed. Because she so consistently prefers the easy way out, she can be very difficult to motivate.

Perfectionist

When you think of the word *melancholy,* which some people use to label one aspect of Perfectionist's personality, you think of a long, deep sigh. Perfectionist can indeed be moody, insecure, even depressed. She can sulk like you wouldn't believe. But she also really wants to do everything right, thinks deeply and clearly, and is extremely conscientious and idealistic. Orderly and thoroughly organized, she gets a lot done and some would even call her a genius at times. She complies well with authority, making her a joy for parents, teachers, and bosses. She enjoys the routine, the predictable, the rigid schedule. Try not to spring stuff on her unawares.

This sensitive introvert sets herself such high standards and is so perfectionistic that she may have trouble getting started on a project for fear that it will not turn out just right. A charming cartoon sequence on *Sesame Street* portrays a dancing, zinging, shape-shifting triangle in conversation with a stolid, steady square. Perfectionist plays the square to Fun-Lover's triangle.

Unfortunately, these personalities don't always get along.

Personalities in Conflict

Said a friend of ours (call him James) to his bride as they left the church immediately after the wedding, "I was going to write this into the vows, but the pastor talked me out of it. No 'dinner at five,' you hear? We can eat at six or six-thirty or five-thirty or seven or five, but not right on the button. Understand?"

James had grown up under a Perfectionist mother who had dinner on the table promptly at five, day in and day out, and you had just better be there. She had to have the kitchen cleaned up and shut down by six-thirty. James, Mr. Fun-Lover, couldn't stand it.

He illustrates two factors in the consideration of personality types: one, they are not shaped entirely by environment or he would not have emerged from his childhood such a strong fun enthusiast, and two, when personalities clash, they really *clash*. Temperament makes a big, big difference in how smoothly a home functions. All sorts of bad vibes can develop when personalities cannot mesh.

Us-Against-Them

Similar personality types might align themselves into "us-against-them" factions. Let's pretend for the moment that James's father was, like James, a Fun-Lover. Through the years, James and his dad might drift into a conspiracy of getting one over on Mom, either willfully or by unconsciously destroying her careful scheduling. Mom wants the yard mowed and trimmed this Saturday; they want to go fishing. A real struggle of wills ensues, with the family divided. Whatever, it erodes Mom's authority and, deep down, doesn't do a thing for Dad's either. At its core, of course, this is a control issue.

Opposites Don't Always Attract

In contrast to the popular saying that "opposites attract," opposite personality types may really grate on each other. Try matching a Controller with a Peaceable. Being the control freak, Controller doesn't have much trouble dominating Peaceable. Peaceable by nature yields. Underneath, though, Peaceable deeply resents the pattern. Fun-Lover's relentless good cheer can really irritate Perfectionist—"Can't you ever be serious?"—and may also get to Controller big time. And so on and so on. Strong personality types repel and attract strongly.

Power Struggles

Controlling types tend to lock themselves in power struggles. William was an interesting mix; he had a cover layer of anger, and he was hungry for both control and perfection. He pitted himself in a power struggle with his father and drew a large measure of the Perfectionist's depression without the balancing optimism the true Controller enjoys. What his father perceived, and rightly so, as obstinacy and opposition, appeared from William's viewpoint to be more a need to maintain sufficient control to keep his wildly spinning world from flying apart completely. Were reason to prevail, William would have realized he could not exercise that sort of control. Reason and ADD do not mix well however. And that brings up the final point:

ADD Greatly Intensifies Problems

When ADD is added to the mix, the problems multiply. ADD kids tend to overdo everything anyway. An ADD Fun-Lover is not just fun-loving but wildly, crazily fun-loving. And because ADD kids are fairly slow to mature, ADD Fun-Lover's sense of humor is going to be pretty hard to appreciate by people who are more grown-up, and that's just about everybody. An ADD Perfectionist is intensely moody, flaring up and expressing impatience for apparently no reason. An ADD Controller is not only Controller magnified but intensely frustrated because he or she cannot control either himself or herself or the world. ADD Peaceables are just as frustrated because they find themselves constantly at war within themselves. An ADD child who is strongly of a particular temperament is not a happy child. Almost certainly the child is not able to understand what is happening inside himself or herself, and that multiplies frustration.

And nobody understands any of them.

The first step then to using temperament in positive ways is for the adults in the child's life to make some major adjustments in thinking. *Change must begin with the adults.*

Adjustments on the Parents' Part

Gunther Steinfelder did not believe much in this psychobabble testing stuff, but he was going to have to wade through it, humoring the testers, until he reached what he wanted—good ways in which to change William into a model son. He studied the results of this latest exercise, an exploration of his and William's temperaments.

Jana Carella beamed. "Mr. Steinfelder, I've been doing this for fifteen years, and I've never seen a more perfect Controller type in my life. You are classic!"

Was he being flattered or insulted? That was one of the worst things about this psychology stuff; you never quite knew. He smiled enigmatically. "And William?"

"A mix. Beneath the anger, Mr. Steinfelder, your son really does want to get along with the world. He just doesn't know how to go about it."

"Amen to that."

Mrs. Carella sat back and studied her desktop in that thoughtful way of hers. "I trust you've noticed an improvement in William's studies since he rearranged his room."

"Yes, and it amazes me. Science fiction could not devise a more alien culture than his room."

"There's a reason we began with his surroundings. It's one of the best ways—"

"Wait. 'We?' You are in contact with Dr. Warren?"

" 'We,' Mr. Steinfelder, means Dr. Warren and myself and you and your wife and William. We are all a team with a single goal: to make William's life better. Considering how high a percentage of ADD kids end up in jail or dead or on the streets, I would go so far as to say our goal is to save him. But that would be overly dramatic."

"He's in a good family."

"That's not always enough, though it helps immensely. *Immensely!*

In fact, if we were to list ways to help William, that would probably be the first item. A good family provides emotional security and a strong team."

Form a Team

Jana Carella, Dr. Paul Warren, Jody Capehart, William's parents, Andrew's mom, Amy's bewildered folks, Amy, William, and Andrew—all must become members of their respective teams. The team must include the teachers involved with each child, as well as significant adult relatives and friends.

Gunther was not accustomed to team play. He understood the power of a team thoroughly, however. Five people running aimlessly around a basketball court accomplish nothing; five with a common goal and a pledge to work together win championships. He knew that. Still, he was going to have to adjust his thinking in new ways, yielding a measure of control and working in concert with others in order to become, for the first time ever, a team player.

Beth had no trouble at all building a team with Mrs. Loring and Jody Capehart. She knew, though, that Andrew needed a strong man on his team and would need one even more as he got older. She regretted that Andrew's father would not be a part of it. As she thought about the past, she could not remember a single time when the man had worked cooperatively with anyone else.

Twelve-year-old Amy's parents read the books and studied the latest in magazine articles, gathering information. Then Peter made appointments with Amy's teachers to sit down and work out study plans and to brainstorm ways to help her. They did not consciously set out to build a team, but they built one all the same.

Gunther was going to have to shift his thinking in some other major ways as well. One of them was to get to know his son well enough that he could see the real child below the annoying, frustrating exterior. This, as you can imagine, would be extremely difficult for a man of his temperament. He would have to lay aside his own preferences and his approach to the world and put himself, as it were, in William's shoes.

What factors of William's behavior, attitude, and appearance were significant and which were simply artifacts of Gunther's annoyance? In other words, was William really "bad" in a certain way, or was Gunther perceiving the behavior as badness because it was not the sort of behavior his own temperament would engender? In order to see William's behavior objectively and then help William change what had to be changed, Gunther had to filter out his own attitudes or at the very least recognize that they were there coloring his view. So getting to know himself very well could make the task much easier.

Know What's Going on with Yourself

You—along with Gunther and Ellen, Beth, and Peter and Viveca—cannot see a child objectively without putting yourself aside. But what attitudes—what mind-sets that must be put aside—are caused by temperament? To better see what your own temperament is and how it colors you, compare yourself to the lists of characteristics below. You won't fit any of the lists 100 percent, but they will give you an idea of what your prevailing temperament might be. Then we'll suggest some things you might want to either minimize or filter out as you look at your child.

The Fun-Lover Parent.   If you're a fun-lover, you are looking for an opportunity to share some laughter with those you love. Here are some other traits of Fun-Lover's parenting style:

- You are loving, sensitive, and upbeat. Kids—yours and others'—enjoy hanging around your house. A friend of ours once told us, wide-eyed, "I came home from town one day and there were ten kids in the yard. I counted them. And none of them was ours; ours were in the backseat!"
- You make home a fun and comfortable place to be. Your child can probably be pretty noisy and active without being reprimanded.
- You can be forgetful . . . but will also be forgiving of the child's forgetfulness.
- You easily turn disasters into humor. You're good at finding the silver lining around every dark cloud. The kids will gravitate to the fun-appreciating parent who can mute with humor the frightening aspect of a scary situation.

While these characteristics lend themselves to good parenting, there are also some things the fun-loving parent of an ADD child has to watch out for:

- The home can be chaotic. The parent enjoys spontaneity so much that the home has no underlying structure. The ADD child needs strong structure. This may require a complete shift of focus on the parent's part. ADD kids' lives are chaotic as it is without adding a disorderly home scene to the turmoil. An orderly environment helps the child keep order, and the child needs all the help possible in this area.

- Fun-loving parents have a hard time providing consistent discipline. Again, this is something an ADD child greatly needs. And yet the Fun-Lover parent is very good at tempering discipline with love and understanding, also something the ADD child needs. Play to the strength—love but not laxity—and build up the weakness by working on consistency.

The Controlling Parent.   Controlling parents have strengths in other areas:

- If you have a controlling personality, you are goal oriented. You believe the primary purpose of any activity is to achieve an end.
- Discipline is important to you. That's how you achieve goals— discipline. There is a chain of command. Use it.
- You are solid. ADD kids in particular need stability, and the Controller parent provides that beautifully.
- You make things happen. The parent may order others around or initiate group projects, but activity increases in the family because of the parent's input.
- You exert active leadership. This is the parent who will build the child's team.
- You thrive on opposition. Here's a curious anomaly; the controlling parent hates disobedience and yet does not in the least mind bucking heads with school officials, teachers, doctors, and even the parole officer in order to get what the child needs.

The ADD child needs a Controller hero, parent or otherwise, to champion his or her cause. Guts and determination are often the only advantages when the child's parents face indifferent schools. Moreover, the controlling parent must understand the shortcomings of the temperament, especially where ADD kids are concerned. Gunther and others of this temperament must guard against:

- insensitivity,
- impatience, and
- a domineering attitude (ADD kids fight domination desperately).

This parent may be insensitive to other family members. "Gunther just charges right ahead," Ellen complained, "without even thinking about what William or I might need." It's a valid complaint.

Oftentimes he or she may fail to recognize and ask forgiveness for personal shortcomings and mistakes, and exhibit a strong tendency to control *everything*—to manipulate just for the sake of being in command.

As Gunther read that last item, the tendency to control, he saw himself. After that he caught himself constantly starting to give an arbitrary order. At first he'd give it, and then when William or Ellen protested (usually with a petulant, "But Dr. Warren said . . ." or "But Mrs. Carella said . . ."), he would rescind it. Eventually Gunther reached the point where he could frequently catch himself when he was flexing authoritarian muscle merely for the sake of flexing it and not to improve the situation. He didn't see his progress in that area; Mrs. Carella had to point out to him that he was actually in much better control, for he was now controlling himself, the hardest job of all. And that improved control was bearing good fruit in the form of smoother family relations.

In contrast, a peace-loving parent of an ADD child has other things to guard against.

The Peaceable Parent.   When you're looking at the characteristics of good parenting, you find many that are also typical of the peaceable personality.

- The peaceable parent is competent, steady, and works well under pressure.
- He or she is usually a good listener, something ADD kids need very much.
- This parent exercises good internal organization and runs an orderly house.
- Most importantly, the peaceable parent takes time for the children. He or she is a nurturing parent.

This is exactly the kind of temperament an ADD child needs in a parent. However, the peaceable parent may also have some traits to be on guard against. For example:

- The peaceable parent may well be lax on discipline. The child needs loving discipline, informed discipline, nonrigid discipline, but it must be there. The peaceable parent tends to let things slide, taking the easy way out. Wise enforcement is rarely the easy way out of any learning or other disciplinary situation.

- He or she is indecisive. The opposite of a controller, the peaceable parent may waffle on things that need a strong response.

Peter Eglund was a peaceable parent, though not extremely so. Amy insisted on lots of TV, and Peter gave in—the easy way out. It was also an expression of love and concern, however; he reasoned that cutting her off cold turkey after a lifetime of TV was cruel and unusual punishment. Frequently Peter caved in rather than risk a confrontation. And yet, when it came to finding a solution to Amy's problems, he worked tenaciously. That's typical of peace-loving folk.

The Perfectionistic Parent. A perfectionist parent, depending upon the temperament of the child, can be a wonderful mentor for an ADD kid. Here are some of the perfectionistic parent's strengths:

- Not surprisingly, given the label we've applied, he or she tends toward perfectionism. That can be a drawback for an ADD kid who by nature is anti-perfection and has the short-term memory of a butterfly. On the other hand, the last thing this child needs is the goal of slipshodness.
- Perfectionistic parents are well organized and run a tight ship.
- They are not afraid to make sacrifices for the kids.
- They are good at encouraging talent. They set high standards.

ADD kids really need structure, and this parental temperament provides it. ADD kids need encouragement, and this parent, along with the Fun-Lover parent, is good at offering it. Raising ADD kids well demands sacrifices beyond what most kids need.

Now here's the downside of Perfectionistic parents:

- They tend to suffer moodiness, depression, and insecurity. These attributes rub off easily onto ADD kids. The child, already moody and prone to depression and frustration, certainly doesn't need an extra dose of them!
- They may become rigid in their search for perfection. ADD kids need special flexibility within a strong structure. For example, an ADD child may be called upon to clean his or her room—no ifs, ands, or buts. That's structure. But the child may be allowed a longer span of time than usual, may be allowed a break other kids

would not get, or may be allowed to perform the task in smaller increments. That's flexibility.
- And, to put it bluntly, these parents may sulk. Perfectionists are good at laying a guilt trip on you. That also is something an ADD kid never needs more of.

Once the personality of the parent, then, is taken into consideration, with attendant attitude adjustments that ought to be made, we can turn to the child.

Know What's Going on with the Child

In our respective practices, we have come to realize that there is always a reason a child does the things he or she does. In some strong-willed children who know exactly what they're trying to pull off, it could be obstinacy or hostility. Much of the time however, the reason is usually *not* that the child is oppositional. It's that the child cannot handle the world the way most people can, and from infancy the child has been expected to do just that—age-appropriately, of course. Unable to meet that expectation and driven by impulse, ADD kids behave in unwanted ways.

Sorting out deliberately ugly behavior from acts of desperation or defense requires that the parent observe the child and most of all become a close mentor to the child. This isn't easy. ADD kids tend to repel others with their behavior, their energy, their infernal forgetfulness, their immaturity, their impulsiveness. Success for the child, though, requires a strong relationship between parent and child, and that relationship is well worth attaining. It starts with understanding.

Try to Understand How the Child Functions

Understanding the child's personality type is one step. Kids do what they do from unseen motives deep within. Temperament provides one set of those motives. It's easier to become close to a child when you can see a motivation besides plain stubbornness.

Once Gunther got into personality types, they fascinated him. He had that analytical turn of mind anyway, and here was a new and fruitful method of analysis. He was not good at building a relationship. What he thought was a relationship was actually a fossilized set of role expectations: "I am the father; therefore I relate in this way. You are the child; therefore you relate in that way." He never did get really close to

William, but he managed to understand the boy a lot better. And as second best goes, that was a strong second best!

Beth found it a lot easier to become closer to Andrew once she understood how he and she both viewed the world, how they functioned as regards temperament, hemisphericity, and learning style. Behavior in Andrew that once had been inexplicable now seemed explainable. Sometimes, at least. It was a start.

Another aspect to be understood, which we will examine in greater detail later, is the child's home life.

Try to Understand the Effect of Family Dynamics

ADD kids can disrupt a family terribly. The anxiety that disruption causes can then intensify the signs and symptoms of ADD. The situation spirals downward. In part, Andrew's problems and extreme activity level were factors in his father's exit from the home. These were actually minor factors, despite what the man claimed. We do not—we *never*—suggest that an ADD child causes a family's breakup. That's not so. An ADD child can be a contributing factor, but the breakup always, always remains the sole responsibility of the parents. Andrew's dad made the decision; Andrew himself was helpless in the matter.

Still, an increased anxiety level adversely affects an ADD child (any child, for that matter), and the parent must take that into consideration. His father's absence intensified Andrew's ADD characteristics. Conversely, reducing family friction can do wonders for reducing ADD and ADD-like signs.

It is important that the whole family understands not just that an ADD diagnosis has been made but also the special characteristics of the ADD or ADHD child. This includes understanding the child's behavior patterns, what impulsivity does and how to avoid being affected by it (locking your bedroom door against an impulsive, overly active younger sibling may not be a bad idea), and what a child's poor attention and organization do to others.

In fact, we'll deal with family dynamics in detail later. For now, we'll look at it only as it influences parent-child understanding.

Family harmony is not the only consideration. Understanding how surroundings affect the child is important too.

Try to Understand the Influence of Immediate Surroundings

For Andrew's behavior, as well as his safety, Beth must know which situations put her son at high risk and which situations are merely stressful—busy malls and distracting, gaudy grocery-store aisles, for example. For an ADD child, the danger of getting into trouble lies in places where there is less structure, more stimulation, and a lack of consistent rules.

At home, this could be free time with large groups, for instance at a barbecue or party, or just free time in general. Andrew could be expected to behave at his worst if Beth had friends in for an evening of cards—high stimulation, you see, and reduced structure as Beth paid attention to entertaining her guests with an essentially grown-up pastime of scant interest to the child.

At school, Andrew would behave his worst in a stimulating environment such as the playground (especially an unstructured or loosely monitored playground), the lunchroom, music classes, physical education, and perhaps going to and from the auditorium for programs and rallies. "Worse behavior" also means "getting on others' nerves." Get on a fellow pupil's nerves, and you could end up with a bloody nose or a painful "accident." Minimally supervised situations are jungles for any kid, but especially so for ADD kids.

Watching out for potentially risky situations is a defensive strategy. Parents can make certain adjustments in attitude in order to develop positive, proactive parenting skills. These skills will count for far more in the long run than constantly striving to avoid risk. Whereas they resemble the skills you'd use for any child, they are especially important, and must be used to an extreme degree, for the extreme of the ADD child.

Using Positive, Proactive Skills

Parents, like their kids, can benefit from a little immediate gratification now and then. Therefore, one of the best parenting skills to concentrate on is to build upon success.

Capitalize on Successes and Try to Multiply Them

Before Gunther inadvertently redirected Mrs. Carella's train of thought, she was going to say, "You see how rearranging William's room brought about improvement. We like to get some successes going to provide encouragement—a little immediate feel-good feedback, if you will, so parent and child can both see that making changes can make a difference. Then we build upon them. That is one success. Now let's enlarge upon it."

Enlarging upon that success would require still more changes on Gunther's part. For example, he could see a difference when William's room was altered. But he could not possibly see how William could concentrate when he was wandering around the house as he read his book. To accept this new concept, Gunther was going to have to force himself to allow what appeared to him to be nonsense. He was going to have to allow William to move at random through the house when ostensibly the kid was studying.

You already know why William tootled about, on the move, as he studied, because you now know about the pearl divers. William is a kinesthetic learner. He learns best when he is moving. The hyperactive aspect of his ADD keeps him from sitting still, but his kinesthetic learning style gives him the alternative means to learn, all the same.

Gunther solved his own dilemma of having to watch William roam by leaving the house. "I can't stand it," he was fond of fuming. "And that music . . . !"

Actually, *that music* was now the Philadelphia Symphony's so-called "rock" record; William realized that music with lyrics distracted him during reading, and he had voluntarily switched to instrumental. He just didn't tell his father.

How did William realize that musical lyrics distracted him? A lot of attitude change must be the child's as well as the adult's, although the adult takes the lead. William talked to Mrs. Carella independently, getting tips on how to study more effectively, and that was one of them. But Gunther could never have forced William to take that step. The change comes from within the child, and it is the parent who goes ahead to show the child the way.

Parents must carefully employ the tool of assigning consequences to children's behavior.

Understand the Importance of Immediate Consequences

Gunther was big on applying immediate consequences for infractions. He took naturally to tough discipline. He would have to consider toning down a little perhaps. Peter and Viveca, however, had to adjust their attitudes by learning to tighten up.

By nature, both Peter and his wife were pretty easygoing. Moreover, his wife never disciplined her children directly; that was the father's job. For most kids, this could possibly be effective because the long, drawn-out dread while waiting for Dad to come home can be almost as much punishment as Dad's arrival itself. Not with ADD kids. They're likely to forget the infraction moments after it occurs.

As Viveca laid out before the newly arrived Peter just what Amy did or did not do, Amy would stand there genuinely confused. She could not remember disobeying or whatever it was her mother was describing. She had no idea what Mom was talking about, and she didn't see anything wrong anyway. When she denied wrongdoing, she was accused of lying. She felt betrayed then by the people closest to her, for she really did not remember doing what they claimed she had done.

ADD kids operate almost exclusively in the present moment. The parent who plans and reflects over a span of hours, days, and years has an awful time keeping that in mind. It's a major adjustment on most adults' part to shift to a greater immediacy of thought.

If something happens now, the results should occur now. This does not apply only to negative happenstance but to positive occurrences as well. ADD kids need all the affirmation they can get, and they need it immediately because they function almost exclusively in the now.

Here are some examples of how this idea could be carried out:

- Viveca reminds Amy to take out the trash. In a bad mood anyway, Amy mouths off. Viveca should not respond with, "Wait until your father gets home, Miss Bigmouth!" Viveca responds immediately with a consequence appropriate to the infraction—sending the sullen Amy to her room, perhaps, or sending her to her room after she takes out the trash.
- Beth warns Andrew to quit picking at the bit of wallpaper that came loose in the kitchen by the door. Andrew, with his one-track mind, keeps returning to it, fascinated, peeling off pieces. Beth should respond immediately and well. Perhaps Andrew should glue those strips back on. Perhaps he needs a time-out. While we certainly do not recommend a swat for an infraction of that sort—swats on ADD kids are minimally effective in the best of circumstances—if Beth resorted to that in frustration or impatience, at least it would be an immediate consequence.
- William is supposed to be studying for the test next week. He does a dozen other things, but he doesn't study. Either Gunther or Ellen (but not both) should promptly administer whatever consequence they've decided upon for that particular behavior.

Immediate consequences do much toward extinguishing inappropriate behavior. But squelching bad behavior is only half of a child's training. The other half, and the more effective part, is to encourage appropriate behaviors.

Encourage Appropriate, Desirable Behavior

Although negative behaviors show up instantly, kids do a lot of positive things that generally escape notice. While this is true of all children, it's particularly true of ADD kids.

Gunther would wrinkle his nose at that. *William? Positive behavior?*

"Well, how often has he been arrested?" Dr. Warren asked one day.

"Arrested!" Gunther almost went ballistic, ready to thunder, "No child of mine is . . ." but he caught himself. Children of very nice parents get into trouble at school and/or run afoul of the law. More than 40 percent of untreated ADD kids end up in detention, as do 20 percent of treated kids. They rarely set out to do so or deliberately invite being handcuffed by unsympathetic cops. But it happens. William, however, managed to keep his nose clean, a big plus for an ADD kid.

"Does he try to get decent grades?"

"Well, yes . . ."

"Is he respectful toward his mother?"

"Most of the time."

Gunther received an assignment then. Find at least ten good things a day, specific things, to praise William for.

Said Gunther, "I don't think I should have to make a big deal out of good behavior. It's what he's *supposed* to be doing."

Gunther's opinion, a very common one, does not accommodate ADD kids' very real need for encouragement. ADD kids require positive reinforcement and lots of it for positive behavior. Read that again. We're not saying they "would like to have" positive reinforcement. We're saying they *require* it. *Need* it. *Thrive on* it. In any case, when bestowing praise, then, be very specific about what you noticed. We can offer some suggestions to get a parent started in this affirming, positive encouragement:

• "Thanks for taking the trash out the first time I asked you."

That could easily evolve into . . .

• "Thanks for taking the trash out without being asked! That was great."
• "You've been playing quietly for fifteen minutes. That's really good. I appreciate you!"
• "I notice you just finished all ten math problems. Here's a cookie. Take a break."

Usually, simply noticing and commenting on the positive behavior is sufficient. It's always nice to know one's efforts are noticed. (By the way, treats as a reward are appropriate on occasion. If they become habit, though, they start to become expected. They are a thank you, not a bribe.)

And most of all:

- "Thank you for obeying promptly. I'm really proud of the way you did that!"

Children's disobedience brings instant recognition. ADD kids' obedience should be given similarly instant recognition along with lavish praise.

ADD kids are generally shortchanged on praise. And yet they really do come up with a lot of praiseworthy stuff. Gunther found that out, though, only after he started analyzing William's behavior in detail, actively looking for the positives.

Parents can do a lot of little things, seemingly insignificant things, to help children respond more positively to commands and instruction. Thinking the way the kids do is a biggie.

Try to Think Multisensory

We remind parents that ADD kids normally respond best to multi-sensory input, and that includes commands. For example, touch is usually big with ADD kids. Beth will probably have much better luck getting her requests through to Andrew if she lays her hand on his arm when she speaks, holds him eye to eye, and uses strong voice inflections. Sound, sight, touch. In Andrew's case, they're *much* more effective than sound alone or a note on the fridge.

Pointing to an item on a list of things to do is far better than simply speaking it. For younger kids like Andrew, holding his hand and using *his* finger to point is quite effective. That pointing, you see, then combines tactile, visual, and auditory clues simultaneously.

Even William at sixteen can do better with tactile reinforcement, a touch appropriately made.

Another technique parents can use at home with excellent effects is to make certain they are providing strong, clear structure. This, too, may require some major shifts in thinking, particularly for the more fun-loving.

Provide Adequate Structure

KISS. It could also stand for Keep It Solid and Strong. A lot of parents remember it as Keep It Simple, Stupid. The lesson it teaches is that it's the parent's job to provide structure. "Wait," Gunther might protest. "Isn't that the kid's responsibility?" It is not, because the ADD child is not capable of providing the structure, and yet the child cannot function without it. In the ADD child's case, the parents provide necessary structure just as they provide necessary food and shelter.

To do this effectively, the parents really have to know their kid. No two children are capable of the same amount of accountability. It's something that comes with age to an extent, but there is wide, wide variation. Some younger ADD children are more responsible than a lot of older ADD kids. To test accountability, try giving the child simple orders. When the child remembers more often than he or she forgets, move on to more complex directions with somewhat less structure. As the child grows, the structure will loosen. Again, observe! If the child can provide structure, we do him or her a disservice by imposing ours. If the child cannot and yet we expect it, failure results—an even greater disservice.

To sound melodramatic, we might say that structure is a boost up the ladder to success. It is the framework of the child's day.

Objectives, goals, directives, and expectations made obvious—that's structure. All this must be communicated clearly, ideally by multisensory means and written reinforcement. Time limits, duties, and consequences both positive and negative should be unambiguously spelled out (although the clever ADD child, squirming to evade a task, will be able to find ambiguity in the clearest of orders).

Structure can be defined as providing sufficient order for the child to function normally—and "normally" does not mean "perfectly." Ordinary kids forget, neglect, refuse. Give ADD kids permission to be normal. Some aspects of structure:

Clearly Define Time Limits. "Clean your room today," would work on most kids, at least in theory. They grasp the order and understand the time frame. That instruction is far too diffuse for an ADD child. The ADD child needs, "It's Saturday morning. Let's have your room clean by nine. Go down the list. Then you will be free to do whatever you want today."

That expanded statement, you'll notice, provided a time limit, the obvious place to start (with the list), a specific directive about how to do the task (consult the list), and a promised reward—freedom on a Saturday morning. And it hinges on the list.

Clearly Define Tasks.   The list. With his girlfriend's help, William had compiled a list of steps to do to clean his lair. At sixteen, William could do that. Andrew at seven would not be able to take that kind of initiative.

An ADD child might need a carefully thought-out list of minitasks to help him or her satisfactorily complete such chores as taking out the garbage:

1. Get the trash can out from under the sink.
2. Empty the bathroom wastebasket into it.
3. Take the can out and dump it in the big container.
4. Haul the trash container out to the curb.
5. Bring in the can.
6. Put a new grocery-bag liner in it.
7. Put it back under the sink.

Notice that none of these items is theoretical or nebulous. Each is a specific act, black and white, that is either done or not done. ADD kids don't dwell on theory and abstracts.

A child Andrew's age might earn a star for each of the seven steps whereas an older child would earn recognition only for the completion of all seven. Gunther was expecting William to do that spontaneously. William was simply not capable of taking all seven steps in order spontaneously. Somewhere in that seven-step process he would forget a crucial step (or forget the task altogether) or stall out, distracted by something else, and get yelled at for not completing so simple a job.

Lists and time limits might be combined for children capable of little responsibility. For example, Beth might break down Andrew's "clean your room" list of sub-tasks into:

1. Pick up your shoes—you have 3 minutes.
2. Pick up your clothes—2 minutes.
3. Pick up toys—5 minutes . . . and so on.

"I can't follow Andrew around forever with a stopwatch," Beth might wail.

And we would respond, "For a while you may have to. If the child never succeeds in these small things, he won't succeed in the large ones."

Don't String Orders Together. ADD kids can only do one thing at a time. In fact, that's often true of us all. A friend's son-in-law recently told her daughter, "Wait. That was four things you want. Which three do you really want?" He had learned that even in adulthood he could handle three tasks, or three grocery-store items, but not four. With an ADD kid, it's one. Period.

"Andrew, get your coat and bring your books. School time."

He might get his coat from the hall closet. He might get his books from his room. Not both. Remember in our first chapter where we introduced Andrew and his mom, Andrew was sent back to pick up a pencil and a book. He got the pencil.

Always one thing.

Don't Underestimate the Importance of Your Presence. The parent may have to walk from room to room, may have to stand there directing operations or simply stand nearby to help the child succeed at these assignments.

Having said that, we know what answer to expect:

"I don't have time!"

For these kids, your taking the time to enforce structure with your physical presence will actually save time as the child learns to handle the sub-tasks unaided. The alternative is to expect the child to comply, and after all the nagging and cajoling and yelling is done, everyone concerned will still be angry hours later. Count on it.

Tailor immediate payback—specialized consequences, if you will—to the child's preferences.

Provide Payback

For kids in general but ADD children in particular, there must be some immediate payback. Telling the child he or she now has "a nice-looking room" is not a payback. The kid couldn't care less. Facetious sarcasm—"Good. Now the health department might leave us alone for another week"—doesn't cut it either. There must be a return that is of value to the child or the child will have no incentive for performing required behavior, let alone for internalizing all this and learning to do it unaided.

Many parents of ADD kids build elaborate weekly charts with chores and ministeps down the side and the days of the week across the top. The child receives a check or star for each completed task or sub-task. Brightly colored metallic star stickers work well. They are attractive, they stand out prominently, and they tell the world, "I did this!"

Stars may not suffice by themselves. An excellent addendum is to offer a special reward for every so-many stars completed. Perhaps you might say for every twenty (or some other number) stars your child earns you will take him or her for a walk in the park or an hour at the playground or a frozen yogurt or a trip to the library. Whatever.

The very least of secondary rewards are material; they should never be money. Money is too abstract. It disappears instantly. A new something, whatever that something may be, loses its luster almost immediately. Of moderate value is some special privilege earned—staying up later or doing something special. The very best of rewards are relational, involving social experience, especially with the parents. Reading an extra book together at the close of day, walking together, playing a game, enjoying time together as parent and child—those are the rewards that will mean most. The most important thing in any child's world is relationships. Always.

Please note: Such rewards must *never* take the place of normal parental interaction and affirmation—*never* "Earn three tokens and we'll play." The parent and child will play together anyway. The reward must consist of a significant addition to the normal or usual interaction.

Dr. Russell Barkley, a pioneer in the identification and treatment of ADD and ADHD, developed a system of reward using tokens. In fact, he's famous for it.

The tokens can be poker chips or something similar. For young children, just about any token will work. For older children, make certain the tokens cannot be counterfeited.

The youngest child understands the immediate, concrete reward of a token bestowed on the spot for meritorious behavior. The child is then allowed to cash in tokens for some clearly defined prize or reward. Elegant in its simplicity, the token system can work wonders.

The best token system is thoughtfully tailored to the individual child with a careful balance between easily obtained and hard-to-get. Earning tokens should be a bit of a challenge but attainable fairly quickly.

For most ADD kids, accumulating chips through an entire week is too long a time increment. Tangible rewards ought to come daily or more often for some kids, every day or two for most. Again, we're trying for immediate gratification.

What if a child fails to reach a goal—perhaps of accumulating the magical number of stars or chips in order to attend a special function (a movie, the circus, a special event at the sports arena)? It's not so bad that a child might occasionally fail to reach some goal. Kids don't learn to walk without falling down a few times. However, if rewards seem too slow to come or take too many days to accumulate, ADD kids quickly grow discouraged.

The system should also be tailored to age. Actual tokens may be too babyish for the child age ten or older. A point system, not unlike some states use for driving infractions, may appeal better to preteens and early teens. These points would reflect positive strokes, however, not shortfalls. For those in their midteens, a written contract might do better. In fact, for the adolescent, a written code is absolutely necessary. Kids get addled and don't remember guidelines clearly. Often the ADD child has one or more ADD parents who also get muddled. A mutual agreement in black and white with expectations, rewards, and punishments all spelled out minimizes arguments.

Can a child lose tokens because of bad behavior? "I tend to say no," suggests Dr. Warren. "A token earned is earned. It represents something done right. It's extremely discouraging to a child, particularly to a young child, to see tokens build up only to melt away. If you must subtract tokens for unacceptable behavior, subtract tokens not yet earned. 'Okay, the next token you would have earned is forfeited because you behaved extremely disrespectfully just now.' Then stick to it. I suggest writing it down.

"If at all possible, avoid giving these kids negative anything. They have so many negatives in their lives already."

If you must bestow negative tokens, so to speak, "bad" tokens for incidents of clear disobedience (not forgetfulness), disrespect, or dishonesty (again, not forgetfulness), use tokens that do not in any way resemble "good" tokens—sticks, perhaps, or marbles dropped into a jar. So-many negative tokens—a number agreed upon beforehand—might result in a loss of privilege. They must never ever result in a loss of relationship or a relational activity. (Threatening, "three sticks and we don't read a book at bedtime" is a no-no.)

Regardless of the child's age, everything about a token system must be put down in black and white. How many tokens does it take to earn such-and-so privilege? Write it down. Exactly what misbehavior results in a negative token? Say it. Also, the list of privileges to be accrued should have six or more items, minimum. ADD kids become quickly bored, so a variety of positive reinforcers becomes necessary. Negative consequences needn't vary in nature the way positive consequences should.

The big problem with this system (or any other) is that the parents must be consistent—and it is rarely convenient to administer the system consistently.

Parents may say, "I don't think my kid will go for this," or, "I tried it. Zip."

To that we would respond, "Don't forgot who's in charge. The parents are. It doesn't matter whether the kid goes for it." The system works if the parents maintain consistency, awarding tokens or whatever according to the written plan, and they keep at it.

But the goal is not to turn the child into a model of behavior, much as Gunther and Beth and Peter might dream.

Keep the Goal in Mind

The ultimate goal of all these efforts is to help the child somehow internalize the process of following directives and structuring his or her own world. It is not simply compliance. Never is compliance primary. Poodles at the circus can be taught to comply.

All children must internalize the skills that are at first forced upon them from the outside as discipline. In that way the child becomes *self*-disciplined. An external system of rewards and punishments, such as tokens or gain and loss of privilege, can help children learn to govern themselves from within. ADD kids need the external system even more than ordinary kids do. They can't internalize without it.

More than others, ADD children, in order to internalize long-lasting appropriate behavior, need those short-term tangible rewards such as some sort of token system. Simple affirmation, plus ignoring (not rewarding with attention) inappropriate behavior, is not effective by itself. The ADD kids need something here and now. At its core, this is another aspect of the kids' multisensory needs—something to hear about, see, touch, hold on to, talk about.

And always remember that whereas the goal is to internalize self-monitoring, self-discipline, and self-control, relationships are the way to achieve success best.

Relationships, relationships, relationships! As much as ADD kids need and crave relationships, they are not real good at developing and maintaining them. They need help in that area. There are times, though, when the relationship crumbles as ADD kids go head to head with Mom or Dad in a Godzilla-scale power struggle. What then?

DISCIPLINE

*A*MY WORRIES ME," Viveca confided to Peter over breakfast. "She's
almost a teenager. She should be starting to look at boys about now,
but she doesn't seem to be. And she—"

"Praise God for small miracles," Peter muttered as he buttered his
toast.

Viveca pressed on, undeterred. "And she doesn't seem to have any
friends. You know, real friends, the way girls her age ought to have."

"How about Becky and Janet and that little girl in the blue house
on the corner? What's her name? Rose?"

"Rose. A lovely girl. But they're not intimate friends. Amy doesn't
have anyone to share her soul with. I think that's important at this age."

"Sharing one's soul is very special. I can't see that happenstance is
always going to dump a special friend on your doorstep at exactly the
time you need her. Sometimes that happens and sometimes it doesn't.
Given time, she'll find a soul mate. And remember, an inordinate interest
in boys leads to all sorts of problems. There's plenty of time for that—
say, fifteen or twenty years."

"Oh, Peter," said Viveca wearily as she got up to refill their coffee
cups.

Meanwhile, over in Irving, Beth Mulroney sighed as she hung up the phone. Mrs. Hastings had described in disturbing detail the medical bill she paid to repair the gash in her Sonny's head. Apparently without provocation, Andrew had corked the innocent lad with a croquet mallet, and it would be very nice if Beth would pony up for the expenses. Beth took her number and promised to call her as soon as she got her next paycheck.

Every time Beth listened to Mrs. Hastings' voice, she burned with fury all over again. At the time of the mallet incident, Mrs. Hastings had explained in loud, excruciating detail (she seemed to have a real gift for delivering these litanies) exactly what she thought of Beth's defective parenting, and how, if Beth simply imposed a little discipline on her serial-killer son, innocent children wouldn't be injured like this.

Discipline and social skills. They are united closely, and in ADD kids neither of them comes easily. The best discipline improves social skills as it internalizes the lesson to be learned. It is never considered simply as a lid for a garbage can, keeping the little twit's behavior controlled until he or she is old enough to leave home.

Unfortunately, ordinary discipline methods, as well as the usual ways to build social skills, do not work as well for ADD kids as they do for most. ADD kids need an approach tailored just to them.

A key to this approach is to maintain control without engaging the child in a contest of wills. Many ADD kids may seem oppositional, hostile, defensive, and confrontational. They have very little turf to defend, so they defend it to the hilt. They have very little power to wield, so they wield it to the hilt. They get very little positive feedback, so they rebel with anger.

By age five or six the child is starting to develop quite a head of anger. By the age of twelve, the sarcasm, the invective, are securely in place, and the child is itching for the chance to use them. He is learning a sad, unfortunate phenomenon: To build yourself up, you tear everyone else down. It's one of the very few defense mechanisms these kids have. But that attitude doesn't do a thing for social interaction.

Discipline is most effective when the parent manages to avoid triggering the child's fury, sarcasm, or confrontation. In the process of disciplining without engaging the child in a power struggle, the parent teaches the child by osmosis, if you will, that there are better ways to get along successfully in the world. And that, essentially, is socialization.

Avoiding Power Struggles

Consider this scenario:
Ellen: "Will, you didn't put away the canned goods like I told you to."

William (harshly): "Aw, come on. I forgot. Gimme a break."

Ellen (her voice rising): "You always say, 'I forgot.' You just didn't want to do it. Now go do it!"

William: "That's not true! I just forgot; that's all. And if forgetting's such a horrible sin, how come Mama Perfect forgot to put the thickening in her cherry pie last night, huh? Why are you so wonderful that you can forget but I can't?"

Ellen: "Once in a while is one thing, Mr. Smartmouth. You forget constantly! Now go do what you're told!"

As you can see, confrontation quickly escalates into shouting (at which an ADD kid is very, very good).

Now consider this scenario:

Ellen: "Will, you didn't put away the canned goods like I told you to."

William (harshly): "Aw, come on. I forgot. Gimme a break."

Ellen (evenly): "I'm sorry you forgot. I forget too sometimes. Nevertheless, you know what we agreed."

William: "Yeah, but it doesn't apply this time. Besides, it's only this once."

Ellen (quietly): "An agreement is an agreement. Put the canned goods away now, please."

William would no doubt wiggle and squirm some more, but there was no room left for argument. The confrontation was gone. Ellen needed only to stick with her quiet, "Do it now, please."

So to what agreement was she referring?

A written one.

Setting up the Ground Rules

When discussing point systems, token systems, and similar devices for bestowing rewards, we recommended writing down the rules. Now let's expand that into discipline in general. Written rules are unambiguous. They take away the power of the excuse, "I forgot."

The source of most power struggles between parents and kids, and remarkably young kids at that, is "Which will prevail? My will or yours?" The struggle is between two (or more) persons. When the guidelines are in black and white, the power struggle evaporates, replaced by, "Have the guidelines been met or haven't they?" The question is no longer personalized. That takes a lot of fire out of the fight right there.

In the first scenario above, Ellen let William's anger stir up her own anger. It happens automatically unless you are well practiced in guarding against it. When William made it personal with an attack on her, she returned in kind with an inflammatory charge of "You *always* [fill in the blank]." The other bit of hyperbole guaranteed to enflame is "You *never* [fill in the blank]."

Written rules invite rigidity unless you monitor their use carefully. We're not promoting rigidity. There are such gifts as grace and mercy. But we do most highly recommend firmness, as Ellen demonstrated in the second scenario above. There were no extenuating circumstances in that situation that would invoke grace and mercy. William was asked to do something. He forgot to do it. Simple.

Here's one way you might begin the task of setting up a rules system.

Identify Infractions

What infractions are important in your home? A list of such would necessarily be individually tailored to an extent for each home. Here are some suggestions to start you out:

• **Failure to perform a task or chore when asked to do so.**

Note that no blame is laid. The child may have deliberately refused; the child may have forgotten. Whatever the motivation, the rule rather than a person has been slighted. We're keeping persons and personalities out of this.

• **Deliberate prevarication.**

We do not offer excuses for lying, nor do we condone it. But there are reasons ADD kids are usually particularly prone to fabrication. When self-esteem is at stake, an impulsive cover-up looks pretty good. These kids have esteem trouble anyway. Frustration may be a motive; the kid may be past caring. ADD kids being notoriously poor at planning and strategizing, even at the most basic level, they will lie without considering the situation or the consequences. They say impulsively whatever they want you to hear without thinking about the absurdity of their position.

For example, Beth saw Andrew kick the neighbor's dog one day. She confronted him instantly. "Andrew, for crying out loud! Why did you do *that?*"

"I didn't do it."

"I just saw you!"

"No you didn't."

"If you didn't do it, how do you know what I'm talking about?" Beth by now was totally frustrated. This was not the first time by any means that she had caught him in a lie. He would lie when it seemed there was no reason to, when the lie was bare or transparent. He didn't seem to recognize that his lies weren't going to work. That's typical of the ADD kid.

ADD kids may not be calculated liars. Usually they are pretty much impulsive liars interested primarily in covering their tails. As they get older, though, they may well become calculated liars.

• **Theft, pilferage, using personal items without asking.**

Again, "I forgot" is no excuse. Neither is "I borrowed it," even if the child actually did borrow without asking. The key word is *asking*.

• **Failure to obey a direct command.**

"Go upstairs to bed."

"Get ready for dinner."

"Turn off the TV."

"Stop that."

Many are the commands of childhood. Make certain that all commands are clear. And make certain, particularly for younger children, that a command embodies only one act or behavior. Remember that the child cannot sequence two things at once.

Continue along these lines to formulate rules appropriate to your household and your convictions. Note that they are definite and clear and fairly comprehensive but not so detailed as to invite loopholes. And don't think the kids won't seek out loopholes.

Consider Making Companion Promises

As you build your household code, you might also wish to make some companion promises. These are things you will do on your part, expecting, then, that the child will come through on his or her part. These companion promises are nice in that the child now feels included in a partnership rather than as the sole victim bearing the brunt of a disciplinary code.

For example, when you make a rule such as the one just above—to obey—you could also frame a promise to go with it: "In return, I will try not to issue orders that are unnecessary."

"You will not lie, but in return I will give you the benefit of the doubt whenever I can."

Make every effort to first tell the child what to do before mentioning what not to do. That's not as easy as it sounds. "Don't do that!" rises quickly to parents' lips. Positive suggestions tend to lie hidden in the soul. You must purposely bring them out into the golden light of day.

Next, lay out what happens when the rules are violated.

Identify Consequences

So what happens if Andrew breaks one of the rules? Structure and consistency require that for each action there is a simple consequence, either positive or negative. That's easy to say but incredibly hard to enforce. After all, parents are human, and they reach the ends of their ropes earlier on some days than on others, and it is so easy to let the consequences slide "just this once."

Peter, as you can imagine, would be prone to this more so than Gunther. Here again, personality type comes into play. Guard against the weaknesses; promote the strengths.

What are consequences? That's what you must decide, preferably in conference with your child or a consultant. Jody Capehart, for example, is always eager to sit down with parents to work out a good system for identifying infractions and consequences. School counselors, a teacher who understands ADD, a friend who deals with the problem well—many helpers are available. Don't be reluctant to use them!

Please let us offer some suggestions for getting started, beginning with this caveat: This list is not—we repeat, *not*—intended as a guide for you to impose blindly upon an ADD child. It is an illustration, nothing more, of what works for some ADD families. Please, please, please do not thoughtlessly parrot it.

Infraction:	Consequence:
Striking a person or animal	Immediate time-out. Separate.
Second time it happens	Banishment to room for [ ] minutes.
Happens again	Loss of privilege as determined beforehand, plus banishment for [ ] minutes.
Failure to obey command	Negative token, perform command.
Deliberate second or subsequent refusal	Negative token, perform command plus time-out.
Backtalk when commanded	Perform command, banishment for [ ] minutes.
Deliberate disrespect toward authority figure (parent, person such as baby-sitter who has been identified by parent as authority)	Time-out or banishment for [ ] minutes.

You see how it works. The child must know what is going to happen immediately when the rules are breached. That is structure.

But guidelines are certainly not limited to misbehavior.

Identify Positive Behavior and Rewards

Equally important, you should identify positive behavior. This is as much discipline as is extinguishing negative behavior, for good behavior is generated from within, and that's the very goal we're trying to achieve.

How about (and again, this is an illustrative guide, not a dictum to blindly follow):

Feeding the pet when asked: *one token.*

Feeding the pet at the appropriate time without being reminded: *three tokens* (note that the phrase "appropriate time" prevents the pet from being fed whenever the child happens to pass the empty food dish).

Picking up toys when asked: *one token.*

Picking up toys when through, without a reminder: *three tokens.*

If the child had to be reminded repeatedly or suffered consequences for backtalk or whatever before performing a task for which a token is usually forthcoming, positive affirmation is certainly in order, but he or she should understand that there will be no good-behavior token—not when the situation had to come to an impasse.

Accumulation of ten tokens in one day: *read two extra books at bedtime.*

Accumulation of ten tokens before lunch: *very special privilege to be decided in conference.* (Kids love that phrase, "in conference." It sounds so official and grown up!)

Accumulation of five negative tokens brings [fill-in-the-blank loss of privilege].

You may wish to define the privileges to be earned, perhaps even labeling A through H or whatever. "A" might be an extra book at bedtime while "B" might be X minutes of extra TV time and "C" is making cookies (which includes licking the bowl).

This is all set up before infractions and good deeds have actually occurred.

Define the Consequences Ahead of Time

Note that nowhere do we refer to *punishment,* a word that suggests revenge or parental retribution. There may be a place for revenge and retribution somewhere, but discipline and behavior modification is not the place. Punishment also implies a personal stake, and you'll recall we want to keep this procedure of disciplining as impersonal as possible. A consequence is simply what happens as a result of the child's particular behavior choice, just as a loud crash is the consequence of pitching a stone through a glass window.

Again, there is to be no room for ambiguity. The ax falls predictably, sure and swift. However, older children especially may be given opportunity to shorten the "sentence." This gives children the experience of using their power of choice in a positive way. Usually, we suggest that a positive act of restitution, something above and beyond normal expectations, could reduce the loss of privileges or cancel out negative tokens, or something. We don't like the implication that if the child acts real, real good now, we'll cancel the consequences of past bad behavior. That's not the idea. We are tempering the justice with mercy.

An example might be, "You lost your bicycle privileges for four days. If you clean out your closet and get rid of last summer's mess, we can reduce the loss to two days. However, we won't remind you again; it has to be on your own. And we won't help."

Here, you see, is a chance to take the initiative in something with positive, immediate payback. The more such chances an ADD child has—legitimate chances, of course—the more that child can learn to control actions. Such opportunities should not completely eliminate consequences.

One warning is sufficient. "I asked you to do this [defined exactly] job. I won't ask again."

Include restitution in the consequences. When the child breaks something he or she should at least symbolically be in on its repair or replacement. A young child cannot help glaze a broken window, of course, but that child can be present during the repair, perhaps holding tools. Older kids can pay for damages, at least partially. Monetary payment without a hands-on payback is of limited use, though. The child should physically, actively, take part in a plan of restitution.

If the child is responsible for another person's injury, both written and oral apologies should be an immediate consequence. Further restitution may include visiting the person, running errands, and/or helping him or her in some other way.

Keep consequences and rewards immediate, short, and to the point. Do not impose consequences or gratification any further ahead than twenty-four hours and ideally, not that long. "Next week when we go to such-and-such . . ." means nothing to ADD children. They cannot project into the future any more than they can learn quickly from the past. An effective goal is to at least begin consequences immediately for young children, within six hours of the infraction for kids like William and Amy.

Reinforcing the Ground Rules

Reinforcement means a written version and periodic review. "Periodic review" is not a situation in which the parent and child sit down together and recite all the rules as reminders. That may have worked when Moses was reading the law on Mounts Ebal and Gerizim, but it doesn't work on ADD kids. Rather, "periodic review" means identifying the rule when it is broken and also frequently *when it is observed.*

Beth would be reviewing the "Thou shalt not lie" rule in, for example, this situation:

"Andrew? Did you brush your teeth?"

"Not yet."

"Do you remember last night when you lied to me and said you did when you didn't? You could have tried to lie to me again just now, but you didn't. You told the truth, and that's very important. Thank you, Andrew! I really appreciate it. Now go brush your teeth, please."

Definition of Terms

Some definitions we use in counsel that you may wish to modify or adopt:

Time-Out. This is a cooling-off and separating procedure, particularly for squabbles. Since ADD kids cannot govern their emotions or their actions well, this gives them time to bring themselves under some kind of control. Sitting on the sofa three or four minutes may suffice. Perhaps a special chair can be the time-out place. This is a humane and more effective version of the old go-stand-in-the-corner punishment.

How long does a child stay there? Some would say ten minutes is the minimum, and others will say, "Until you're calmed down." Just as some prescriptions allow unlimited refills, time-outs can be repeated until the child has a handle on his or her emotions and behavior. However, for a time-out to also be a consequence, there should be a minimal figure.

A rule of thumb might be that the child separates and sits for at least one minute for each year of his or her age. Andrew would sit there for at least seven minutes. William would sit for at least fifteen (although he was sixteen, he and his parents agreed ahead of time that fifteen minutes was the minimum and maximum). This shows flexibility, tailored to the specific child.

Grounding. Grounding means limiting the child to a particular area with (usually) a reduction or elimination of privileges. Grounding as a rule won't work on kids under age seven. Their world isn't all that big to start with. As they enter school and make friends away from home, however, being denied access to those friends and to other play areas begins to take on importance.

Grounding Amy might mean taking away her phone privileges for two days, something she would claim as being disastrous to her social life. In contrast, phone privileges would mean nothing to Andrew and even to William, who was generally indifferent to the phone. The grounding and attendant losses must be carefully tailored to the child.

For a serious infraction, grounding a kid like William for five days to a week would not be too onerous. Three days is usually a standard sentencing guideline, and for younger kids, even shorter times would be appropriate. There are no clear rules or even suggestions. It all depends totally upon the severity of the infraction and of the child's ADD, as well as upon the child's temperament. Fun-Lover may feel grounding keenly, and Perfectionist, perhaps, hardly at all.

Banishment. This is a hardcore version of time-out, wherein the child must isolate himself or herself in a particular place. Usually the child's room is the place. This is not just a time-out in order to regain control but also a time-out from outside reinforcement. The parent removes both the stimulus to inappropriate behavior and also the external check on it. Here is the time wherein the child can impose upon himself or herself a degree of self-control.

For a child Andrew's age, the standard of one minute minimum for each year of age is pretty good, though we recommend against isolating a child under age two or three. For young children, time out in the presence of an adult is appropriate. Not only are they still working on figuring out relationships, they are not capable of fending for themselves and they know it. Besides, isolation is extremely scary for a young child.

Banishing a child to a separate room also changes the venue of an argument or potential argument. This in itself can help defuse a situation. The parent either releases the child or else knocks and enters the child's room, but only after there is some assurance that the child is back in control.

If it doesn't "take" the first time, it should be repeated.

Fine Points

May we suggest some refinements on both time-out and banishment?

The location of the time-out—chair, stool, sofa, whatever—should be in a position that does not provoke everybody or draw attention to the child. Attention for improper behavior is the last thing you want. You also want to avoid further escalation of a hostile situation. Putting the child near another child's room, for example, would be counterproductive. So would putting him or her in the middle of the living room.

If the child is isolated in his or her room, play is an appropriate activity. In fact, it helps by diverting the child's interest and therefore anger and provides time to think. Oftentimes, we do our best thinking, you know, when we're otherwise occupied.

Does the frustrated child cut loose and destroy things in the room? If it's the child's toys and other possessions, let him or her take the consequences, not trying to stop it. Destruction to the room or to the self, of course, is different. Then the parent must resort to physical restraint. In any case, destruction is the child's responsibility, and the child should take part, at least symbolically, in any repairs.

What if the child won't stay in the room? The parent has several options. One might be to lock a younger child in and stay nearby, right outside the door. An even better option is to loop a bungee cord around the doorknob and secure it, perhaps even to a hook set in the wall. That way the child can open the door a tad, something that can be extremely important for insecure children because it lets them keep some sort of contact with others. But the door is not to stay open.

The child escapes the parent's clutches and runs out of the house? Unless there is a clear concern for safety, it's probably wisest that the parent not go after him or her. Chasing after the kid destroys dignity, and the child has nowhere to go anyway. The anger fades quickly in most ADD kids.

If the child is isolated or seated for refusal to perform a task or obey, the parent reissues the expectation as soon as the time-out has ended. "You still need to do this."

The child has no choice. The time-out or isolation will be enforced. Period. If the child refuses to yield, we suggest two possible courses. The better one is to count. By prearrangement, the count is, let's say, to five. It should not be less than five nor longer than ten. If the parent reaches the end of the count and compliance has not begun, serious consequences will result. All this is prearranged, of course.

The count gives oppositional, argumentative kids a chance to save face, to rebel and yet obey. This can be extremely important to some kids. It's a concession on the parents' part, a bending, and deep down, it's acceptable on the kids' part. Counting gives them time to think a moment about consequences.

The child still refuses to cooperate? "Go to your room on your own, or I take you to your room."

The child refuses and is too large for the parent to physically force him or her to obey? Beth was facing that in a few years. Ellen had it now with William. An alternative will be to shut down all privileges until the child has served the time.

If the child continues to provoke, to come at the parent, the parent should remove himself or herself from the child's presence. Does this mean the parent is backing down? In a way it does, and it's not a solution for everyone. Gunther could never in a hundred years back down before William. But that is exactly how that fight resulted, and the fight nearly brought grief to everyone.

In extreme circumstances, call for help. In the ultimate-ultimate case, dial 911 and summon the police.

The point in all these worst-case scenarios is to avoid remaining in conflict. A power struggle with an ADD kid never subsides on its own. Someone has to win or lose, and neither winning nor losing serves the interests of the child.

How It Works

Let's consider this scenario, a Saturday morning in the life of Beth Mulroney. For the first time that month, Beth had no Saturday morning appointments. This afternoon she had two and tomorrow would be hectic, with a number of open houses to attend and clients lined up to see homes, but this morning she was free to catch up on housework.

Andrew usually did not take Ritalin on weekends. That was Beth's first hint that today would not go smoothly. When she got up at six Andrew had already been up an hour. His blocks were scattered clear across the living room. His little office was littered with unfinished homework. Most of his breakfast cereal had apparently missed the bowl, and the kitchen floor was sticky-crunchy with sugar.

Out in front of the apartment building, his skateboard, bicycle, basketball, and bike helmet were spread all over the lawn. Beth knew the manager didn't like clutter. In the backyard Andrew was busily digging a hole under the oak tree. What for, Beth could not guess. She didn't want to know. She could just imagine what the manager would say about *that*.

Barefooted, she hurried out back. "Andrew! What do you think you're doing?"

"Building a dirt track." Andrew didn't slow down a moment. "I'm going to use this dirt to build a dirt track."

"Give me the shovel, please."

Andrew gripped it tighter. "I can do it, Mom."

"No you can't. The manager will throw a purple fit if he sees this hole. Give me the shovel. We have to fill it in."

"What with?"

"The dirt you took out, of course."

"No! That's why I'm digging the hole, see? I need the dirt to make this hill here, and then you run the track up over it, and you race your bike on it."

He imagined it as being just like the dirt-bike races he had watched on the sports channel last night.

Beth snatched the shovel and was startled by the strength of a seven-year-old's grip. "This is not an Astrodome full of dirt, and we have to fill it back in before the manager sees it. Now stop being stubborn, Andrew! Go inside." She jammed the shovel into the dirt pile.

Before she could tip the shovelful into the hole, Andrew shoved her away, instantly furious, instantly yelling.

She would just have to risk the manager's wrath. She dropped the shovel, grabbed Andrew around the waist, and hauled the kicking, flailing, screaming child back inside. Above the ruckus she shouted, "Time-out!" and stuffed him into his room and slammed the door. She shot the bolt, locking him in, but the flimsy door molding into which the bolt was screwed would never take this kind of punishment. She leaned full-weight against the door as on the other side, Andrew kicked and pounded on it, shrieking. With horrendous *whumps* he flung himself against it.

Now she was sobbing, too, deep shuddering gulps. She couldn't control him at seven. What was she going to do in five years? The lower-right door panel splintered and pushed outward, poking her in the leg. Andrew's next kick broke the panel into an open hole.

Beth realized even as she stared at the break that not all the pounding was coming from Andrew. Someone was pounding on the door also.

The manager burst in the front door. "What in blazes is going on in here?!" He stopped and stared at Beth, at the bedroom door, and at the gaping hole with the child's foot kicking it bigger.

Through her tears Beth begged, "Help me!" But she knew from the look on his face, she absolutely knew, that no help would be coming from this source.

Glaring, he moved in close enough to be heard above the din. "The front yard is a mess! Clean it up immediately. And fill in that hole." He stepped in another foot closer. "This is it! Finis. You two will be out of here by the first of the month, do you hear?" His voice rose as Andrew began wailing. "And that door will be fixed before you go!"

The Beginning of the Episode

What could Beth have done differently?

A basic rule, remember, is to avoid a power struggle. This is not pandering to the child or caving in. It is avoiding pushing the big red CONTROL button so many ADD kids have. An ordinary child will engage in a power struggle and give up when the situation becomes hopeless. The ADD child cannot act that sensibly.

Beth invited the power struggle by snatching the shovel away from Andrew. She could have done better by either calling (usually doesn't work), luring (works sometimes), or distracting Andrew into the house. Once his attention was elsewhere, she could redirect him to picking up in the front yard, perhaps, or catching a favorite TV program while she filled in the hole.

In counseling, we ask parents to work on developing a sort of radar that is turned on to a developing situation. By observing and analyzing, parents can develop a sense about when a power struggle is coming on. Often the ADD child will invite it. They're great manipulators when it comes to control issues.

Parents who sense a situation coming on must remember that their first and foremost responsibility is to keep themselves in firm control. Unless they do so, they have no hope at all of controlling the child or the consequences.

Beth had no rule written down to specify, "Thou shalt not dig big holes in the backyard." She and Andrew did, however, have an understanding about leaving his bike and toys scattered out front. There is where she might better have directed her energy and Andrew's.

"There's a bunch of stuff scattered out front, Andrew. You know the rule; bring it back inside. Let's go get it before the manager throws a fit or worse, someone steals it."

She would then draw the line for expected behavior, remind Andrew of the appropriate consequence, and work from there, always keeping the impersonal rules at the center and not personality.

Always she would watch where she walked, lest she step into the trap of letting power become the issue.

The Middle of the Episode

Beth handled the middle about as well as she was able, separating the child and isolating him. She remained firm, not letting him out, not going in to him (which would have availed nothing anyway in his agitated state). Beth needed a helpmeet here. She needed her apartment manager. It is to his great disgrace that he did not respond favorably to her plea.

When an ADD child is out of control, the child is totally out of control and helpless to pull himself or herself back. That's hard for a non-ADD adult to grasp. The manager saw Andrew's behavior as willful, the escalation as deliberate. But it was not.

The End of the Episode

Two hours later, the day's two afternoon appointments canceled, Beth called her counselor, Jody Capehart, and the situation finally began to turn around. Call it luck or providence, but Beth painstakingly commenced stitching her world back together. For one thing, Mrs. Capehart was actually home and able to talk to Beth. Her speaking engagements take her so far and wide, that rarely occurs.

Beth described the episode, and they discussed ways the problem could have been resolved less dramatically, the power struggle evaded. Mrs. Capehart concluded with, "Now Auntie Jody here is going to get very stern with you, Beth. Listen to me. You are kicking yourself for not handling the situation differently from the start. Don't you dare do that! It's the easiest thing in the world to decide what to do two hours after the fact."

Beth smiled through her tears. "Monday morning quarterbacking."

"Exactly! You're going to blow it more often than you're going to do it right. That's just the way it is. Expect it. You'll learn from your mistakes, but circumstances are never the same twice, so the lessons are limited. Do your best, and never look back. Don't beat up on yourself for doing what comes naturally, hear me?"

That out of the way, they discussed the restitution Beth should elicit from Andrew. Restitution from a seven-year-old? Absolutely. Even a four- or five-year-old is not too young to understand justice and cause and effect.

That afternoon the two of them together took the door off its hinges and stuck it in the back of a neighbor's pickup. Andrew helped with the screws and hinges. They took the door to a big hardware store where they purchased parts, stain, and finish, and then they were directed to a cabinet shop. Andrew sort of helped the cabinetmaker set the new panel. At home they rehung the door before staining and finishing the panel. Beth would have liked to work on it as it lay down flat, but she needed that door up in case Andrew went ballistic again.

What galled her most in the whole episode was Andrew's good cheer of all things. Once the storm passed, he was totally, absolutely sunny again. He put the event behind him, seemed to care nothing about what he had just done, didn't even appear to have remembered it. Sure, he kicked the door panel out. But he didn't remember details, and he certainly did not perceive the grief he had caused his mother.

Weeks afterward, his lack of concern still dogged Beth. "He didn't show a bit of remorse. He just doesn't care."

Andrew was not being perverse. He was not capable of grasping the things Beth considered so important. ADD kids live the movie of their life, remember, one frame at a time.

Avoiding power struggles is only one spear in the full armory of discipline techniques to apply to ADD kids. Another is to avoid negative reinforcement.

Avoiding Negative Reinforcement

"Picture this." Beth sat in the powder blue easy chair facing Jody Capehart's desk. "A mother and child go into the grocery store for half a dozen items. Not much, because they're moving in another week or two. Within five minutes the child is throwing a tantrum, screaming loud enough to wake the dead, and two different old ladies are telling the mother how she should have handled the problem and what they would do if it were their child."

Jody nodded. "So where are you moving to?"

Beth burst out laughing. "All right. What should I have done? He gets these ideas in his head, and he won't shake them. He wanted a particular kind of cereal, and I refused. He went into orbit. One woman told me I should beat it out of him, and another said, 'Give him the cereal; it's not like he's asking for a Mercedes or something.' But Mrs. Capehart, that particular cereal seems to make him hyper. I don't want him to have it."

"Who's in charge?"

Beth grimaced. "I insisted on staying in charge, and two different floor managers offered to help me out to the car and check out my groceries for me. It was quite a scene."

"It's past. Now let's work out a course of action so it never happens again. And the first thing we discuss is negative attention."

Negative Attention

Abel offered pleasing sacrifices, and Cain committed murder. Both men caught God's attention.

All kids crave attention, but none more than ADD kids. All kids will to some extent seek negative attention—attention for doing something bad or annoying—if they perceive that that's the only kind of attention they have any hope of obtaining. They'll repeat the improper behavior just to be noticed. ADD kids usually don't even grasp that it's bad and annoying. It's attention. That's sufficient. So they go for it.

Negative reinforcement, like negative attention, is a payback for undesirable behavior that tends to perpetuate that behavior. Quite often, negative attention *is* the negative reinforcement.

ADD kids tend to behave their worst out in public for several reasons. One is that a public outing such as a grocery run is usually not very tightly structured. You prowl the aisles and pick up items. ADD kids need more lockstep structure than that. Another reason is that this is of practically no interest to an ADD kid, who bores quickly and readily anyway. A third is that public places are usually quite open and spacious, inviting the kind of gross motor movement—running, jumping, climbing—most ADD kids specialize in. Still another reason is that it's a marvelous venue for attention. At home the audience is comprised of one or two caregivers and maybe a couple of siblings, and they're all pretty jaded. Here in the grocery store, dozens of people provide a large and welcome audience.

Does the child deliberately present a "show" for that audience? Probably not consciously. But the audience is there, and deep down, the attention-hungry child knows it. In short, the public venue is a perfect place for negative attention that, to the ADD child especially, is hardly less desirable than positive attention. So let's look specifically at moderating and controlling public behavior. How would Beth, or any other harried parent, minimize the situation?

First, Establish Parental Attitude

For starters, as Mrs. Capehart pointed out, Beth should think out her own attitude and adjust it if necessary. The vast majority of parents, particularly parents who have been dealing with ADD, are self-protective. *What will the relatives think of me? What will the neighbors think of me? What will total strangers think of me?* This self-protection is natural to human beings. Deep down, we all want to be well thought of. But the ADD parent has a particularly nasty goad to self-protection.

The rest of the world is right in their criticizing that person's parenting skills.

ADD antics, if we could call it that, mimic the antics of non-ADD kids—spoiled kids, entitled kids—who are out to get negative attention. Everyone is certain he or she could handle the situation better than the parent is doing. For some reason, bystanders feel no compunctions about stepping in and telling the parent what he or she ought to do or ought not do. A woman who would never dream of telling another woman she's driving a car poorly will eagerly chastise a mother she thinks is parenting poorly.

The parent of an ADD child, then, should have firmly in place a useful set of personal attitudes *ahead of time*. Those attitudes ideally should be unselfish.

I'll Not Be So Self-Protective.   The worst thing Beth can do is nothing. And yet, embarrassment often drives a parent to do nothing. The harried mom or dad hopes the situation will simply fade away if ignored and blessed anonymity will return. It almost never goes that way.

As Jody Capehart put it, "Public opinion is lovely, but there comes a time when you step beyond worrying what other people think."

And Beth replied, honestly, "I don't think I can do that."

"That's right. You can't abandon that self-protective desire to be admired or approved. But you can reduce the tendency quite a bit. I suggest substituting a worthier aim: to raise Andrew well. Put that ahead of self-interest."

"I've been doing that my whole life."

"Exactly. It's a lifelong investment you're making. So protect your investment by going one step more."

Beth sighed heavily as only the parent of an ADHD child can sigh.

The Child's Best Interests Come First.   It would not be in Andrew's best interests to enjoy the fruits of negative attention—negative reinforcement of his unseemly public behavior. And yet, he lacked the ability to regulate his own behavior. He was nearly eight now but not mature enough to get a grip on his impulsivity. Beth's primary goal would best be to help him learn to control himself in public.

There it is again: easy to say, terribly hard to do. But this one attitude adjustment, to put Andrew's best interests first, can be a splendid enabling mechanism for Beth to move ahead and act decisively instead of cowering beneath the glares of all those total strangers. It can be broken down into self statements:

• **I will be willing to give up something here.**

The sacrifice might be to abort the store trip and simply go home. It might be to hire a baby-sitter and shop in peace. It might be to go without eggs and bread a day. Andrew had good days and bad days. Beth might better postpone shopping for a good day.

• **I will act immediately and proactively.**

Back home, Beth ought to have a written rule that says, in effect, "If you act out in public, I get to set whatever consequences I want to set." A companion guideline will be, "You get extra [tokens or privileges] for behaving well in public." Home rules need not apply exclusively to the home.

In public, then, the moment the parent sees the potential for an escalation and scene, he or she is wise to instantly intervene. That has to be an attitude, an automatic response, and it doesn't come naturally. In a public place the parent is usually reluctant to jump on a behavior that has the potential for escalation.

Second, Establish and Enforce Expectations and Consequences. Here are Beth and Andrew in the parking lot, locking up the car. Andrew bolts for the grocery-store door, but Beth grabs his arm and hauls him to an instant stop (her grip is partly restraint and partly physical contact. Andrew listens better with her firm touch—tactile/kinesthetic, remember?). "I'll expect you to help me when we're in there. We have a lot to do, but we can get it done if we work together. It should be a fun time."

Hear the positive spin? No "I'll expect you to settle down," and no "Don't do this and don't do that." Those are negatives and are generally remembered for less than ten seconds. "Fun time" should stick in Andrew's memory better; it means more to him. So does "Help me." That's what we mean when we say the first guideline is to keep expectations positive.

• **Try to keep expectations positive.**

Andrew resumes his bolt for the door, slams inside (there's that word again: *slam*), and has a cart yanked free by the time Beth gets there. Andrew runs. Beth whistles him back and lets him ride by standing on the bottom rung and hanging on the side. She knows it's frowned upon, but she also knows it won't last more than a few moments. It doesn't. Andrew heads for the soda shelf.

Our second guideline is to nip trouble in the bud.

• **Anticipate problems and head them off if possible.**

This requires a sacrificial mind-set, as we discussed above regarding attitude adjustment. Beth can't give her whole attention to her grocery list. She has to tune her radar not just to what Andrew is doing, a difficult enough job, but to what he's going to do next.

What he was going to do next was ask for soda pop. She could see that clearly enough, so she anticipated him. "Let's get some soda. What's on special?"

They discussed price. They discussed flavors. Beth had heard that caffeine sometimes helps ADD kids, so she permitted a cola. They put a six-pack in the cart.

Andrew: "I want one now."

Beth: "Okay. As soon as it's ours and not the store's, you can have some. We have to pay for it first to make it ours."

There's that positive spin again. Andrew didn't have anything negative to bounce off of and dropped the matter. Be advised that that doesn't always happen, but it's worth trying for.

Beth then diverted him to the milk case. She asked him to muscle a gallon of milk into the cart, quite a struggle for a seven-year-old. She praised him highly, lavishing attention on his strength. She dearly wanted to comment on the strength required to break a door panel in a fit of fury, but she demurred.

There came a moment in the grocery-shopping adventure, though, when the foregoing guidelines fell flat. ADD kids simply do not fit into any management plan. Andrew was back after his forbidden cereal—and they hadn't even gone down the cereal aisle. Now Beth had to apply authority and decisiveness.

• **Be authoritative and act decisively.**

This time, Beth had been talking to Jody Capehart, and she felt confident about what to do. She laid a hand on Andrew's arm (the arm not wrapped protectively around the cereal box). "Andrew. You're going to put that back and not ask for it anymore. End of discussion. Thank you for obeying."

It set him back a second or two. But experience had taught him that he could either get his way or at least get a lot of attention if he pushed the matter loudly. He began his litany, his escalation.

She interrupted him. "Stop immediately or we leave." It was so, so hard to keep her voice low and firm. She had delivered the expectation and the consequence. Now the ball was in his court.

He volleyed with a tantrum.

She unceremoniously scooped him up and marched the length of the store, out the doors, across the parking lot. She felt mortified, absolutely mortified. All those people watching . . . and yet she felt a certain heady exhilaration too. She had minimized the situation. She had shown Andrew that this kind of behavior avails nothing. The negative reinforcement was minimal this time. And she remained in control.

As Mrs. Capehart had pointed out, trying to force an ADD child into a behavior (or cessation of a behavior) or trying to convince the child of some adult point of logic only reinforces what we call hostile dependency. Hostile dependency is a love-hate relationship between persons, in this case parent and child. The child, and usually the parent as well, although parents hardly ever admit it, feed on the emotional energy of the situation, even though it is negative energy. Removing the child from the situation without arguing or cajoling extinguishes much of the energy.

Beth would find that with time, this solution would become easier to enforce. Her no-nonsense position of removing her son from negative situations would take the form of an attitude on both their parts, reducing the need to actually take that step.

As Andrew finished his fit while strapped into the backseat, Beth sat in the driver's seat. There was a symbolism here. She was in the driver's seat. She sensed somehow a turning point. For the first time in years, Beth Mulroney could see light at the end of the tunnel.

Now she could look to ways to provide good attention.

Third, Maximize Positive Reinforcement. ADD kids never receive quite enough attention. A solid twenty-four hours of constant attention is not quite enough. However, lavishing positive attention has the advantage of minimizing (not eliminating, but minimizing) negative attention.

If you use a token system, providing opportunities to earn extra chips or tokens is good positive reinforcement. Children might earn them for staying close to the parents in public places, avoiding argument and fussiness, helping with parcels and parking meters.

The overriding rule, the rule of rules, is to control only what you can control.

Finally, Control What You Can Control and Drop the Rest. The corollary of controlling what you can control is: Don't try to control what you cannot control. This is the basic principle behind all discipline as well as most social skills.

Beth cannot control her child's thoughts, attitudes, and, to a large extent, behavior. In a few years, when he's bigger than she is, she won't be able to control it at all. She has no power over the words Andrew says or the look on his face, or whether he'll argue or be compliant.

Her job is to teach her child how to control those things himself.

She can do that by maintaining control of the two things she can handle: herself, and the consequences of Andrew's actions.

Recite after us: "I control how I respond when my kid is behaving and misbehaving. The child does not."

Now repeat it.

Gunther lost control when he got into that physical fight with William. He let it get away from him. During the shovel incident, Beth controlled the situation as well as she could, but she minimized her ability to creatively plan what to do next when she let emotion overcome her. It may not have been possible to do otherwise—the situation was traumatic for her—but she did not think of controlling herself.

Parents also sometimes forget that they are the ones who control the consequences of their children's behavior. Their kids choose a particular behavior; the choice demands a response. And rest assured the child will try six ways from Sunday to change the consequences.

"Aw, come on! That's too harsh! I only forgot this once."

That's not an effective argument.

"Okay, just go ahead [and impose the consequence]. See what I care. I don't care."

The response? "It doesn't matter whether or not you care. This is the consequence."

Notice that throughout, we avoid the word and the concept of *punishment*. If the child is to learn self-control, the child must realize that for every action there is a reaction, for every behavior a consequence, both at home in the family and out in the real world. And although you, the parent, control what the consequences are, the child can control which consequence pertains.

Self-control. It's an immensely important life lesson, a fruit of discipline, and the root of social skills. Let's look at that next.

SOCIAL
SKILLS

I VISITED AMY'S SCHOOL today and watched her in class awhile. Amy is so—so flirtatious." Viveca Eglund looked ready to melt into the rug as she thought about her twelve-year-old daughter. "Oh, dear. I didn't mean it to sound like that. It sounds so terrible. It's not sexual. At least I don't think it is. But it's—well, it's nonsexual flirtation." She frowned. "Is there such a thing?"

For want of a better term, there is. Many girls with ADD do not display the loud, overly active behavior we usually associate with the condition. Hyperactivity that in boys emerges as ramming around, fighting, and yelling—socially unacceptable behaviors—may appear in girls as more socially acceptable histrionics and impulsive social behavior.

From an early age, these girls, like Amy, live to socialize. They're the ones who will be caught passing notes, who talk incessantly, who will be known as gossips and flirts. Viveca Eglund guessed right; it was not at all a sexual flirtation, but it was a striving to be noticed and attractive and desired at an emotional level, all the same.

Social skills in ADD kids, then, take a turn that other people rarely understand and may not even tolerate. Although we may not know just why ADD occurs or how it functions, we can see how ADD kids' social interactions take that different path. The path is determined by conditions within and outside of the child. This is true of all of us; it is true in spades of the ADD child. External influences are family interactions, interactions with others, and cultural conditions. Internally, the ADD child's different wiring provides a whole different outlook on life and relationships. Let's look at the internal wiring first.

The uniqueness of ADD children manifests itself socially in several distinct ways. Understanding those ways helps immensely in learning to understand, tolerate, and yes, love an ADD kid. It's next to impossible to drum up genuine affection for a strongly ADD child unless you can see how that brain ticks and know what's probably going on inside it.

Influences from Within

The ADD child's wiring peculiarities—the inability to sequence as well as impulsivity, excessive activity, poor short-term memory, and late maturation—all combine to do in the social graces.

Inability to Sequence

You will recall that one of the hallmarks in most cases of ADD (but by no means all!) is the child's inability to think in linear ways—A plus B equals C. Most ADD kids also have problems associating things that ought to go together, another sequencing function. For instance, the child cannot associate a thoroughly familiar rule—Don't run in the street—with the activity of the moment, running after a loose ball.

At a social level, the inability to sequence prevents most ADD kids from recognizing that their actions are having an adverse effect on others. To them, A plus B equals A and B in any configuration. No C. No effect. "I'm clowning around," which is A, plus "People are getting upset," B, does not equal C, "Maybe I'd better cool it." When the situation escalates and eventually explodes, the ADD child, bewildered, cannot see that his or her actions precipitated the explosion. He or she is hurt and angry that other people act like that without provocation. The sequence simply does not come together the way it does in most people.

And yet, ADD kids can be quite sensitive to the moods and feelings of other people, but it's a disassociated sensitivity. The ADD child detects the effect of irritating social behavior, but not the cause. The non-ADD person, to whom sequencing cause and effect is not only important but natural, cannot understand this apparent insensitivity in the ADD child.

Now combine this sequencing difficulty with most ADD children's extreme impulsivity.

Impulsivity

The social implications of impulsivity are also sequence related. ADD kids blurt out without thinking what the effect of their words may be; they act without pausing to assess the possible outcome. By saying whatever comes to mind, whenever it comes to mind, the ADD child comes across as grossly insensitive and thoughtless, caring not a whit for others.

But that's just not true. In fact, the child cares deeply. He or she simply does not think the same way most people do. Stop and consider this for a moment. Most of us have very little of the sequencing and impulsivity problems we've just discussed. We look at the world from our natural mind-set combining cause and effect. We know that's how the world works. We use caution in dealing with others, understanding that we can hurt them with a thoughtless remark, an impulsive action. We listen with some care, keying our responses to the other person's remarks and actions. Certainly, no one is 100 percent perfect at dealing well with others, but at least we grasp the mechanics.

Not so the ADD child. ADD children look at the world from *their* unique mind-set, which is not at all like ours: To them, there is no strong relationship between what just occurred and what is going to happen next. It does not occur to them to expect such a relationship. They don't cater to it. They don't use it to analyze what has just happened. They are going at life from an approach totally opposite to most people's, and neither group of people, ADD or other, appreciates the other group's mind-set. That's why ADD kids can offend deeply and then be so surprised by others' reactions.

Now put all that together with another hallmark of over half of all ADD kids, hyperactivity.

Excessive Activity

Picture your senior prom. Most of your classmates probably attended. There were loud, obnoxious guys and maybe some loud, obnoxious girls. Maybe you wanted to pull a bag over their heads and stick them in a corner. They embarrassed everybody. Most of the kids, though, interacted normally, talking, dancing, mixing, having a good time. And then there were the wallflowers, the shy ones. They sat at tables and didn't talk much, didn't dance much. The majority wondered why the shy ones bothered to come, and then they forgot about them.

The in-your-face kids were annoying, the shy ones forgotten. It's that way with ADD kids. A hyperactive boy buzzes around your ears for a few minutes and you want to bop him with a hammer or tie him to a big iron anchor. An overactive girl seems even more annoying because girls aren't supposed to be like that, loud and unruly. The kid's going to end up in prison; you just know it. Neither child is very high in the running for the Most Beloved title. The shy ones will earn the crown before these two do.

Socially, both the hyperactives and the shy ones suffer deeply. Again, the overly active kids don't understand why everyone is bent out of shape at them. They soon come to expect the world to treat them differently, yelling at them when others are not yelled at, snapping and snarling at them when others are treated kindly. That doesn't do much for a kid's social development.

And the shy ones? A lot of ADD kids are classed as spacey, or "out of it." They are the forgotten ones. Again, their social development lags, undernourished.

One more hallmark of most ADD kids, short-term memory malfunction, provides its negative contribution as well.

Poor Short-Term Memory

Most people dwell on past hurts. The more recent the hurt, the more intense and painful the dwelling. Most adults can remember injustices and wrongs done against them as children. It's the way we are.

But it's not the way ADD kids are. They have a lovely gift for putting the past behind them—of forgetting hurts and arguments. This was the case when Beth smarted for weeks from Andrew's hideous kick-the-door-down scene and Andrew forgot about it almost immediately. "He showed absolutely no remorse," said Beth.

"He had absolutely different wiring," would have been a far more accurate analysis.

Ordinary people deeply resent what appears to be the ADD child's total lack of remorse, of feeling sorry for committing a wrong. Ordinary people do not realize that to an ADD child, blowing up is natural. Rage is ordinary. People yell at him or her, and the child yells back. No big deal. The child can explode in fury, cause harm and hostility all around, and five minutes later be sweet and loving as if nothing had happened. As far as the child is concerned, nothing significant did happen. Others, their memory seared, cannot dismiss the behavior so lightly. They may feel smoldering resentment—but the ADD child does not.

Late Maturation

The basic nature of most ADD children, then, can damage and limit their ability to develop social skills. Added to this is the fact that these kids usually mature more slowly than most. Their juvenile behavior in itself is a deterrent to good social skills. Add it all together, and you no longer doubt why these kids cannot connect well in happy relationships with the rest of the world.

And it seems appropriate to repeat here what we've said before: It's not perversity on their part—at least not to start with. They're simply wired differently and are not at fault. There is no fault.

Outside conditions and situations can also adversely affect an ADD child's social skills and social development, intensely so.

Influences from Without

Says Paul Warren, "Watch some of the videos on television these days, and that includes the Christian ones. They're constantly moving, with a new shot, a new angle every second or two. On television the frenetic activity becomes constantly more frenetic. We worship the art of all this fast-paced action and then criticize the youth who do it. We like impulsivity and quick snapshots of life and claim that's what sells. But when we see kids like that, we label them 'disorderly' and put them on Ritalin."

Says Jody Capehart, "There's a new child out there. He's aggressive. He can be mean. He's not as sweet. It's hard to be a good, godly kid today. Everything is pulling kids in the opposite direction."

Strong external pulls include cultural influences, family influences, and peer influences.

Cultural Influences

Dr. Warren muses, tongue in cheek, "Back when I was a boy in the good old days, we walked five miles to school through the snowdrifts, then came home and plowed the back forty and milked the cows. I'm being facetious, but my point is that in another culture, including America in her past, overly active, kinesthetic kids have been considered an asset. They would be on the go constantly, tirelessly working. That kind of person was greatly admired. Now we drive our children to school, and they come home to sit in front of the TV, Nintendo and all, with little physical outlet. That ups their aggression level without providing any constructive physical way to burn it off. People bewail the number of hours kids spend with television and look at the intellectual effects. But that's not all of it; there's this other aspect as well."

Single parents and families in which both parents must work have to use day care in a child's early years, the television set later. It has been demonstrated that both can accelerate aggression in susceptible youngsters. ADD kids, with their reduced social skills, are especially susceptible.

Besides that, society itself is far more aggressive, and this also rubs off on children. To quote a woman who has worked for eighteen years in the police department of a major American city, "Out on the street, when I first entered the department and was assigned to patrol, if a gun went off or even if there was just a backfire, every cop in the city descended on the spot. Today, we don't bother to respond at all unless someone reports physical injury or damage."

A ten-year-old boy, injured in a drive-by shooting in a "nice" neighborhood, told the paramedics attending him, "This is the first time I got shot." He had already accepted the probability (not just the possibility—the *probability*) as a way of life. He is not alone.

Every reader of this book can tell similar war stories about the kind of society that has developed over the last few years. Pause a few moments to think about how that dangerous, confusing society must look to an impulsive, socially inept ADD child who is constantly ranked upon by everyone.

Family Influences

It would be bad enough if cultural chaos were the only outside influence applicable to the ADD child, but add to that the fact that almost half of ADD kids have an ADD parent and you start to realize the extent of the problem. The prevailing wisdom used to be that a person outgrew ADD at puberty and was expected to be a "normal" human being from then on. Now we know better. ADD extends into adulthood. Even when it abates with maturity, and the great majority of ADD does indeed subside, adults feel the residue throughout life. In fact, some profit from medication well into adulthood.

ADD parents tend to be disorganized, and the child needs organization. ADD adults polarize: Either they can't stand to see their child go through what they went through (Andrew's father's case) or they empathize. If they empathize too closely, they may actually get in the way of progress by trying to shield their child too much. In addition, non-ADD spouses of ADD parents may not be capable of raising a child who displays all the most annoying attributes of an oftentimes annoying spouse.

When the ADD child begins that final giant step of separation and individuation (becoming his or her own person and not just a member of a family) in the early teens, the parents and other adults with whom the child is supposed to identify may well seem impatient. When your so-called role models think you're just lazy and need to straighten up, you don't have much to work with to shape a concept of what a loving adult is all about.

Dr. Warren usually finds himself working with children who are entering this crucial life stage, the twelve- to fourteen-year-olds. The parents see these children slipping backward, negating whatever progress they seemed to have made, and the kids consider themselves broken, their brains stuck. They've had lots of negative social experiences, and that sort of thing feeds on itself, producing negative social attitudes. They have not yet learned how to get along with their parents or anyone else, but they're expected to take their place smoothly into the social fabric of their world.

They can't even fit into the fabric of their immediate circle of acquaintances.

Peer Influences

As a child like young Andrew grows, criticism and failure to achieve what is demanded of him drive his self-esteem deeper and deeper into the ditch. By the time he reaches William's age, the midteens, he will have suffered some heavy-duty damage to his concept of self. When they are in their early teens, children's peers are supposed to be the new stabilizing group, the support structure to help them bridge the gap between child of the family and independent adult. In the ADD child, that avenue is restricted, for the kid is not well received by his or her peers. Too often he or she is the nerd, the weirdo, the loose cannon. The child is too impulsive and generally too obnoxious to develop the kind of bonds a child that age requires.

While all children at this age feel a need to get out from under the parents' thumbs, as it were, ADD kids feel the need so more intently, for the "thumb" has pressed heavier on them. Usually, it's Mom who has been monitoring so tightly, trying to force the child to remember, to behave, to grow up, to shape up. Separating amicably from Mother is difficult under the best of circumstances. For the ADD kid it can be traumatic and painful. In William's case it was Dad, good old Controller

Dad, who was so utterly different and so firmly in a position of authority.

The breakaway attempts, in which a child tries to find a place as an adult or tries to engage in what the child thinks are adult activities, often lead to failure. Although most kids are about ready for the work permit and part-time job, the driver's license, maybe even the outside love interest, the ADD child has not yet matured that far. He or she tries and fails.

You don't keep getting kicked in the teeth without ending up injured. Emotional overflow, loneliness, the feeling that you are different, feeling rejected and not knowing why, often drives ADD children to more extreme behavior. They may choose to handle social situations by taking control, being bossy and dominating, and that leads to further social disappointment and disapproval.

All this failure causes a still greater adverse impact on social growth. And again, we remind you, this maturity level and brain function are as much a part of the child as are hair and eye color. Failure comes not because the child is wrong but because the child is being wedged into a culture that is not designed to accept him or her.

Though nothing is broken, there are steps we can take to fix things.

Building Social Skills

Having just moved to a new apartment, Andrew Mulroney was now going to a new school. He hated it. He felt like the only Martian on Jupiter. He'd been here in his new class maybe an hour and his teacher had already yelled at him a dozen times. She wanted him to settle down, she said. He *was* settled down. It wasn't his fault they were working on subtraction. He hated subtraction.

Finally, here came recess. Everyone was supposed to stand beside his or her desk. Andrew bumped his desk standing up, and it rattled. The gaunt and elderly Miss Pruitt glared at him. The kids on the far side of the room began filing out. Andrew headed for the door. At last! Try out those big swings!

"Andrew Mulroney! Come back here!" Miss Pruitt had lost none of the power and vivacity with her obvious onset of old age—she appeared to be at least forty-five or fifty.

Andrew stopped, confused. "I was just going outside."

"You'll wait your turn. Return to your desk."

He did, and noticed that none of the kids in his row had moved yet. They just stood there like fenceposts. Now obviously it was his row's turn to go outside. Here they came, marching out, brushing past him. He headed back toward the door.

"Andrew!"

"But it's my turn now."

"You need to learn how to wait your turn. You can sit at your desk for five minutes."

But he fidgeted, so he was assigned another five minutes. By the time he was allowed out, only five minutes was left of recess.

He headed for the swings, but they were all occupied. The two guys who sat beside him in class were playing in the sandbox. With a mighty leap he jumped into the sandbox and landed with both feet on a pile of sand. He cackled merrily. "I'm the great dirt jumper! Look at the pile flatten out!"

"That's my hill, you jerk!" The kid named Billy put his truck down and began impatiently rebuilding his dirt track.

Andrew dropped to his knees to build a hill of his own. The kid beside him shoved him back. "This is my place! Go find your own place!"

Billy blew a raspberry. "Andrew Kangaroo. Always jumping around! Boing, boing, boing!"

The other kids seemed to think that was hilarious. "Andrew Kangaroo! Boing, boing, boing!"

"That isn't funny!" Andrew jabbed at the kid closest to him.

"Sure it is. Even Miss Pruitt says you jump all around! Boing, boing, boing."

"Why are you picking on *me?!* Cut it out!" Andrew took a swing at Billy and missed. Then the other kids really laughed. The bell rang just then, or he would have nailed these stupid kids for sure. All he wanted was to join these guys. Andrew couldn't understand how this happened.

Miss Pruitt stood in the door, humorless, to watch them line up. Andrew figured out that he ought to get in line between Harry who sat ahead of him and Mark who sat behind him, but Harry was clear up in front and Mark was the last one in line. Oh well. Andrew slipped in between a girl with pigtails and someone named Sally. They were standing toward the back, about where his seat would be if they were inside.

"Andrew!" Miss Pruitt's glare told him he'd done it wrong again.

It was a long, long, long, long day.

The ADD child needs several powerful boosters in order to shore up his or her social skills. Primary among these is the parents.

The First Booster—Parents

Miss Pruitt, unfortunately, was a controlling left-hemisphere lady with little patience for anyone of different persuasion. She had scant enthusiasm for the children who did not toe her rigid mark. There was not a thing wrong with Miss Pruitt—unless you call not understanding kinesthetic kids a fault—but she was not the best match for Andrew. Andrew's best recourse would be his mom.

Remember that children are essentially powerless. About all they can do is get in trouble because the adults set the rules and it's up to the children to fit into that pattern. The adults pass all the judgments; the children have none. The adults believe each other; as a rule they never believe the kid. Andrew had nowhere to turn. He had to fit in or else, and in this case, his wiring forced the "or else."

Beth assumed, and logically so, that the school was doing its best for Andrew. That is not always a safe assumption, particularly in these days when schools are beset by so very many mandates and horrors that did not exist a generation ago. The school's faculty may not have the time to read the child's nature and fit him or her into exactly the right situation. The school may not even have the right situation, a teacher sensitive to the needs of right-brained kinesthetic or auditory learners.

Beth's best course of action, at the very beginning, was to talk to Andrew's new teacher for half an hour. She also might have observed her class awhile even before Andrew entered it. Then she could consider whether this was a place where Andrew could learn, maybe even flower. Observation would tell Beth that Andrew was going to have a hard time here. Although he needed close supervision and tight structuring, Miss Pruitt's Controller, left-brain style was not what he needed. Beth would have three choices.

If possible, she might be able to move Andrew into a different class. There might be a teacher more aware of Andrew's needs and learning style. If not, she could ask for a special-ed class to help Andrew get started well. The school might balk and talk about budget restraints, but the bottom line is that they must provide a venue for effective instruction for every child, and if Andrew really needs it, it must be forthcoming.

Her third course would be to develop a strong team with Miss Pruitt. Help Miss Pruitt see what Andrew needs, help structure homework and extra work, help in the classroom itself if possible. "Team" effort means teacher *and* parent, two braves and no chief. In any case, regardless of the teacher Andrew ends up with, the team effort applies.

A person of Miss Pruitt's temperament is likely to misinterpret ADD as deliberate arrogance, bossiness, and lack of courtesy, and not without reason. There are a lot of kids out there who are arrogant, bossy, and almost totally untrained as regards courtesy. Beth would do well to watch for signs of personality misinterpretation as well as lack of appreciation for alternative learning styles, and address them.

At home, Beth can do much to help Andrew get a grip on positive social interaction. First she must remember that the problem with Andrew is not that he doesn't know what to do. In the cases of Amy Eglund and William Steinfelder, for example, they absolutely knew what the rules were, for they'd been around years longer than Andrew, hearing the rules twice as much. The problem is that at any given moment, Andrew is likely to impulsively fail at remembering what to do. Therefore it avails nothing for Beth to say over and over, "Why didn't you do so and so? I told you a hundred times!"

A better response? "The rule, as you know, is [state it]. It applies here." Beth would strive to convey authority without being adversarial. She is not trying to tell Andrew what to think but to be able to think effectively.

Jody Capehart tells this case study of the most personal sort— herself and her Damon. Being fiercely opposed to medication at first, she chose instead to spend an enormous amount of time, essentially teaching Damon compensatory behavior. Because the success of lessons of that sort depends upon the ability of the short-term memory to blot them up, ADD kids have trouble learning them, and they also have trouble sequencing them later.

Says Mrs. Capehart, "You can't teach those behaviors when you're in the midst of a problem because the child's self-esteem is already in the ditch. So when Damon was growing up, late at night, I'd sit with him and we'd make a list of what happened in the day. I'd scratch his back or snuggle with him, and we'd go through the list and talk about the events. What happened? And how could Damon and we have made the outcome better? Not just Damon. Any and all of us. This wasn't a 'dump-on-Damon' session at all. It was lessons in social skills."

As they rehashed the day, Mrs. Capehart used playacting a lot. Playacting is extremely effective with a kinesthetic learner. "Okay, Damon. When I asked you to take your plate out to the sink after supper, remember? This time, I'll be you and you be me. Go ahead. Ask me."

Then, in an argumentative tone of voice dripping with sarcasm, she reproduced as much as possible Damon's nasty-mouthed retort. "What would you think when you heard that?" Damon's memory and the feelings of it brought to the surface now, she would press her point.

"Now how would you want that person to respond? What are a couple things you might have said differently and still be funny?"

Mrs. Capehart smiles. "He didn't mind the whole-body playacting. We might go over it and over it and over it, coming at it from various angles."

She also used just plain telling. This was more effective as he grew older. "When you do [this], Damon, people feel [this way]. Therefore it would work better and you'd get further, if you did [this]."

She also worked with Damon to determine some responses in advance. That sort of preparation routinely fails to work with ordinary people, and the failure rate is much higher for ADD kids with their hair-trigger impulsivity, but a success now and then is a sufficient foundation upon which to build more success.

"One of the things you have to pre-decide," Mrs. Capehart suggests, "is to not mouth off every time you feel like it. Instead, try to not say anything rather than trying to figure out what's appropriate. Not responding cures another social skills problem, the fact that ADD kids are such easy targets for other kids' jibes.

"Because most ADD kids have such an off-the-wall view of life and boundless creativity, they are more prone than most to do weird things and adopt idiosyncrasies. The worst thing in the world if you're a kid is to be idiosyncratic, especially when you start into puberty. ADD kids overreact to the teasing the way they overreact to everything else, and that gets other kids on their back even worse. As a result, the ADD kids go ballistic.

"At these close-of-day sessions, I was careful not to let myself off the hook. We critiqued my performance, too, mine and Damon's father's." That simply gesture, that willingness to be put under the microscope as well, quelled Damon's feeling that he was being unfairly picked on.

"When Damon was young," Mrs. Capehart continues, "short of wrapping our hands around his throat to get his attention, he just didn't focus on what we were saying to him. We would reach such a high degree of anger trying to grab his attention that by the time he finally got it, he assumed that anger was the level of life we interacted on. He'd miss the ten times we were patient; anger was the first level he keyed in on with any kind of cognitive awareness. There's not an easy answer to that.

"Two partial and difficult answers were to admit a lack of patience and to attempt to develop a signal system of some sort to rein in his attention short of hitting him on the head. A hand on the arm, a snap of the fingers, clapping the hands, a sudden startling motion—we worked out some signals."

Another one-on-one ploy Mrs. Capehart used was to teach compensating skills for those times when Damon did have to make a reply. "For years he would not answer gently. He over-everythinged. He was loud and condescending, speaking inappropriately, and then he didn't understand why everyone was so irritated with him. So my husband and I would sit down with him after the fact and teach compensating skills to show him how to deal with people. We kept them basic."

- Always turn down the volume on your voice.
- Stop and pray for guidance.
- The madder you get, the quieter you speak.

At the deepest level, these one-on-one methods provide what nothing else can, a personal relationship. No technique or ploy or threat or cajoling can substitute for a close personal relationship. But social conduct also requires working with others outside the close familiarity of family. Parents can do much toward helping their child with group interaction.

There are groups and groups within groups to help the child—groups in which the parents participate and groups that aid the child's growth.

The Second Booster—Groups

Gunther Steinfelder insisted upon calling support groups WEWs—Whiners Encouraging Whiners. He pronounced it "Wooze." What good could come of a bunch of self-pitying people getting together to out-ADD each other? he wondered. "My kid is ADDier than your kid."

Nonsense. He therefore greeted with considerable alarm his wife Ellen's insistence that they attend a Parents of ADD Children support group meeting.

In fact, Ellen herself was beginning to alarm him. She had always been so easy to govern. Previously, her few temper bursts had subsided quickly. She had never insisted on anything, never seriously questioned his decisions. Now she was making decisions of her own contrary to his and sticking to them. Like a bloodhound hard on a scent she was relentlessly pursuing this new avenue. Gunther's carefully structured world was restructuring itself without his permission.

They sat now in the church's adult-ed room, the dregs of last Sunday's spirited discussion of Romans 7 still chalked all over the blackboard. Ellen seemed animated, as if she'd found the key to a new life. In contrast, Gunther felt smothered. The other nine people here seemed comfortable in this milieu.

One person assumed the role of an informal moderator. "For those of you who have not attended before," and he stared right at Gunther, probably the only person here to qualify, "this group has a purpose. We swap stories about what we've found that works, and what we've tried that hasn't worked. We know, however, that our kids are all so different that what works for one of us may not work for others, and vice versa. Also, we swap information we've learned recently about ADD."

Information? William was lazy and inattentive. Period. What was there to learn? Gunther smiled noncommittally and introduced himself and Ellen when invited to do so.

The moderator continued. "At our last get-together, Irene suggested we talk about helping our kids get along in groups. Anyone want to open?"

The Parent Support Group

In our various practices and counsels, we always recommend that parents of ADD kids do two things that will help bring success for themselves and for their children. One is to become intimately involved with the kids (this is exceptionally difficult to do with ADD kids, who so often disappoint parents' pre-set expectations, and parents just don't realize how far apart they are) and the other is to communicate with other parents of ADD kids on a regular basis.

Getting together with others achieves what the moderator was describing in the meeting Gunther and Ellen attended—it helps parents learn about the condition labeled ADD and find out about possible coping skills. Not the least of the benefits, however, is that it also greatly relieves beleaguered parents to know that someone else suffers the same kinds of trials and tribulations. Finally they realize they are not alone after all. Also, it is immensely comforting to hear others reassure you that they understand what is happening and that they know it's not your fault. Beth was not a lousy, rotten parent. God was not out to get her. She needed that kind of reassurance, and she needed it frequently.

Most major communities have parental support groups. To find one in your area ask at the public library reference desk, call a local counseling center or your school counselor, or consult the resources mentioned in Appendix A of this book.

The Child's Support Group

In the loosely supervised playground situation at his new school, Andrew was a walking time bomb. ADD kids, likely to blow up at any moment, usually are. Although there are group situations wherein they do very well, many should be avoided. The playground is one such.

Group Situations That Don't Help. The adult supervising Andrew's recess, be it Miss Pruitt or someone else, had several key concerns. One was keeping tabs on a rowdy, enthusiastic, churning, yelling, vociferously interacting, diverse gang of kids who didn't want to be supervised. Another was to prevent major weeping and bloodshed. A third was to maintain a rough-and-ready discipline—no shoving, no fighting, no grabbing.

The supervisor did *not* have either the time or the resources to monitor the social interactions of Andrew or any other individual kid. If he or she (we'll use "she," assuming it was Miss Pruitt who was out there) did indeed observe his behavior and the resultant teasing, and if she did indeed have the time and backup to intercede, she would probably let the situation play out without interference anyway. The theory would be that Andrew must learn to handle himself and others, and you learn that only through experience, through various wins and losses.

That is usually true. Children learn social skills through trial and error. ADD kids, though, present a complication. Their self-concept is constantly being trampled by both adults and peers. They routinely lose by being teased, ignored, sometimes ostracized. They just don't get the occasional social successes other kids enjoy. Everything they learn is negative.

There is another unspoken item on the playground supervisor's agenda. It exists at the back of most adults' minds as they work with kids: the appearance of success. An unruly, chaotic playground where kids are always tangling and getting hurt would be a discredit to any supervisor. Miss Pruitt and most anyone else would be concerned with how the total situation looks to an outside observer, regardless of what they might say. Keeping the place looking good leaves scant time for helping kids like Andrew make it through the jungle. If anything, Andrew will be the one removed from the picture. ADD kids usually don't add much to a scene.

The problem of the "How do I look?" factor crops up in a most unlikely place that is also a bad place for ADD kids—church and Sunday school, and kids' programs such as scouting and children's clubs. The leaders and Sunday school teachers in these programs are volunteers the organization desperately needs. If you head up a program in which volunteers are your lifeblood, you want them to feel good about their jobs. Keeping the lid on a disruptive ADD child who needs the program just as desperately as the program needs the volunteers is not a positive stroke for the volunteer. Compounding the problem is the fact that very few volunteers such as Sunday school teachers and scout leaders are trained to deal with ADD kids.

The result: In Sunday school, scouting, and other programs, the ADD kids are looked upon as troublemakers. Do they perceive the rejection? You'd better believe it.

Incidentally, that practice in some communities of organizing neighborhood play groups won't work, and for the same reasons. Most are minimally structured, the very idea of them being to allow children free creative time. And the last thing in the world an ADD child needs is lots of free creative time . . . not as inventively creative as that child's mind is. In no time at all you'll have terrified cats in trees, kids in tears, equipment in shambles, and an occasional arm in a cast. Instead, ADD kids need structured activities supervised by adults who understand the kids' needs. These are adults who are affirming, who plan activities of interest to the kids, who remember that most ADD kids must keep moving. In short, successful scout groups, choirs, Sunday school classes, and sports teams need the right adult leadership, rife with structure. These are the contacts that will lead to social growth.

Group Situations That Lead to Social Growth.   "Mrs. Mulroney." Miss Pruitt, gaunt and grim, did not in the least resemble a team player just now. "Your Andrew is not a credit to this school. In class he is bad enough, constantly annoying the serious students, but on the playground he is a wild animal."

Deep inside, Beth cringed. She tried to maintain a businesslike exterior. She was about to say something innocuous when the enormity of Miss Pruitt's attitude hit her. She really should maintain a team spirit about this, work something out to help her son. Instead, she exploded, something she had never ever done before.

"Miss Pruitt!" Beth made her voice every bit as gaunt and grim and sharp-edged as Miss Pruitt's. "Andrew has trouble controlling himself, particularly when he has time on his hands. I strongly suspect that's the case at recess and lunch—unstructured free time. But I assure you—no, I insist!—Andrew *is* a serious student. I've worked with him enough to know that he genuinely wants to learn. Don't you ever put him in some other category or contrast him with your other so-called serious students. You will treat him as a serious student and find a way to help him learn. Need I remind you, teaching children is your job. Not just 'some children' but all children, including mine."

Miss Pruitt's lips, not quite as full as Mick Jagger's, flattened out into a paper-thin white line. She drew a deep breath. "May I suggest we shelve this discussion until we can both approach the subject with less rancor."

"Good idea. I'll drop by Friday between clients." With the barest of good-byes, Beth marched out, furious.

Disturbing the serious students! Bah!

The eruption did nothing to help Andrew's foundering social skills, unfortunately, and Beth knew it. She knew, too, that without social skills he wasn't going to be able to succeed as a student. She had been referred to Jody Capehart back when she first considered medication for Andrew. Now she made another appointment with the educator. For Thursday.

Mrs. Capehart's advice to all people, parents and teachers alike, is this: "If kids are going to have positive social experiences (and positive experiences are the key to social growth, to learning how to cope with social situations), you have to attend specifically to *their* needs. Not to what your class or group looks like from the outside but to what the kids need."

During their Thursday session Mrs. Capehart told Beth, "There are two other criteria for a good social group for ADD kids. One is that the child must have some interest in what's going on. The other is that the experience will offer the child some modicum of success socially. It doesn't have to be a lot. It doesn't have to be a constant string of positive experiences. But some positive outcome must be there."

That's the theory. How is it put into practice?

The Planned Activity Group. At the Minirth Meier New Life Clinic, we periodically run activity groups specifically for kids having social difficulties. They will be fairly homogeneous groups—children of similar age with similar problems. These are not children who are emotionally disturbed or in need of psychiatric attention. They're ordinary kids such as ADD children who have to learn to get along. In the groups, children receive between eight and twelve weeks of positive interactions in a social environment. They meet once a week.

The goal of these groups is to provide positive social experiences. That's all. These kids already know what they should do to make and keep friends, to fit into situations. But they can't do it. You might say the head knowledge is there but the heart and body must be trained. Rarely have any of them known acceptance and respect by their peers.

In these controlled situations, we let the kids experience success rather than be preached at. In the course of the eight or twelve weeks, they end up learning valuable social skills, even though that is not the aim.

You don't need specialists in order to set up something like these groups. You do need supervisors familiar with the special needs of right-brained, kinesthetic youngsters, ADD kids, and shy ones. Parent support groups may be able to provide such persons. In any case the group will be highly structured by the adults who run it. That is, activities will be carefully planned, and the operating rules will be firmly in place before the first child enters the door. Our rules are:

1. Keep your hands and feet to yourself.
2. No put-downs. As Thumper the rabbit used to say, "If you can't say something nice, don't say anything at all."
3. You cannot get up and leave without an adult.
4. No interrupting.

The nature of the group is to emphasize interpersonal and interactive social situations. At the end of each of these group sessions, we talk about what happened during our time together and what it was like when So-and-so did this-and-that. Certainly, we don't make fun of each other (rule 2). We do, however, re-live the positive events, rehearsing them orally, laughing and reminiscing. We rarely talk about interaction. The projects do that without words.

Activities? Given the propensities of the group members, we make sure their hands have something busy to do. We pick strongly interpersonal and interactive things, such as a game of Uno or projects they work together on. Those might be trooping off on a scavenger hunt or making a radio program that we tape.

All this is keyed into a point system. Again, the guidelines for earning and spending points are all firmly in place before the group first meets. Kids earn points for working together, for sharing feelings, for remembering and observing the rules. They are allowed to pool their points (the ultimate in cooperation) in order to reach some overall point goal, such as amassing a thousand points to go to an amusement park.

"Take a group of boys like William to the amusement park?" Gunther would recoil at the idea, aghast. "All I can say is, masochism becomes you."

By leading the children through tightly structured cooperative activities then helping the kids share their feelings at the close, we are helping them build true and stimulating friendships. By the time the group sessions end and they go somewhere public, they're a unit, comfortable with each other, capable of really enjoying a positive experience in a wildly stimulating environment. It happens, though, only because equally stimulating friendships are already in place.

The wrap-up gatherings at the end of these eight- to twelve-week activity groups constantly surprise and touch us.

"This is the first time I ever had a friend," said one eleven-year-old.

A twelve-year-old guy brought gifts for everybody, saying he had never had friends before. He wasn't quite sure how to present his gifts; he'd never done that before, either. The group-mates helped him, but of course, they had a vested interest.

Other Activities Promoting Social Growth.   Not all activities have to be so thoroughly planned and executed. The right school and community programs, effectively administered, can be invaluable for an ADD kid.

Constantly, parents ask Jody Capehart and Dr. Warren about the value of martial arts training. Often the subject comes up because the ADD or hyperactive child wants the training and the parents cannot imagine teaching a kid like that to create mayhem and then turning the little killer loose on an unsuspecting world.

Actually, it's not like that at all. Martial arts training focuses not on destruction but just the opposite—on self-control and self-regulation, which are exactly what an ADD child needs. Martial arts require good concentration, another area in which the ADD child benefits from training and practice. The skills—learning and practicing them—drain all sorts of action and energy, and ADD kids need an outlet for their built-up steam. They need a powerful arena in which to express their intensity. Further, martial arts instructors are a bit larger than life, people easy to revere. ADD kids need adults of that caliber as role models and heroes.

We do see a few ADD kids who didn't seem to benefit much from closely structured activities such as martial arts training. In some cases, at least, the activities may have been misused. As a whole, boys seem to particularly benefit, and those benefits far outnumber the nonbenefits.

Team sports require the learning and honing of social skills simply because teammates are people. You have to get along. But individual and competitive sports also provide practice in social interaction. The distance runner who races alone, the swimmer who's out to beat the clock, still must relate closely to the coaches, the opponents, the sponsors, and the well-wishers. All such contacts help.

Other structured activities might include drill teams and sports offering plenty of movement with direction, sports catering to the positive aspects of impulsivity—that is, the ability to think and act quickly. Basketball, for instance, would serve well so long as it were played spontaneously without the memorization of set plays. Other appropriate choices might be soccer, swimming, most track and field events, and tennis.

Ice hockey, with a good coach and good team, burns lots of energy and provides plenty of movement and the need for quick thinking. Says Dr. Warren, "I have some boys in my counsel who have really found a niche playing hockey. We're building ice rinks in the suburbs, and that's a great thing, especially for ADD kids. Roller hockey, using in-line skates, now is getting really hot, too. We have leagues and all levels of teams. Professional people have been very generous with this. I applaud them."

Ice skating itself is also a good sport for ADD kids, although the level of competitive figure skating that requires the mastery of school figures is not. Typically, skaters develop a bond of shared enthusiasm.

ADD kids frequently being daredevils anyway, skiing is also a favorite. Dr. Warren smiles. "This may date me, but I remember the televised pictures of Franz Klammer winning his Olympic alpine ski event. He came hurtling down the course with total abandon, frequently out of control. He was going to either win or flame out brilliantly. No middle ground, no caution. Most ADD kids would relate to that completely."

By and large, football may present more difficulties for the ADD kid, either for social growth or self-concept improvement. There's too much standing around, too much memorizing of playbooks. Football requires a great deal of sequencing and not a little sitting on the bench. It can lead to impulsivity in a negative way for it's a high-contact sport with moments of high emotion, inviting that little jab, that elbow in the belly, that deliberate kick or gouge. All such temptations work counter to development of social skills. With the right coach, however, football allows the expenditure of lots of energy and can provide an excellent opportunity for polishing self-discipline.

Even more difficult for many ADD kids, couched in terms of general experience, is our national pastime, baseball. Ninety-five percent of the time, the baseball player is either perched in the dugout or standing in the outfield, doing nothing. Distractibility takes over, and blades of grass become as interesting as the action at home plate way over there. Attention wandering, the fielder misses the ball and may even get bopped by it. Errors and messed-up plays bring down the fury of teammates, coaches, and fans (i.e., parents). Positive social experience? Zip.

A well-knit team in an ADD-appropriate sport, be it the cross-country or track team, the swim team or the soccer team, serves the

ADD child in a positive way quite apart from the heady joy of winning. The child may not be mature enough to socialize on the level the teammates do, but the team's momentum both carries the child along and teaches skills by osmosis, so to speak. Socially, the child can live and perform at a level somewhat above his or her natural degree of maturity, and that in itself is highly positive.

Some community organizations notwithstanding, the sports to which most children are exposed are school sponsored. In a large, large way, school is the child's whole life.

Parents can do much to make the school experience positive, to enhance learning. Teachers must be equally diligent with the children assigned them.

We will address the next chapter, "The ADD Child in School," to teachers. But remember, parents are the child's first and most important teachers, and our comments will also apply to them. Moreover, they will be working to build a team with their child's school and thus must know what the child needs in the classroom setting.

But most of all, parents and teachers alike must know what works and what does not work, how to maintain effective discipline that leads to self-discipline. Parents and teachers must know how to keep the child from disrupting the learning process for himself or herself as well as for others. Last (but not least, let's admit) teachers and parents together must hone effective methods to prevent the child from driving everyone else bananas.

THE ADD CHILD IN SCHOOL— GENERAL THEORY

M*ISS PRUITT, I* understand you have a problem." With a wave of the hand, the principal, Ira Chapin, invited his senior teacher to sit.

She sat. "I do. His name is Andrew." She sighed. "Nearly every year I've been teaching—and that will be thirty-two years this June—I've had a problem child or two. Restless children, defiant children, children who refuse to sit still and obey. But these last few years have seen an avalanche of such children, an absolute avalanche. And Andrew is among the worst I've ever encountered."

"Is he abusive? Do you feel threatened?"

"Threatened? No. Frustrated. Terribly frustrated. His mother seems to think she knows more about teaching than I do. She's a *real estate agent,* for pity's sake!"

Chapin pushed himself back farther into his Naugahyde chair. He knew where this conversation was going to end up and he didn't like it, but he had no real options. "What do you want me to do?"

"He's been in my room a week. Moving him to another room will hardly be traumatic for him. He's made no friends."

"I can't. Each of the other two teachers already have four more pupils than you have."

Miss Pruitt's narrow, bony face hardened. "I want him out, Ira. He is disruptive and compromising my ability to teach."

"I'll see what I can do. Do you happen to have his mother's phone number handy?"

"In my desk. I'll call it to you on the intercom." The recess bell rang. She excused herself and left.

So far today, one bus had lost a brake line and another had backed into a closed bus-barn door, the health inspector had just made a surprise visit and festooned him with a list of seventeen alleged violations—all insignificant nuisance infractions—the custodian had gone home with the flu, the textbook rep was two hours late, and Chapin's wife had just called to say their cat was at this moment giving birth in the newly upholstered backseat of the '56 Chevy he was restoring.

And now, Miss Pruitt.

Identifying the Problems

Miss Pruitt.

Miss Pruitt believed that some children were inherently lazy and some oppositional, but she didn't really grasp the nature of attention deficit disorder and she did not intend to bend her standards to accommodate this particular shortcoming. She did intend, if possible, to redirect, force, pressure, or otherwise shape such errant children into a proper frame of mind and behavior. Miss Pruitt and Andrew were on a collision course, and Chapin could see it, as bright and clear as a new paint job on a classic Jaguar.

In the past he had been pretty much able to shunt kids like Andrew into other classes, not as a favor to Miss Pruitt but as a favor to the children. She didn't have enough patience to deal well with them. This time he was stuck.

Ira Chapin was challenged not just by the problem of how to get Andrew and Miss Pruitt somehow to mesh but also by more pressing and practical matters. According to federal civil rights legislation as defined in section 504 of the civil rights act, all public schools must provide modifications for ADD children, even though many never have. In short, by law Miss Pruitt had to teach Andrew effectively.

This is not the horrid burden it first appears. This is not a mandate for a big program of special education. In most schools, implementation occurs in several ways. One is simply helping the teacher with volunteer assistants or other aids. Another, more costly option, is a separate content-mastery class for the children who need it or support such as a tutor or aide to help the child grasp the material and provide an opportunity to catch up to his or her grade level.

The school may be able to make minor alterations that will produce a major improvement in the child's progress. For example, allowing the child to take tests in a less distracting environment can work wonders and may open the door to other simple modifications.

The law exists primarily to ensure that the ADD child has an advocate. We encourage parents to speak to their principal or counselor about this.

In any case, the team we talked about earlier—parents, teachers, and kids working in concert—is crucial to success. A lot of teachers, though, have no idea what ADD is or how to deal with it. The first step in many cases, therefore, is to help teachers understand and recognize the problems and challenges that go along with ADD. Equally important, teachers and parents together must see what ADD is not.

Identifying at-risk children is a necessary first step in getting a complete overview of the problem to be solved.

The At-Risk Child

ADD is not to blame for everything that goes wrong with a child's life, nor is addressing it the answer to everything. The ADD kid possesses all the normal quirks of any growing child *plus* the unique challenges of ADD.

Some children are learning disabled both with and without the additional problem of ADD. We call them at-risk kids. For what are they at risk? Everything. Success, happiness, effectiveness, contentment. There are sources that claim that half of all learning-disabled children are also ADD; other sources say it's closer to 25 percent. Regardless, four-fifths of them will fail at least one grade. That in itself is an unacceptable risk.

The problems for these at-risk kids start pretty much when school starts, in large part because the children themselves change at about that time of life.

When Risk Begins

Beth Mulroney reminisced, "Andrew was always incredibly active and bouncing off the walls. It really bothered his father, although I didn't understand why at the time. I didn't take much notice. Healthy babies are active. He was climbing, running, and go-go all the time. His troubles didn't really begin until he got rolling with kindergarten. And first grade? It was a disaster!"

Most ADD kids can get through preschool and perhaps also kindergarten fairly smoothly. First grade is where the sheep and goats part ways. A big shift occurs in every child around age six or seven.

During infancy and into the preschool years, children learn pretty much with all five senses. They taste everything they can jam into their mouths, feel everything they can reach, hear and make noise, see, smell, and do. Constantly doing, constantly exploring. By taking in the world through all their senses, these brand-new organisms can learn at a particularly fast pace.

Knowing that tiny children learn this way, we design preschool curricula as multisensory. Preschoolers play with blocks and clay, with paints and crayons, with bright colors and toys to climb upon. A good kindergarten curriculum is also multisensory with lots of activity.

But about this time, children's learning styles shift. Taste is the first to go. Preschoolers don't stick stuff in their mouths the way the one-year-old did. By age six, give or take, the child's hard-wired learning style has settled into what it will probably be for life. The child who learns best by hearing will from now on prefer auditory cues. The visually oriented child will do best with things to see and study by eye. Tactile-kinesthetics become full-blown tactile-kinesthetics, learning best when in motion and touching the material.

At this same time, along comes first grade. Suddenly, this child who has been moving, touching, and doing is expected to sit at a desk with a workbook for six hours. The visual child without a particular penchant for tactile-kinesthetics, and that is the majority of children, will be able to handle the change in teaching technique. The in-motion kid and the auditory kid are in trouble already.

Most ADD kids are in-motion and/or auditory learners, and for these frustrated kinesthetic and auditory learners, love of learning fades from first grade on.

Second grade: "I like recess."

Third grade: "I don't like school."

Fourth grade and on: "I hate it!"

The problem? Schools simply do not set the environment and curricula up for the way children other than visual learners learn. For the most part they don't have to. Kids who are mildly at-risk can still learn visually even though it's not the best way to learn. They won't do as well and the work will be harder for them, but they survive. Frequently, the ADD child, burdened by so much additional baggage, cannot function adequately at all.

What super-hero will rescue these kids? Enter "The Team."

Accommodating the ADD Pupil

Miss Pruitt. If Ira Chapin so much as breathed a word about teaching old dogs new tricks, she'd skewer him with a blackboard pointer. And yet, that was the only solution he could see. Help her come to terms with the kid somehow and somehow learn to accommodate him. Removing the Mulroney kid from her room just wasn't possible. Whoever got Andrew would scream bloody murder, and with good reason.

Mostly to placate Miss Pruitt, he would ask Andrew's mother to come in for a chat. But there was a curiosity factor also. So she was telling Miss Pruitt, the veteran teacher, how to teach, was she? Maybe she knew a few more tricks than the teacher gave her credit for. After all, she'd been dealing with Andrew for eight years, give or take, and Miss Pruitt was stymied by him in one week.

But first he called the district office to line up someone from counseling. There were numerous batteries of tests available for evaluating kids. He might as well take advantage of some of them.

To work effectively together, parents and teachers must be on equal footing. This is not to suggest that each knows how to do the other's business. Parents make the best parents, teachers make the best teachers. They're not going to tread upon each other's toes or, Lord willing, tell each other how to do the job. By "equal" we mean that both are equally aware of the needs of the student, of the peculiarities of the student, and of the student's strengths and weaknesses.

(A word of caution to parents of ADD kids who themselves exhibit ADD tendencies: Teachers often report that parents who tend toward ADD come across as militant, aggressive, demanding, and thoughtless. They never say, "Can you talk a minute?" They call at all hours and hardly ever get the hint that the teacher might have something else going on. So be sensitive, okay?)

Frequently, school-sanctioned testing tells the parent little that he or she does not already know. But it tells the teacher a great deal about a pupil who enters his or her life a virtual stranger. Also, because parents often have blind spots when it comes to their kids ("My little Johnny isn't a bad boy; he's just a bit careless of others' life and limb. I'm sure that blood will wash right out."), teachers tend to trust test results further than they trust the parent's observation.

Ira Chapin, then, was on the right track when he brought the parent in from the outset and scheduled tests for the brand-new pupil who was giving Miss Pruitt such fits.

Testing, a First Step

"When I evaluate for attention deficit disorder," says Dr. Warren, "I do all the standard things, such as look for signs of depression and other conditions that can mimic ADD. But I also look at learning style and learning problems. I ask the child for a handwriting sample. I ask him or her to write the alphabet, draw a picture. I look at nominal recall, fact recall, short- and long-term memory, task memory—that is, can the child remember and perform a sequence of commands—and visual and auditory memory. What does the child remember of what he or she sees and hears? All these factors can be indicative of ADD as well as clues to some other problem. In either case I must know if they are present and to what extent. However, technical tests of actual learning I request from professionals who have made learning problems their field of expertise."

Most common learning differences involve difficulty with math and numbers, difficulty with reading mechanics and reading comprehension, difficulty with handwriting, and difficulty with speech and language skills. Most people don't often think about handwriting as an indicator, but it tells revealing stories.

ADD kids are not only slow to mature, they often display a disparity between their intellectual level and their performance level. That is, there is a great gap between what they know and what they can adequately express. The ADD child may actually know a lot, having blotted up both school material and what might be called life skills. But the child's performance as measured by the ability to articulate what he or she knows may be delayed. Writing and handwriting can reveal that.

Beth Mulroney could understand that. In Principal Chapin's office, she studied her son's essay, completed as part of the testing procedure. She wagged her head. "He can tell the most elaborate and fanciful stories. I don't mean lying, although he sure can do that too. I mean fairy tales. The counselor asked him to write a fairy tale, right?"

"Right. Make up a story. I'm sorry to say this, Mrs. Mulroney, but what he wrote here isn't even first-grade-level work. Simple words are misspelled, letters are poorly or incorrectly formed, sentences are badly constructed. He put down, what, thirty words? Not that much."

She looked near tears. Chapin hated it when mothers started crying in his office. It happened a lot; that's why he kept the box of boutique tissues on the corner of his desk. He shoved it toward her, anticipating the waterworks.

But the waterworks didn't come. Her voice remained firm. "I learned in our support group a couple of weeks ago that 75 to 80 percent of boys with ADD have written language difficulties. I mean they can't get what's in their head onto paper. Like Andrew here. And the more they try, the more frustrated they get. It's a vicious circle, so that by the sixth grade or so, they don't bother to try anymore. Mr. Chapin, I don't want that to happen to Andrew."

I don't want that to happen to Andrew. The words struck a chord in Chapin somehow. He was talking to a woman who knew what she wanted for her son and maybe a little bit of how to get it. School administrators constantly complain that parents not only fail to get involved in the education process, they don't seem to care about their kids' education. Now here was a woman who was informing herself about her son's particular needs and willing to work to help him get them. He wasn't going to let this rare opportunity slide by.

He smiled, in part to allay any tears that happened to be waiting. "Miss Pruitt may be a little slow to come around. You have to realize she's been doing things her way for a good many years. However, I think we can put together a program that will benefit your son. Now let's go through the rest of these results."

Learning difficulties, like those revealed in Andrew's case, can cause ADD-like behavior all by themselves. Remember that actual ADD is biological, a variation in the hard wiring, if you will; it is not purely behavioral. Learning difficulties cannot cause ADD. But they, together with clashes in learning style (again, as between Andrew and Miss Pruitt), can greatly worsen biologically induced ADD behavior. Language problems, particularly as regards writing, spelling, and comprehension, are a strong indicator of those learning difficulties.

It works the other way as well. A clear diagnosis of attention deficit disorder from outside the school indicates that learning problems and perhaps emotional difficulties as well will probably also be part of the package; a great majority of ADD kids experience them.

The school would also look at behavior rating scales. Such tests are taken with a grain of salt. They are not measurements; they are observations, albeit valuable observations. Because they are biased by the tester's unconscious attitudes (Miss Pruitt, for example, would test Andrew much more harshly than would Mr. Chapin), all these tests give confirmation of the educators' suspicions as well as trends toward which the child bends, but they are not diagnostic in themselves. Mr. Chapin would also use the tests Andrew and Beth took in the past.

At the end, Mr. Chapin would essentially make a judgment call. "Andrew seems to need such-and-so, so we will try this, this, and this." He would probably feel pretty good about his judgment call, too, for he arrived at it from several different angles—various tests, other experts' opinions, and Mrs. Mulroney's own experience and knowledge.

Convincing Miss Pruitt was going to be the real challenge. Teach an old dog new tricks? He couldn't even make his cat respect his brand-new upholstery job.

The Next Step: Adjusting the Child's Environment

In Chapter 4, we looked at the effect of the ADD child's comfort zone on behavior and learning. Everything that applies to the child's comfort zone at home also applies at school. But there is a big kink in that plowline. Teachers in a classroom do not have the flexibility to vary learning environments that parents at home do. The teacher is dealing with several dozen kids, and each child has unique needs. ADD kids' needs are often not compatible with the needs of the class's overachieving left-brainer or the child who thrives in quiet settings. In other words, accommodations for the ADD child must be tempered against the needs of the other two dozen pupils. It's a balancing act to tax Solomon's wisdom.

Chapin screwed his courage to the sticking point, as Lady Macbeth put it, steeled his nerves with a double-tall latté, and called a conference with both Mrs. Mulroney and Miss Pruitt. Having the three of them together in one room was almost certain to invite fireworks. Chapin gave his secretary orders that if she saw a mushroom cloud billow out of his transom, she was to call 911.

Miss Pruitt, stiff as a crutch, kept her nose high and tried not to look at Mrs. Mulroney. To her credit, Beth Mulroney didn't seem at all put off by the teacher's cool behavior.

Chapin began. "You're aware, Miss Pruitt, that Mrs. Mulroney has Andrew on medication upon the advice of a physician, and Andrew is under his care. In addition, Mrs. Mulroney has been receiving the counsel of an expert on learning differences; incidentally, the woman she's consulting also happens to be the founder and former principal of a highly successful private school. The suggestions that counselor made seem to have improved Andrew's behavior and study habits at home."

Miss Pruitt appeared to be waiting for an ax to fall. She sat unmoving and unmoved. Obviously, she wasn't going to make this a lick easier than she had to.

Chapin continued. "I spent some time after school yesterday sitting in your room at Andrew's desk. Just sitting. Thinking about it."

Miss Pruitt's face softened slightly into a smirk. "I can hardly picture your knees fitting under his desk."

Chapin smiled. "Okay, so I was sitting *on* his desk. He's right under a fluorescent fixture near the back of the room. For starters, just as an experiment, I'd like you to move him up beside your desk. Up into the northwest corner of the room there."

She studied him with no hint in her face of compromise or approval. "That reminds me. The light is out over that corner. I've put in a repair order."

"I know. I took the tubes out. Apparently fluorescent overheads have a seriously negative effect on the behavior and learning curves of kinesthetic children, ADD kids—in fact, any kind of at-risk students and learning-disabled kids. They say it's physiological, and there's research to back it up. I suggest you put Marsha's desk there also and Whittaker's. From what you've mentioned about them, they seem to be kinesthetic also, and Whittaker's on the edge, what with his parents divorcing. It's worth a shot."

"Why that corner? Why not at the back where he won't present a spectacle to the other children? And Marsha and Whittaker? They're wiggle worms. They'll disrupt everyone if they sit up there."

"I want you to put Andrew in that corner so he's not distracted so much by activity around him and so he can concentrate on you better when you teach because he's closer to you and to the board. Also, in that corner you can reach him and touch him when you want to get his attention. And the subdued lighting might help him and your other wiggle worms."

"I can't see that it will make any difference." Miss Pruitt cast baleful eyes upon Beth, obviously the cause of her travail. "It will just increase disruption."

"Let's try, all right?"

The Problem of Teacher Resistance

Miss Pruitt was not trying to be difficult. She was not out to cause Andrew a hard time. But her attitude is a common one.

For one thing, teachers teach according to their own learning style, and the majority of teachers are left-brained. Like parents, teachers assume there is a right way to learn, and their own style is it. As parents try to shoehorn their children into their own learning styles, so do teachers, and for an additional reason: The left-brain learning style of sitting quietly at the desk *looks* good.

Miss Pruitt would be mortified if her class were noisy and unruly when an outsider happened by. And heaven forbid the supervisor's visit during a compromising situation such as free time during rainy recesses. Miss Pruitt, like the vast majority of teachers, wanted her class at all times to appear well controlled and conducive to [left-brained] learning.

This is a justifiable attitude. The vast majority of school administrators expect to see quiet, perfect order, the pupils all sitting nicely in their little chairs. The churning, active world of kinesthetic right-brain learners scares most teachers and administrators because classroom control is not obvious. And that kind of wild and hairy atmosphere is detrimental to the left-brain learners in the room.

"There's an answer," says Jody Capehart, "at least a partial answer: cubicles and learning stations."

That answer requires a teacher like Miss Pruitt to drastically alter her whole attitude toward learning and order. A quantum leap of that sort for a left-brain teacher will be excruciatingly difficult. Wrenching! But if he or she can make it, student achievement will soar, and not just for ADD kids. Right-brain learners and other kinesthetic kids will blossom as well.

Children whose attention easily wanders need a place of their own that offers minimal distractions. A cubicle with plain walls may be the answer. Children who require quiet in order to concentrate may also benefit from a cubicle or cubbyhole in which to curl up and separate themselves from the mainstream.

Tactile and kinesthetic kids who profit from hands-on action learn best at a station—a table or bench—where they can manipulate blocks, clay, sticks, and figures. Auditory learners need to discuss what they are doing and learning, and a station may also serve that purpose. Computer terminals should be located in situations that are comfortable for both left- and right-brain learners; a terminal and monitor down on the floor might be a good idea for some kids.

In short, Miss Pruitt would have to rearrange her room to fit not her own sense of order and correctness but the needs of a broad spectrum of children with different learning styles. Quite frankly, many teachers like Miss Pruitt cannot bring themselves to make that paradigm shift. The concept is too radical, the loss of order and straight lines too frightening.

Let us emphasize that this is absolutely *not* a fault or shortcoming on the teacher's part. In order to function well, the teacher, like her pupils, must work within his or her comfort zone. Because the teacher's comfort zone and natural proclivities must also be served, a classroom geared to right- as well as left-brainers can run so firmly counter to those proclivities that the teacher's productivity is compromised. That must not happen.

Our Miss Pruitt, however, was made of staunch stuff. She did not last thirty-two years in this profession by being rigid and unchanging. She held out for the removal of Andrew for another week. Then she finally resigned herself to the fact that it wasn't going to happen and began looking at options.

Because she didn't quite trust Mrs. Mulroney to get all the facts straight, Miss Pruitt herself made an appointment with Jody Capehart. Two minutes after they sat down together in Mrs. Capehart's frilled and teddy-beared office, Miss Pruitt knew she was dealing with an alien. Mrs. Capehart's credentials aside, the woman bubbled and bounced. She talked about the Gregorc model, about abstract random and concrete sequential learners. This was definitely not Miss Pruitt's style.

And then Mrs. Capehart ended her lengthy explanation with a statement that stuck. "Several of my daughter's friends own horses. One girl rides flatsaddle, that is, English style—helmet, quirt, the works. She gets a lot of ribbing and good-natured grief from the others because they ride western style—cowboy saddle with the horn and everything. And there are a few kids who like to ride bareback. Which way is right, and if so, is the other way wrong? There is a right way to teach and a right way to be taught, but it varies incredibly with the child. That's the fascination and challenge I find in teaching—to celebrate the diversity."

Celebrate the diversity. Miss Pruitt accepted some journal reprints and several books on the subject of different learning styles. They chatted a few minutes longer, then Miss Pruitt took her leave.

Celebrate the diversity. Throughout her lengthy career, Miss Pruitt had done her best to minimize the diversity and homogenize her children, teach them order and discipline, show them the path to success. Some of Mrs. Capehart's resources here suggested that certain children could not follow that path.

Celebrate the diversity. Miss Pruitt thought about the children she had failed over the years, children like Andrew and Whittaker. And Lucy Mae. Little Lucy Mae, so bright in some regards and so totally unteachable in others. Lucy Mae would be in her late twenties now. Miss Pruitt wondered what ever became of her.

Celebrate the diversity. Miss Pruitt was retiring in a year, when her 80-percent pension schedule kicked in. She thumbed through these studies and books again. And then Miss Pruitt made a paradigm shift in her thinking. She had a bit over half a teaching year to go. Already she had proven herself many times over. Already she had triumphed. For the balance of this school year, she would play. She would experiment. If Mrs. Capehart's resources were accurate, children like Whittaker, Marsha, and Andrew might blossom. At least they would avoid repeating the grade.

Yes, that's it. She would continue to cater to the concrete sequential children, the orderly, analytic learners, and she would also work to accommodate the others as described in these books and papers. On the brink of retirement, she was the perfect person to conduct this noble experiment.

Beginning tomorrow, she would celebrate the diversity.

Deciding How to Adjust the Surroundings

So how might Miss Pruitt, hampered by severe space and time limitations, perform her noble experiment? Her classroom was fairly small and her teaching time limited. She could not set up tables and odd furniture just anywhere she needed it. She would have to squeeze things and do a lot of rearranging. Also, she simply could not afford to lavish time on a few when the many required instruction. Obviously, this was not going to be as simple as it first seemed.

Most of the time, external environment is not fully manipulatable. ADD children are particularly sensitive to certain outside influences such as, for example, barometric pressure changes. Grandma may be able to tell when a storm is coming by noticing whether or not her corns ache; ADD kids may go ballistic for the same reason. Also, as strange as it seems, they sometimes need a stronger managing hand when the moon phase is ascending toward full. Interestingly, that's when mental institutions and police blotters see their craziest activity as well. While you can't do anything about the weather or the phases of the moon, there *are* many things that can be controlled in the ADD child's environment.

Jody Capehart suggests, "For starters, use the child's own instincts. If you free up the child and get rid of the *shoulds* and *ought-tos,* that child will adjust his or her environment to what is needed. So I ask the child, 'Which way helps you feel smarter?' Then in his or her own way the kid can find the way that makes him or her feel smarter."

Mrs. Capehart recommends abolishing "seatwork," as such. Her umbrella rule is: "Work where you work best, but try to work quietly." Most of the children will sit at their desks to do, for instance, math. She provides standing desks for children like Andrew who have to move while they work. Some kids do ten times better stretched out on the floor with a clipboard.

Mrs. Capehart maintains order in this diverse atmosphere by cruising. She roams around the periphery, watching, helping, gently correcting, laying a hand on this shoulder, tapping that arm. Often a touch is sufficient to bring an errant mind back to the work at hand. On the move, she directs and redirects, keeping the kids on task.

She smiles. "I always wear skirts with pockets. A child brings forbidden toys to school—those POGs that are so popular now, for instance, or super-bounce balls—I ask them once, nicely, to keep them put away. If I see them out again, I confiscate them. My pockets get some pretty incredible contraband."

Miss Pruitt was amazed by which children gravitated to the indirectly lighted corner—not just Andrew and Whittaker but Mercy and Jeff and Regina too. She had the custodian remove two more fluorescent tubes to enlarge the "darkened" study area. When Mercy stretched out on her tummy there to write her story about a pony that would not eat green grass she turned in the best work she'd ever done.

Within a few weeks, Miss Pruitt had installed several stand-up desks for the more restless of her pupils and two tables by the window. It crowded the orderly rows of desks under the lights, and that bothered her. But she managed to endure.

A week before the Thanksgiving break, she stood by her doorway and gazed out the windows across her bejumbled room. Beyond the glass, children were streaming out the gate and clambering aboard buses.

The principal stepped through her door and stood beside her. He looked around. "I'm curious. You mentioned that one of your new goals was to say something nice about each child every day. How is that coming?"

She snorted. "With most of the children, it's not a problem. But Andrew? The only good thing I can say is that he doesn't come home with me."

"However, he's making passing grades." Chapin pointed to the darkened corner, the tables by the window. "That's a big change."

"Quite so. Frankly, Ira, I can't wait for the learning-stations part of my experiment to fail so I can remove the tables and open up the rows a little better. Look how close those desks are."

"Still, I've noticed considerable improvement in several of your kids. Whittaker, especially. I've worried about him. And of course Andrew." Chapin watched the gaggle of departing kids a few moments. Out there, happy bedlam. In here, silence. "You've raised the level of your whole class—the poor students are better, and the good ones haven't slipped."

For the first time in her life, Miss Pruitt hated having to admit to success. So she didn't. "Besides, I have no idea what to use the stations for. Everything the books recommend is play, not work."

"Isn't that the idea? Learning through play?"

"Learning through drill and repetition is the key, Ira."

Not necessarily. Not all children can carry that load.

Adjusting Workloads

"If you want to drive ADD kids absolutely crazy," Jody Capehart claims, "make them write some sentence five hundred times."

What about the idea that diligent practice makes perfect?

Sometimes it works. And sometimes . . .

Diligent practice in the form of drill, repetitive work, and large numbers of problems or study questions do not teach ADD children anything except frustration. A child whose sequential skills are strong will receive three pages of math problems, sit down, and zip through them, one at a time. It might take awhile, but the child's attention and linear thought processes will be up to the task.

Not so the ADD child. A page of problems row on row is confusing and disconcerting to an ADD child. A global learner doesn't see a row of problems to be ticked off one by one but a whole page crying out all at once. The child sees only the whole job, not the do-able increments, and mentally he or she freezes up. Thus paralyzed, the child hears, "You're lazy," from the presiding adult; as a result he or she becomes further paralyzed. Sometimes the child will skip around, doing this one and that one and perhaps missing some altogether. Far too often, when the child's analysis becomes, "I can't do this!" he or she will race through the exercise with no thought to getting the right answers. There has to be a goal, and if the goal cannot be to finish well, it will become one of finishing first.

Miss Pruitt's linear thinkers could do two pages of subtraction problems and earn praise thereby. Her global thinkers would accomplish just as much comparatively by completing half a page.

In particular need of consideration are the many ADD children who have difficulties with writing skills. Their fine motor coordination, slow to bloom, may cancel out speed and neatness. Like any other come-from-behind factor such as hearing loss or vision difficulties, this physical inability to write swiftly and accurately deserves modifications. What modifications? Less written work. More one-word answers. Multiple-choice and matching tests instead of long sentence-writing. Shorter essays. Earlier computer work and more of it. These kids also profit if the teacher avoids requiring needless copying. The teacher may need to provide the older child with an outline or syllabus of lectures. A tape-recorder can save the day; we'll discuss that idea in detail later.

Obviously, ADD kids, in particular, need workload adjustments. The ADD child will learn no more from a hundred questions and problems than from fifteen. This child's penmanship will not get better by executing rote loops and swirls line after line after line. The only thing drill accomplishes in an ADD pupil is to further sour the child on school.

ADD kids need adjustments in homework assignments also. Andrew was still too young to be assigned extensive homework, but preteen Amy and midteen William were struggling with tons of it. Basically, the key is to individualize the homework program for each child. This is especially crucial for ADD kids.

If the ADD child can work ten long division problems in twenty minutes, let him or her do ten problems. Many teachers think that if ten is good, fifty will be better. Not! Tired, swamped, and frustrated, at-risk kids just can't cope with the same load most others can.

Indeed, the most common complaint of ADD kids in our counsel is that they can't keep up. This is not the load carrier's fault. Putting four hundred pounds on a Shetland pony will not force that pony into becoming a Percheron. The load assigner, by adjusting expectations, can help greatly.

Says Mrs. Capehart, "You have to set up a realistic agreement of what the child needs to do. Not too easy, not too hard. I do a contract with them—with each student. We agree on what needs to be done for the week. Then I break it down to daily parts and show the child how to write it on an assignment sheet. The next week we cut a new contract. Kids have learning 'muscles,' so to speak, that you can compare in some ways with physical muscles. Exercising their learning 'muscles' makes them stronger learners. Last week's contract might not reflect this week's abilities. They really can grow."

We say all this cautiously because we certainly do not believe one ought to excuse the ADD child from the pressures of life. By the same token, if the goal is to learn, by hook or crook, then whatever serves that goal efficiently should be considered.

"And please," Mrs. Capehart stresses, "never give homework for homework's sake. Homework is to teach, not to frustrate."

In the long run, though, neither homework nor schoolwork will determine whether the child will step forth into the world prepared to live a good life. The child's attitude will determine that, and the child's attitude, by and large, will be shaped by the adults around him or her.

Adjusting Attitudes

Three sets of attitudes require fine tuning, then: the child's, the parents', and the teacher's.

Miss Pruitt's attitude change was already well on the road. Once she accepted that some of her pupils needed different teaching methods and a different learning environment, she became much more effective.

Says Mrs. Capehart, "In any classroom, whether or not ADD kids are involved, the wise teacher asks himself or herself, 'What have I done for kids to see? What have I done for them to talk about? What have I given them to touch and do?' You'll hook just about every child on one of them. If some kids can do workbook work, let them. Great. But the others need active learning tools too."

Beth's attitude of becoming involved in her son's life in ways to best serve his needs and interests was a good one. Because she worked full time to support herself and Andrew, she would constantly feel guilty about not doing more. But her heart was on the right track, and her impact was great.

Together, Miss Pruitt's and Beth's attitudes would profoundly influence Andrew's attitude. But not all parents enter the team with that attitude. If a teacher has trouble, the sooner he or she sets up a conference, the better. If necessary, the school may have to drag in the parent kicking and screaming and then work to build a real team.

The overriding attitude for parents and teachers both, especially in conference, is always, "We must help the child learn." Should the parent attack the teacher or vice versa, the flow of progress ceases instantly. The magic words teachers long to hear from parents are, "What can I do to help?"

Jody Capehart not only watches her own attitude, she tries to mold her students' attitudes indirectly. "I love to read. I love to learn. So I always have a book on my desk. Not a textbook. Something extracurricular. I want my students to see a teacher who communicates the love of learning."

Love of learning does not mean the same to the ADD child as it does to most children. Teachers and parents must always keep in mind that the ADD child is extremely insecure academically. Extremely. This kid always feels as if he or she can't do it, whatever it is. A true love of academic learning may lie beyond the child's capabilities; parents and teachers may be achieving total success if they can but instill a tolerance or mild interest in learning.

In general, parents and teachers should do as you would do for any child: Start with what the child knows and does now, then go on to what the child does not know. Because anxiety is a constantly recurring component of an ADD child's makeup, teachers and parents must watch for signs that the child is starting to get fearful and panicky and then work to help get him or her back on safe ground. That in itself will ease the fear and dread of academic learning that so many ADD kids feel.

Keep in mind, too, the ADD child's extreme variation. Some days the child knows the material, and some days he or she doesn't. Saying, "Come on, you know it! You knew it yesterday!" only adds to the fear, because although the child knew it yesterday, today is another story. The parents and teachers then must adjust their attitudes to incorporate what they know about the ADD child's way of thinking and seeing. The shift of adult attitude from "You're lazy and obstinate" to "You're different" is one of the wildest, widest, most effective swings in the world.

Attitudes cannot do the whole job, of course. The conduct of classroom teaching is what makes or breaks the child's learning experience. Let's look at those rubber-meets-the-road details of teaching ADD kids.

We remind you that the material in this chapter—where we've discussed generalities about learning and teaching—and in the next as well—where we'll look at specific techniques for teaching—applies equally to church and Sunday school teachers. All teachers. Keep in mind also that parents are their children's most important teachers. So this material applies to the parents just as much. We will, however, gear it to schoolteachers.

THE ADD CHILD IN SCHOOL— PRACTICAL TECHNIQUES

*I**RA CHAPIN SAW** something he had never in his life imagined he would ever see. He stopped by Miss Pruitt's room after class to drop off the midyear grade forms and a carton of art supplies that didn't fit in her box and found her standing by her window, watching the departing riot. There were tears in her eyes.

Tears. The indomitable Miss Pruitt.

He stepped in beside her and spoke quietly. "Talk to me."

She didn't seem ashamed. She did look very sad. "Whittaker is an auditory learner."

That could not have produced the tears. He waited.

She continued, softly. "In all my years of teaching, I had not fully grasped the differences between what I would call the ordinary child, the one who can do workbook work well, and auditory learners. I found out just recently through reading that most auditory children must verbalize what they are learning. They have to repeat it. Say it back.

"Whittaker's trouble at home with his parents' separation has made him something of a troublemaker here. Not nearly the problem that Andrew is, thank heaven. He's merely annoying, a talker, an interrupter. Lately, in sympathy, I suppose, I've been giving him some slack, to use the slang. Letting him go, letting him talk. Letting him ask silly, repetitive questions. It is the first time I've ever permitted that sort of behavior. And do you know? He's been doing much better scholastically. So *much* better. He has almost total recall of information. It's amazing."

"That can't be causing the tears."

"No. Of course not. Do you remember Jason, Ira?"

"The kid with the green streak through his hair?"

"Yes. I would explain the lesson, and he would seem to be getting it just fine. He was very attentive. But then he'd try to ask a question, and it would always be a silly question, a repetition of what I had just said. So I didn't allow him to speak out—that was disruptive, you see—so the lesson would never actually sink in. I remember telling him, 'If you would just listen, you would get it.' He said one day, 'I'm sure stupid,' and I in my lordly impatience replied, 'Yes, I believe you are.'" The graying head wagged slightly. "I'm not sure I will ever be able to forgive myself for the damage I did to that innocent little boy."

Specific Techniques for ADD Pupils

Because so many kids, ADD and otherwise like Whittaker and Miss Pruitt's Jason, learn in other than the usual ways, the schoolteacher, the Sunday school instructor, the scout leader, and the parent need an arsenal of special tricks and methods. With modifications, these techniques will work at home, at school, in church, and in public venues such as the zoo and even the grocery store. We will discuss them as they apply to the formal teaching of ADD kids, but keep in mind that they are not by any means limited to that situation.

Ideally, methods are meant not just to teach facts, language, and concepts but also to teach self-monitoring, self-teaching, and self-control. We are not merely teaching the ADD child the date when Columbus first reached the New World. We're teaching the child how to cope with the new world. In this regard then, the first and biggest thing ADD children must learn is how to organize and structure their lives.

Imposing Structure

Structure—which is to say organization, reminders, and monitoring—is the ADD kid's bugaboo. William Steinfelder tried to deal with it by getting Mel's input for his clean-my-room list. Amy depended upon her parents to direct her life because she had limited internal structure of her own. Andrew seemed to have none at all.

One of the assumptions adults make is that children are somehow born knowing how to do such things as cleaning up a room, taking notes, doing homework, studying for a test. Most kids muddle through, although they would benefit greatly from instruction. ADD kids can't muddle. It is well worth the heavy investment of time it takes to teach ADD kids the structuring skills involved in processes such as those.

Remembering that the ADD child does not remember well or think in logical, incremental steps, we will make up a system to compensate for the lack of sequencing and short-term memory. The child will fight you on it. You'll no doubt hear, "I don't want to do this!" or "Quit treating me like a baby!" and "You don't do this to my brother!" But he or she needs it, and deep down inside, the kid knows it. This is why successful ADD adults become obsessive about organization and structure in their lives, compulsively tying themselves to their calendars and daily organizers and certain habits. They realize they must impose a structure upon themselves from outside because internally they just can't do it.

Structure in Everyday Activity

Parents and teachers must work together closely to organize the child and then keep the kid put together. This involves monitoring every aspect of his or her life, such as succeeding in school and completing homework, note-taking and outlining (the person preparing a job resume is, in essence, building an outline!), and accomplishing long, complex projects.

Many of the poor grades ADD children receive come not from the lack of learning but from failure to complete or turn in work. The child forgets the assignment, forgets to bring homework back to school, forgets to complete the project. Poor short-term memory and lack of sequencing do the kid in. The child needs monitoring from without, both at school and at home, until he or she can develop a useful degree of self-monitoring (and that may not happen until the late teens). Sure, all kids need reminders now and then. But ADD kids need them constantly. Here are some things you can help your child use as reminder devices:

The Assignment Notebook.   Every kid from third grade on needs a notebook in which to record all assignments at the time they are made. A system that provides a list or assignment sheet right on the child's notebook cover is even better. The parent and teacher will have to show the child exactly how to record the assignments and then monitor him or her constantly for compliance.

The Supply Pouch.   You know those zippered plastic pouches you can buy that fit in a three-ring binder? The child needs one. It will contain all his or her supplies—pencils, erasers, pens, six-inch ruler, and extras, the kind of things that disappear at a constant rate of attrition. To minimize loss, train the child to put all supplies away in the pouch promptly and monitor closely.

The Special Pocket.   The notebook may have a horizontal pocket inside the front and back covers, or you may have to purchase a page-size pouch or envelope sort of gizmo. One way or another, supply the child with a special file pocket. In the child's favorite color, label it in big letters: HOMEWORK. This is where the child puts homework as soon as it is completed. At first, close monitoring will be necessary, but given time, the habit will develop. All children occasionally forget to bring their homework in; the ADD child will still occasionally forget homework, too, but the special pocket will minimize the problem.

The Notebook.   Kids love those manila notebook dividers with the brightly colored plastic tabs. The notebook should be divided according to subject or project. Constant reminders then will prompt the child to file papers in their appointed division. Actually, ADD kids generally enjoy clicking the ring binder open and shut, manipulating the pockets and zippers.

"Did you file your math paper?"

"Did you put your homework in the homework pocket?"

"Did you put your pencil back? Good!"

"You may put your spelling paper back in the pouch."

And on and on. Never assume these children will remember in February what you've been saying from September to January. It will take years, not months, to build the kind of internal structure you are imposing now from the outside.

When do you let up on externally imposed structure? Now and then, cautiously. See how well the child does. When the child keeps making the same mistakes over and over, the parent and teacher might ask, "Do I need to tighten the structure here?" Externally imposed structure is the ultimate treatment for a multitude of ADD-inducing problems. The child who gets in trouble misusing free time needs more programmed time. The child who cannot handle certain privileges must have those privileges revoked for a while, not as punishment but as guidance.

Structure—close programming and monitoring—is essential for the completion of tasks, and that's another area in which the ADD child needs lots and lots of help.

Imposing and Controlling Homework

Here is where the parent-teacher-pupil team really kicks into high gear. Homework can cease to be the pounding headache it so often seems if the team can build a concerted plan of action.

Preparation.   At home, the parent sets up the child by providing the comfort zone we discussed earlier. In the child's supply trove will be notebook paper, stick-on notes in various colors, markers and high-lighting pens in various colors, three-by-five or four-by-six cards in various colors (purchase quantities in those discount office supply ware-houses), lots of pencils and the child's own pencil sharpener—one that really works, not those rinky-dink little handheld blade-in-a-box things.

The child will use the stick-on notes to stick reminders to himself on his wall or desk. He will use them as bookmarks and place-to-study markers. They're fun to use, which makes them of interest to the child.

Although Andrew was not quite old enough to be assigned home-work and Miss Pruitt did not believe in giving small children homework, let's pretend for the moment, just for example, that homework was in fact a part of Andrew and Miss Pruitt's life.

Here we go.

At School.   Shortly before school lets out, Miss Pruitt cruises by Andrew's desk. She makes sure Andrew has written down the assign-ments. She will probably have to show Andrew which books to take home. In essence she is preparing Andrew at this front end of the homework process. She will probably have to prepare Whittaker simi-larly because Whittaker is developing some fairly serious ADD-like char-acteristics. You don't have to be certified ADD for this method to work well.

Because Andrew, like most ADD children, is not medicated after school, his distractibility and attention deficit are at a maximum during homework time. Besides, he's starting to get tired from his day in the trenches. And poor Whittaker is living in a motel with his mom and sister. All in all, homework suffers even under the best of circumstances.

At Home.   Beth is either waiting or has a baby-sitter waiting for Andrew. Several rules kick in automatically.

1. Transition Time.   Andrew need not dive right into homework before he can play. He gets some unwinding time after school. A snack, physical activity, prattling, bouncing off the walls—let it all hang out, as they used to say. Transition time.

Television and video games such as Nintendo are not appropriate transitions. We recommend against allowing the TV set on at all during this break between school and homework.

2. Homework Time.   A specific and unvarying time is set aside for homework. The length of that time has already been determined in conference between Andrew, Beth, and Miss Pruitt: thirty to forty-five minutes. Half an hour may be plenty for a strongly ADD child. During that time, there will be no phone calls, no TV or Nintendo, no running around (unless the child prowls while reading, the way William did). Breaks may be allowed or programmed in during homework time—the younger the child, the more frequent the breaks.

As William built himself a broken-down checklist of tasks for cleaning his room, so the ADD child needs a breakdown for completing homework. This normally falls to the parent. Place the list in a notebook, tape it to the door, display it in the study area. Whatever. The child then has to go through the same steps every day. In essence, the parent is training the child to monitor himself. The steps might include:

A. Bring all books home every day unless the teacher tells you otherwise. Even better, ask the school for copies of the child's texts to keep at home. Schools are usually happy to provide this service; it cuts down on loss between school and home.

B. After the snack break, sit down and go through the whole assignment list first, then break it down into sections. The parent will probably have to monitor this portion. "Get this amount done, and you can take a break. Then do this other little assignment and take a break." And so on.

C. Do what you have to learn. A really kinesthetic kid might read while pedaling a stationary bike or walking on a treadmill with a music stand for the book. (And you thought exercise machines were destined to gather dust!) The auditory learner will be making tapes of his work or listening to a tape. We'll get into that in detail later in the chapter.

A child in Dr. Warren's counsel could not learn math facts. A kinesthetic, she bounced a ball in rhythm with her recitations. (Bounce) three times (bounce) four is (bounce) twelve. When her dad drilled her, she would bounce it to him as he asked the fact: "Three times four." By the time the ball came back to her she had to have the answer. (Teachers are not overly happy to have such shenanigans going on in the classroom, but they do work.)

D. A treat awaits completion. Here Dr. Warren and Mrs. Capehart express a difference of opinion. They both agree that every ADD kid is a Nintendo freak. Once addicted, the kids cannot turn the thing off once they start. Mrs. Capehart prefers that parents of ADD kids not bring video games such as Nintendo into the house at all, solving a number of problems before they appear. Dr. Warren argues another side of the coin, saying ADD kids need as rewards something very desirable that offers instant gratification. They can't wait for goodies promised somewhere down the line. The immediacy of games such as Nintendo serves that function.

As for the game itself, ADD kids need practice with sequencing—seeing causes and effects. Again, video games rely heavily on cause and effect; if you do this, that happens. Besides, the joystick and mouse are excellent tactile-kinesthetic devices. Also, here is something—perhaps the only thing—the ADD child can truly control. Dr. Warren, therefore, suggests that if Nintendo or similar games come into the house at all, they be used as the ultimate treat, to be saved for when all homework is completed. Even then, set Nintendo on a timer. At the end of the prescribed time, the lights go out—no ifs, ands, or buts.

3. Help Time.   Someone—Beth, the baby-sitter, perhaps even a kind neighbor—will be available to help the child. An older sibling can be a blessing here. Andrew is given to know, however, that help will not be forthcoming unless it is requested appropriately. Being nasty or argumentative gets him nowhere.

4. End of Homework Time.   When homework time is over, it's over. Finis. ADD kids as a rule never profit from struggling longer. Forcing protracted homework sessions only increases conflict in the family and frustration in the kid.

An hour of homework for your average kid is at least an hour and three-fourths for an ADD child because ADD kids work more slowly.

Overloaded, an ADD child becomes exhausted, self-defeated, paralyzed. By helping him or her succeed with small, measurable tasks, building up learning muscles if you will, the child learns to take on more.

This is why the team is so important. Beth can tell if Andrew's homework assignments are too burdensome or not burdensome enough. She and Miss Pruitt then will be in constant communication about the amount of work to be done. Need we mention that Beth must be very careful to be objective about this? It's extremely easy to want to let the child off the hook in sympathy or impose extra work in anger.

The most important thing about growing up is not schoolwork and homework, a position Miss Pruitt would probably debate. The most important thing about growing up is learning to forge effective relationships and to become a self-sufficient person who functions well out in the world. Heated arguments about completing quantities of homework are hardly the central theme of an effective family life.

None of the above rules should be chiseled in stone. The child might spend more home time on a special project, modifying the rule about time limits. The rule confining homework to a certain time might be abrogated when the family goes out to a movie. The homework time could shift to some other spot on the clock, but such instances should be rare. ADD kids more than most must be taught to appreciate that rules are rules.

Again, Beth and Miss Pruitt will work in concert, bolstering each other's lessons, to teach Andrew the basics of study and schoolwork. Among them are note-taking, outlining, and completing large projects such as term papers.

Remember that children who experience difficulty with the fine motor coordination necessary for fast, accurate writing—and that's many ADD children—may need some accommodation. However, they still must learn outlining and note-taking if they would get along well in advanced education and the real world.

Teaching Note-Taking and Outlining

Telling most of the kids in Miss Pruitt's class, "We'll take notes" suffices. The kids somehow figure it out. Certainly by the time kids reach William Steinfelder's level of school, note-taking and outlining come normally. But not for ADD kids. They can't pick out the important from the frivolous. Every word carries the same weight.

For the same reason, the child having trouble taking notes will also have trouble outlining. All the information carries equal weight to a global thinker. Mrs. Capehart uses a method of note-taking and outlining that both teachers and parents can employ. In fact, both should. The teacher probably will not have time to walk a child through the process. The parent should be able to as part of the homework.

Says Mrs. Capehart, "Let's say the parents are the ones who are going to do this, but the teacher can use this technique also. The parent and kid run down to the copy store and make a photocopy of the reading material to be outlined. When you get back home, lay out three or four colors of transparent highlighting pens. Highlighters. Then the parent sits with the child (I'll call the child 'him' because Damon and I used to do this). You (the parent) read the paragraph, and as you read it you use greatly exaggerated voice inflections. Emphasize the high spots. Say the key words louder; put more *oomph* in them. This will help the child clue in on the important words and concepts.

"You finish reading. Now you ask him, 'What is the main idea in the passage?' He'll probably say, 'I don't know.' 'Okay,' you say, 'What do they talk about the most?'

" 'Oh,' he says. 'Elephants.'

"Elephants. So you take the yellow marker to the photocopy and highlight 'Elephants.'

"What did we find out about elephants? They have trunks. We highlight that fact in a different color.

"Facts about the facts we highlight with a third color. What about trunks? They're very sensitive, they are used to grasp, and they're used for feeding and drinking. Three facts. We go through the whole set of material that way. Now we're ready to outline. The Roman numeral I is the first color. The subheads are the second, and smaller items are the third. Bang, bang, bang. By manually highlighting, seeing the colors, and reading and reciting aloud, the child is learning through three different avenues, visual, tactile, and auditory. I've watched an awful lot of kids successfully figure out outlining with this."

As the children get older and further into outlining and note-taking, supply them with colored notecards to match the highlighted passages. Putting together a term paper is a snap for an ADD kid using color-keyed notes.

At school, the teacher will probably not have the time to walk through the method above step by step. But he or she can encourage good note-taking by keeping in mind that the child doesn't know what to put down unless told.

Let's say Miss Pruitt is talking about gerbils and she is expecting everyone in her class to take notes (remember that Andrew's class wasn't actually up to that yet; we're just pretending). The children will be told at the outset to follow her cues.

One cue will simply be when she says, "Now write this down. This is important."

Another is when she puts something on the board. Anything written on the board is to go into the children's notes as being important. Miss Pruitt needs to keep that in mind so she doesn't write insignificant things up there.

Outlining is a linear skill, beyond all but the most mature ADD kids. So every time Miss Pruitt changes the topic, she says, "Now we'll talk about [ ]," and Andrew knows to draw a line across his paper. Later, those lines will mark the outline's Roman numerals.

If Miss Pruitt is really good (and teaching an upper grade), she will show her children how to abbreviate some words and take other short-cuts. She might suggest using a symbol for a word that keeps coming up frequently. Being the inventive souls they are, ADD kids will find a symbol. And if they come up with the symbol themselves, they're likely to remember it.

Lastly, Miss Pruitt will show her children how to take their scribbled notes and transfer them to notecards. In the process of transferring them (which for auditory learners should include reciting them aloud or in an undertone), she is teaching the children how to organize.

Teachers can teach study skills in this way and parents can reinforce the lesson at home. That's by far the best way to help a child.

Teaching How to Complete Longer Projects

What's wrong with this announcement? "It's January 20. You have a paper on gerbils due March 15. Do it."

For most kids, nothing is wrong with it. They'll need a few re-minders—"That gerbil paper is due in two weeks"—but they'll manage.

To the ADD child, though, a date nearly two months in the future might as well be two decades away. The child doesn't have that sharp a time sense. Worse, the idea of writing a paper or term project is instantly overwhelming because the child sees the whole job globally—all at once. All the various steps in the process clamor to be the first step. The child freezes, unable to guess where or how to start.

A. A. Milne presented the ADD child's dilemma brilliantly in a poem about a shipwrecked sailor. The fellow decided he needed food and shelter, but he could not decide which survival task to do first and in the end he did nothing. Wrapped in a blanket, he sat on the beach and simply awaited rescue. That's our kid.

To help an ADD student learn how to undertake a detailed project, the teacher must break it down sequentially and *assign* the steps.

"The first step is to read the material. Do that this week, four pages each day." Write it down as an assignment.

"The next step is to outline the material. Finish it by Friday." That goes in the assignment notebook.

"Next, build your file of notecards. Better take a couple of days, using the colored highlighters."

In sequential steps, then, the child will lay out his or her cards on the floor, arrange the information the way the paper will read, skewer the cards on a safety pin or nail, and then write the paper, peeling the cards off the pile in sequence, one by one. The key, of course, is to break the monstrous task down into little steps. And recall at all times that the child cannot do this alone.

Eventually, though, the child will indeed be able to do this kind of thing on his or her own, but he or she will be approaching adulthood when the miracle finally happens. The child will then carry these skills through life.

Parents and teachers can work together in another important way: helping the child study by using a variety of tricks to take advantage of alternative learning styles.

Catering to Different Learning Styles— Little Tricks

Controlling Global Tendencies

People who are global thinkers see the whole page quickly. Thus, when faced with an entire page of problems or test questions, they become overwhelmed and mentally *shut down*. Providing a *window* such as the one described in the next paragraph minimizes the sense of being overwhelmed, and thus helps the student to focus on only one part of the test or worksheet at a time. Tests, particularly achievement tests, are full pages of problems. There are ways to modify the overwhelming effect of a mass of problems or questions.

Now most right-brained global thinkers have strong color preferences. Let's use that. Ask the child to pick a color he or she likes. If a really weird color is chosen—puce or mauve, perhaps—give the kid a choice between two calming colors, blue and green. In a big piece of paper of the chosen color, cut out a window above the middle of the paper. The window should be just about large enough to reveal one or two problems or questions at a time. The child does only what appears in the window. The child then moves the paper down to reveal one or two more problems or questions in the window. Able to see the increments instead of the whole, the child feels less overwhelmed by the task at hand.

Double-Teaming

Rarely would Miss Pruitt have time for this in her class of twenty-five, but Beth at home will find it effective. The double-teaching team is not parent and teacher but parent and child.

Says Beth, "You read the material several times, Andrew, and then you teach it to me."

This is very successful, particularly for kids in the middle grades and up. Buy the child a chalkboard or markerboard (it needn't be expensive) and let the child organize the material and teach it to you.

Another excellent ploy: "Will you make a worksheet for me, please?"

Any of these methods works splendidly on the child who learns best by touching, handling, talking, and moving. Best of all, by becoming the teacher, the child feels in control. It's a heady delight for an ADD kid.

Using a Tape Recorder

What a blessing a tape recorder can be for an auditory learner! Amy Eglund, Peter's spacey preteen, was a strongly auditory learner. She could understand spoken instructions that went right over her head if she tried to read them. From about third grade on, she and others like her would benefit greatly from a tape recorder.

With it she can tape new material, teachers' lectures, and important instructions. She simply turns the tape recorder on when her teacher is discussing something new, then listens to it again later.

She might read her textbook aloud, emphasizing important words—if she notices them. With time, she will learn to read a paragraph and recite aloud only the important point.

Jody Capehart's Damon had to recite from a book into a tape recorder and then make written notes. That middle step was necessary for him because he was an auditory learner.

When it comes to learning rote stuff like times tables and states and capitals, the tape recorder comes through again.

Amy can even make herself a study tape. For example, she has to memorize the capitals of all fifty states, a daunting task. She recites the states and their capitals on a study tape to which she will listen repeatedly. On another tape she will recite "Arizona" then leave enough dead airspace of time so she can later say "Phoenix." Then she says onto the tape: "Arizona—Phoenix" so she can verify the answer she will give when she's using the study tape later. In the same way she would say, "Oregon . . . [dead air] . . . Oregon—Salem." When she can, speaking aloud, fill in the blanks and get it right when checked by the repeat, she has it nailed.

Study tapes work well for spelling words also. "Illusion . . . [three or four seconds]. Illusion. I-L-L-U . . ."

Rewind it and do it again.

A part of the fun with this process is the sheer pleasure of holding the recorder, of pushing buttons, of controlling the machine.

Many ADD kids, Andrew in particular, have to be in the presence of sound. If the child doesn't hear sound, he or she will one way or another create the required noise. Miss Pruitt, then, can cut down Andrew's noisemaking considerably by allowing him a Walkman with earphones and letting him listen to it as he works. Otherwise he will generate the sound he needs.

At all times, the teacher, the parents, and everyone else must emphasize to the auditory learner, "Your tape recorder is a tool, not a toy. Abuse it, and you lose it."

Miss Pruitt would be especially good at enforcing that one.

Flipping Flash Cards and Other Tactile Gimmicks.   Tactile learners and strongly global kids really cook with flash cards. Mrs. Capehart uses pounds of three-by-five index cards in all colors when she teaches. Math facts, for example, lend themselves beautifully to flash cards. Put 3×4 on one side and $3 \times 4 = 12$ (not just 12) on the flip side. Global ADD kids have to see the whole thing.

Amy Eglund would probably benefit somewhat from flash cards, but they do not cater to her style well. "Ohio" on one side and "Columbus" on the other doesn't mean much to her. But it means a lot to the tactile kid who will pick up the card and manually turn it over.

Flash cards make good pop quizzes that are actually fun. The teacher can lay out, for instance, the names of all the states and the names of all the capitals, a sort of Concentration game with all the cards face up to start with. In turn, the children pick up this or that card to properly match the states with their capitals. Great stuff for a tactile learner!

The tactile learner who cannot easily sit or read and answer questions can prepare the cards and use them successfully.

There are many other ways to reach a tactile learner. For example, on waxed paper, Mrs. Capehart spreads sugar-free pudding or whipped topping. She says the spelling word, and the child writes it in the pudding with a finger, erasing it with a stroke of the palm. If the child gets the word right, he or she is allowed to lick the victorious finger. Instant gratification.

A tray of sand is hardly finger-licking good, but it provides a fascinating texture in which to write answers. Shaving cream offers still another.

Employing Motion.   William Steinfelder, the sixteen-year-old, was a kinesthetic learner. He retained visual information—the read word—best when his body was in motion. That it drove his father right out of his tree was strictly a fringe benefit.

In Miss Pruitt's class, dark-haired little Marsha was terribly kinesthetic. Squirmy, jumpy, constantly in need of a drink or a sharpened pencil or a book from the library. She could not handle subtraction.

Much against Miss Pruitt's better judgment, she allowed Marsha to bring a soft foam ball to school and squeeze it for a minute when she couldn't think well. When Marsha was having too hard a time, she could squeeze her ball a few minutes to see if perhaps the answer might come. It often did. Kinesthetic kids can frequently figure out the answer as they're doing some physical action.

"If you throw it, Marsha, or if it gets you off track, you have to keep it in your desk. We only allow in this room things that help you learn. Is that understood?"

That was understood.

Miss Pruitt noticed that all during the Thursday math test, Marsha was rhythmically squeezing her ball in her lap with her left hand as her right put down the answers. Correct answers, as it turned out.

Allowing Minibreaks

ADD kids who feel swamped (and that happens a lot) may benefit from a moment's break. When the press of work gets too hard, it may benefit the child to take out a scratch pad or something similar and doodle for a minute. Mrs. Capehart lets her students have Legos in their desks for that purpose, something Miss Pruitt would never, ever be able to bring herself to do.

Catering to these diverse learning styles solves important problems in student attention and accomplishment, but it also causes a serious problem. The other kids—the ordinary kids who don't need kinesthetic props, auditory gizmos, and tactile tidbits—become jealous of the children who get to play.

"You let Marsha play with a ball. Why can't I?"

The difficulty stymied Miss Pruitt at first, to the extent that she almost revoked all privileges and went back to her old ways. She solved the problem in part by discussing the new techniques with all the parents during the fifteen-minute parent-teacher conferences at the close of the first half of the year, gaining their understanding and acquiescence.

In the end she also allowed each child one privilege. The ground rules: It had to be inconspicuous and therefore not distracting to the other students, it could not make noise, and it was revokable for misuse.

A number of skills do not come easily to ADD kids, and that includes being able to process data the left-brain world thinks they need or want to know (usually, they don't). Encouraging reading, the use of mnemonics, and other tricks help out in this regard.

Encouraging Reading

Andrew couldn't read worth a hoot. William had to walk when reading or it didn't stick. Amy hated reading and loved having people read to her. Reading is a problem with many ADD kids. Rarely will an ADD kid who isn't a gifted reader develop a real love of reading, but the dislike can be allayed.

Here is where parents like Beth can make all the difference. But success may start with the teacher.

Miss Pruitt believed firmly in phonics, and that was to be expected. Phonics is linear, a strongly left-brain method of learning reading, and so was Miss Pruitt. Reading by sight is a global function in which the child naturally takes in the word as a unit. School systems, teachers, and parents often argue about which is better, the look-say method or phonetics. The truth is, both are necessary. One will work well with one child, the other with another.

It falls to the teacher, then, to find a method that works best for the individual child.

But parents like Beth hold a key as well. They can work with the child one on one, and that is very necessary for an ADD pupil.

For a child like Andrew, just beginning to learn to read and spell, those notecards are very helpful.

Beth might print each of the spelling words and Andrew's new reading words on a notecard—let's say, a red one. Andrew then copies the word onto another notecard—green, perhaps. There are now two matching sets. Beth turns her word card over, talking about the word, and asks Andrew to think of a picture. "What comes to mind? Draw a picture on the card." ADD kids are often wonderfully creative and artistic. Drawing the picture, of course, is right up their alley and helps them remember the word.

Beth does this for each of her cards. Now she lays her cards out picture-side up. Andrew must match his word card to her picture card, reciting the word, reading it. When he's done, he turns her cards over and they see how well he did. Note how nice the gimmick is for a tactile learner.

Another method for facilitating reading is to read to the child. Every day. Miss Pruitt can read aloud to her children, perhaps going through a book one chapter each day.

At home, Beth reads to Andrew; her reading sessions usually will not extend much over ten minutes or so. As she reads, Andrew will follow along with his finger or a three-by-five card held under the appropriate line on the book. The finger or card, you see, becomes the tactile/kinesthetic function. Beth's voice is the audio as Andrew sees the words. The higher the degree of voice inflection she uses, the easier it will be for Andrew to comprehend.

You can see, as Beth weaves this process together, how it will profit a child like Andrew with his unique global outlook and special learning style.

Mrs. Capehart suggests that if the child says, "I want to read it," that you let him or her read. If he or she never says that, don't force the child.

Miss Pruitt, frankly, had a great deal of trouble with this whole concept. For years she had been teaching her children that to follow along the written line with their fingertips as they read was a crutch. Dispense with it, she ordered them. And above all, don't move your lips when you read silently. But that's how auditory learners read; they are listening to the written word in a literal way. When Miss Pruitt made these adjustments in her thinking she really was making a major, major shift.

How long does this reading-to-the-child go on? As long as possible. Into high school. And what will Beth hear for her efforts?

"Mom, don't treat me like a baby!"

Her response? "My goal is to help you read better, and this will."

In fact, this method works in spades for older children, kids William's age who have gotten to junior high or high school without ever effectively learning to read. The lack will start to show up now as learning shifts even more strongly to the left-brain methods of listening to lectures and text-reading.

If Beth can persist with this into high school, of course she will do it one on one so no one else knows about it. A child's sense of self, integrity, and ego loom very big during puberty and adolescence. Also,

Beth should pick something at Andrew's interest level. Oh, true, she must draw lines. *Playboy,* no. *Sports Illustrated,* sure. *Reader's Digest, National Geographic,* there's lots of interesting material out there. Even when Andrew is older, she will use her voice inflections to emphasize the important points in the material. She should be getting pretty darned good at it by then.

As her son climbs through the grades, Beth can do both Andrew and many others a service by reading his textbooks aloud. Again, she uses the exaggerated voice inflections to, in effect, give auditory clues to the major points. Then, at the end of Andrew's school year she can donate the tapes to the school, for there are always kids coming up who have trouble learning visually.

Using Mnemonics

The lines of the musical scale—Every Good Boy Does Fine—and the spaces of the scale—FACE—are mnemonics, words or phrases that help us remember facts in sequence. When it comes to memorizing lists, ADD kids are in a world of hurt. Mnemonics can make all the difference.

ADD kids are usually very good at coming up with funny words and phrases, off-the-wall names, and other mnemonics once the teacher or parent clues them in to the trick. Having learned how, then, they become pretty good at recalling the goofy word or phrase and from it calling up the complete list.

ADD kids usually do very well also with gimmicks such as acrostics or alliteration. They need a little help; if the parent or teacher can come up with some key words, the kids will come up with others.

The heat that makes the pot boil is imagination. The child already has an active one; parent and teacher—yes, especially Miss Pruitt—must follow suit. Here are some random suggestions that have worked for Mrs. Capehart and others in the trenches, where it counts. You may wish to use some of them. May we suggest a larger use of them however—use them as springboards to launch your own imagination. Think active, think tactile, think auditory. One way or another you will reach the child and make him or her feel good about learning. And that is the bottom line.

Various Classroom Tactics

Laughing, a friend named Bill tells about going to the cattle auction with his pals when they were in their teens. The moment the bidding started, the guys froze into pillars of salt. So afraid they might accidentally buy a cow, they could actually stop in mid-sneeze until the bidding ended.

Their fears were ill-founded, of course. Buyers who planned to bid registered at the office beforehand and informed the spotters of their preferred gesture—a hand raised, the bill of the cap touched, a nod, a flick of the finger. Subtle gestures they were, and just as effective as jumping up and down would be—or sneezing.

Mrs. Capehart uses a similar system in the classroom. When a child needs her to repeat instructions or explanations, he or she sends her a predetermined signal. Perhaps the child will pull on an ear or scratch his or her nose. Mrs. Capehart can then provide the needed repetition without drawing attention to the child and to the child's inability to catch it all the first time.

Older children particularly need a prearranged signal system for communicating unobtrusively with the teacher, for this is the age when painful self-consciousness rears its smothering head. ADD kids feel inferior during the best of times. Needing repetition or special consideration makes them stand out before their peers in ways they don't want. Attention they love, but only on their own terms.

In geography and social studies, the usual map skills employing pencil and paper can be very boring for the ADD child. It just doesn't seem important. Mrs. Capehart gets children's interest piqued with two square cake pans. To start with, the kids have to make their own clay, which involves measuring and using fractions. That's a lesson in itself, however fun.

A child pushes the clay out flat in the bottom of one pan. With a table knife, another child cuts a circle from the middle, lifts it out, and puts it in the second pan. They pour water into both pans. In the first pan is a lake, in the second an island. "Now let's find all the lakes and islands on this map."

On a grander scale, they find continent and ocean or a cape and a bay, a strait and an isthmus, a fjord or sound and a peninsula, or a mountain and a valley, all expressed in tactile/kinesthetic clarity.

This isn't just schoolwork. At home, Beth can do the same with Andrew in the kitchen. Get out the measuring cup for hands-on fractions. Cut up apples. Break up cookies. Let Andrew literally get the feel of math.

Herald Press, an arm of the Mennonites, publishes several excellent cookbooks. One of them, *Extending the Table,* features recipes from missionaries and others all over the world. Along with the contributors' anecdotes and reminiscences are recipes for ethnic foods made with

American ingredients and measurements. A book of this sort is a splendid study aid for geography and social studies. "Here on the map is Zaire, and in this book is a recipe from that country. And listen to what the missionary from Zaire says . . ."

With supervision, the child prepares the food, hears the firsthand experience, identifies the location, learns with taste and touch, ear and eye.

How can the ADD pupil learn to memorize things for which there is no mnemonic, such as multiplication tables? How daunting it is for an ADD child. This kid finds memorizing math facts staggering because he or she cannot see patterns well. And in the math tables, each fact stands by itself without any obvious relationship to other facts.

We suggest you make a chart of the complete multiplication table. Put all the facts on it in long, scary columns. "We're going to master this!" you say, and the child flinches.

So the child learns the "times twos," and the "times threes." You then highlight the facts he or she knows. "Look! You know more than just the column-full you've memorized. You know three times nine equals twenty-seven, and that means we know nine times three equals twenty-seven. Yea!" He or she probably didn't see that until you pointed it out. Invite the child to literally reach out and touch it, to see it and possess it. A light comes on, and what a beautiful thing that is! Success.

In short, the answer is never just one learning method. Always the effective teacher of ADD kids, at school or at home, must employ an eclectic approach, trusting that something in the mix will sink in.

Jody Capehart's face takes on its happy smile of enthusiasm as she talks about one of her favorite activities. "Frequently I'll invite teachers to ask me into their classroom, if they wish, to teach for a day. It's a break for them and both instructive and invigorating for me. They'll say, 'What do you want to teach?' I'll say, 'Anything you want.' 'Anything?' they ask. 'Anything,' I tell them. And they say, rather wistfully, 'Long division.'"

Long division. The black hole of elementary school.

The Special Example of Long Division

Long division provides an excellent example of the methods we've just been talking about, as well as demonstrating the problems ADD kids have grasping schoolwork.

"All right, boys and girls," says the teacher smugly, "today we learn long division."

Okay, the ADD kid's up for this.

The teacher puts a sample problem on the board.

Now long division is pure left-brain visual. Linear. The numerals have to be positioned just so, or it doesn't come out right. But wait. Look what she's doing. She divides. Good. The ADD child was expecting that. But now she's multiplying. And now she's subtracting, and now she's bringing down another number.

And there sits the ADD child feeling betrayed and confused. *She said it was division, but she's doing all this other stuff.* And because the child's probably not able to think in linear ways well, the kid can't see any pattern or logic. He or she can't keep the sequence of functions straight. Able to handle only one piece of information at a time, the child tunes it out.

But the next thing he or she knows, the child is facing a page of problems to do. As always, the child sees the page as a whole all at once rather than as a series of tasks. In response, the child successfully convinces himself or herself that he or she can't in a million years do all this, and the lights go off.

Meanwhile, the left-brain linear kid, the analytic child who is used to sequencing, is saying, "Cool! Bring on the problems." That's fine for that child, but the others are left in the dust.

"For starters," says Mrs. Capehart, "I bring in test tubes of colorful red and green beads. Hands on, the kids get the idea of dividing things, evenly or unevenly. It's a game. When you make it a game, the kids learn. It's that simple.

"When you teach the kids to divide, multiply, subtract, and bring down, the linear kids see it and you turn them loose with workbooks and problems. The global child cannot do this without help, so we provide a mnemonic, a memory-jogger: D-M-S-B (divide, multiply, subtract, bring down).

"Daddy, mommy, sister, brother.

"Dirty monkeys suck bananas. The kid who came up with that one told me recently, 'That's still how I remember long division. I'll do that my whole life.' The guy's a construction worker now with two kids of his own."

You would get the idea so far that this whole teaching business is a cakewalk. Hardly. All during teaching, even when the best-loved projects such as cutting up clay in square pans are the subjects, there is the problem of control and discipline.

Most ADD kids fidget more than the class can tolerate. Most have personality and social problems that keep them in hot water a large part of the time.

Constantly there is that need to keep the lid on. And yet, for most ADD kids there is also the constant need to move.

Fidget-Busting

Like those nature movies of bighorn rams slamming into each other horns-to-horns, Miss Pruitt butted up against her classroom wiggle worms. Andrew led the pack but Whittaker was nearly as fidgety, and Marsha was constantly moving, sharpening a pencil, getting a book, asking to go to the bathroom. It drove Miss Pruitt nuts, particularly since Whittaker was getting worse and worse. On the days Andrew's doctor asked that he not take his Ritalin so he could be evaluated medication-free, Miss Pruitt felt certain her destiny was an early grave.

A few short weeks ago, during her halcyon days, Miss Pruitt didn't have to worry about such things as kinesthetic children. She nailed them all to their seats, and that was the end of it. All children were alike in her eyes back then. Now she found herself with more than two dozen radically different children, each with a unique style, each needing a special twist on traditional and not-so-traditional learning techniques. The more she studied up on learning differences, the more she saw the variations in her pupils' needs, and the more complex her job became.

And yet, you couldn't fault the results. And all her children, bright and slow, seemed so much more enthusiastic about school.

She learned pretty quickly that she got less fidgeting through the day if she stopped periodically for exercise breaks. The children might clap to music, sing songs, march and move around. It was an excellent, excellent change of attitude on Miss Pruitt's part, and it yielded good fruit.

Most ADD kids really, really need to move. They don't just prefer it. They *need* it. "That," says Mrs. Capehart, "is why I let them move to the floor or to an unconventional desk to do their work if they wish. The child who moves around is not allowed to be disruptive; I make it plain: 'I let you do this as a privilege. Abuse it, and you lose it. When you stop to play with your classmates and bother people, even if they want to be bothered, you can't move freely anymore. That's the way it is. Period.'"

Another way to keep ADD children from disrupting the class is to let them be the helper. ADD kids generally love to help. Give them something to do when they're going into orbit. They can take messages to the office. No messages to send? Make up stuff. Clean a dirty window. Take up spilled paint. Whatever. All these tasks (remembering, of course, to assign only one task at a time) not only give the child a chance to move, they facilitate self-esteem. Thus the two things an ADD child needs most are provided simultaneously.

But there comes a time, and it may come frequently, when the butting rams are more than just a figure of speech. ADD kids, with their warped social gifts, are going to get in your face at school and at home. Caustic, oppositional, disrespectful—that's the ADD child's other side.

Discipline

Let's review some discipline techniques from the viewpoint of a teacher in the classroom. Remember that they work equally well for the Sunday school instructor, the scoutmaster, the club leader, the parent at home.

Cooperation: Plan It One on One.   There are actually two goals here. One is to enlist the child's cooperation from the outset, and the other is to set up the classroom structure solidly, right in the beginning. Though she didn't realize it at the time, Miss Pruitt would have done well to take Andrew aside on his first day in her room for a private tête-à-tête. She would explain to Andrew how the class operates and explain what she as the teacher needs. This puts together a team from the get-go, teacher and pupil working together.

"When I'm teaching new material, Andrew, I need you to be as quiet as you can. God made your body to move, and that's very good. I understand that, and I'll help you to learn. Your job is that when I need you to be still, you try as hard as you can."

Communicate: Set Up a Signal System.   For an ADD child like Andrew, who was prone to excessive activity, Miss Pruitt might set up a signal system. She can show Andrew a sign she might flash him when she needs him to be still.

"What special signal would you like me to give you, a secret sign only the two of us know?"

Andrew might come up with something like tugging at an ear.

"Good. That's our clue. Let's practice." (Here's where the kinesthetic aspect helps Andrew remember.) "But if you forget, and I've been pulling on my ear, what's a second sign?"

You'll probably need at least three in escalating obviousness. It helps also to have the child's desk at school or his or her chair at the dinner table at home next to the teacher or parent. The adult can reach out and touch, tap, or grip as needed.

"And," says Mrs. Capehart, "a bear hug from the back means it's time to pull it together; activity has gotten way out of hand."

Concern: Care and Show It.   As with all disciplinary and teaching matters, it takes repetition, the same thing over and over and over. As a general rule, however, so long as ADD kids feel cared for, they will do their best to cooperate. They don't get all that much care and affection from the world. Instead, the world delivers pain and criticism most of the time. So care and affection become the key for guiding them into a self-disciplined adulthood.

Control Yourself.   You are the only one you can control fully. Once you have yourself in hand, you can work on the child. Here are some guidelines for enforcing full-bore, hard-core disciplinary measures.

First, speak softly and firmly, avoid yelling. An important secret of effective discipline is to always end a statement or order with your voice pitched down. While it's a good rule of thumb when dealing with any child, it is especially important for ADD kids. They are sensitive to intonations of voice and react to them without thinking. When the adult yells and voices go up, the child instinctively becomes more active and more anxious, exactly the opposite of the effect needed. When the adult speaks quietly and firmly, ending with the voice modulated downward, that technique not only stabilizes the child, it makes it easier for the child to hear the words.

Second, move slowly. Again, if the adult walks, talks, and moves too fast, the child is stimulated to greater activity. ADD kids are mirrors and echoes of what is going on around them. The ADD child focused on an out-of-control adult is going to pick up the lack of control instantly and go into orbit.

Work on winning an Academy Award for detachment. You are not detaching from the child, of course; you are detaching from the antics.

When you move toward the child, move slowly and deliberately, keeping your eyes focused on the child's eyes. As a result the child will respond more positively.

Third, when you reach the child, maintain that eye contact. Keep the connection even though the child doesn't want to. There is great power in the eyes. An ADD child may not realize or care that his or her own action precipitated this confrontation; but the child certainly understands the intense one-on-one communication.

Now cup the child's face in your hands gently and look right into those eyes. State the infraction and/or what you want the child to do first. Positive terms. One item.

"Andrew, you may use your hands to help. You may use your hands to make something." (Now dramatically shake your head while maintaining that eye contact.) "You may *not* hit." Your face is in Andrew's face; you are stairstepping your voice down. "Do you understand me?"

You wait for a response, perhaps offering some coaching. "I want to hear, 'yes, ma'am.'"

Fourth, don't turn your back. After you receive the desired response, back up slowly, keeping your eyes on the child. When an adult turns away from a child, an ADD child especially, he or she provides a safe target against which to rebel. It is in the nature of an ADD child to impulsively stick out the tongue or do something rebellious to authority. As you step backward, maintaining the disciplinary focus, you are helping him hold it together and behave less impulsively.

Finally, follow up the incident if possible. Talking to the child one on one outside the classroom—before or after class or even in a separate home visit—can greatly reinforce the disciplinary measure. We emphasize in the strongest terms: The investment of your time in this regard will reap great long-term dividends.

After cooperation, communication, concern, and control, there is a final C to use, and it is the most important of all:

Call Upon the Spirit. The smallest ADD child can drive any sane adult to the wall in minutes. And the sane adult almost always reacts in the flesh. The Christian must learn to respond in spirit. That requires more control than we can muster, and thus the aid of the Holy Spirit enters in. Pray for help to avoid making the human reaction. You can't do it alone.

Let us pause and pretend now that Miss Pruitt simply could not handle Andrew, could not discipline him, could not stand him. Moving him out of the room was out of the question. What about home-schooling?

Some states are more amenable to home-schooling than are others. Beth Mulroney, having to work for a living, might not have the option of home-school even if her state's educational laws smiled on it.

How would she go about it if she did? What are the advantages and problems? Home-school is going to make an impact on family life, but then, the ADD child is already doing that. In the next chapter we'll picture the situation as if Miss Pruitt were impossible to contemplate as a teacher for Andrew.

HOME-SCHOOL AND HOME LIFE

12

I HAVE A SERIOUS problem," Beth Mulroney confided to Jody Capehart. "I'm starting to resent Andrew."

"Tell me more."

"He takes so much more of my time because of his ADD than he would if he were—you know—normal. I resent that. I have so little time anyway. And the reason I have so little time is that I'm alone. I'm raising him and earning a living too, and there's just not enough time. Or energy. And I can't get past the fact that if Andrew weren't the way he is, I'd still be married."

"You don't know that."

"Okay. I don't know it as in 'I'm certain.' But it's a very high probability."

[And here, remember, we are pretending that Miss Pruitt's teaching methods, her traditional sit-in-your-seat-and-use-the-workbook approach, had not changed a bit.]

Beth went on, "His behavior never seems to improve. Never. And his schoolwork is going right down the tubes. Trashed. I've spoken to the principal, but he says there's nothing he can do. And I can't afford the time and expense of driving Andrew to a different school, even if I could make the switch. Lots of times they won't authorize a transfer. I feel like the *Titanic*. My maiden voyage as a mother, and I'm sinking."

The Stress on Families

Quite probably, Beth's assessment of her situation was right. ADD is a primary cause of the breakup of too many families—ADD in the child and/or ADD in one of the partners. In Beth's case, ADD in both father and son was indeed a precipitating factor. Her husband could not deal with his son's ADD, knowing too much about the problems Andrew would face.

Note we did not say reason or excuse. Never do we condone or advocate the separation of a family (except in some other situations, such as physical abuse, which is a different problem we cannot address here). We are saying it happens, and ADD enters into the equation very, very frequently.

Even when separation is not the end, stress can mount to nearly intolerable levels. Meshing diverse family members into a functioning unit is hard enough without a loudmouthed, impulsive, disrespectful, caustic, underachieving, insensitive kid.

Multiply the deleterious effect on family life if the ADD child also suffers a related or overlapping behavioral disorder, as a majority of them do. As we've already said, these disorders can mask ADD, be masked by ADD, or work together with ADD synergistically to make the child's behavior nearly uncontrollable. It all spells *stress*.

Complications Wrought by Other Disorders

"He grunts." A woman we'll call Nell was describing her eleven-year-old son. "Kind of like a pig, although I'm a city girl; I've never actually heard a pig. Other people tell me it's like a pig, though. Just out of the blue, he'll just grunt."

Tourette's Syndrome

Nell was describing her son's Tourette's syndrome. However, the signs her son displayed are the least common indicator of the disorder. The diagnostic symptoms of Tourette's are motor tics. These are twitches, either obvious or not noticeable to the casual observer, that can occur in the face, the neck, or elsewhere. Tourette's produces non-diagnostic symptoms in some children. One set of symptoms is behavior that looks a lot like ADD. Another set is excessive worry and obsessive-compulsive repetitive behavior. Rarest are the phonic tics—uncontrollable blurting of noises or words.

Nell was lucky in a way; if she was embarrassed by her son's grunts, she'd be mortified with this rarest way in which the disorder manifests itself. A few people with the disorder burst out uncontrollably with shocking profanities, and they are not *that* kind of people. On the other hand, others display the more common extremely mild tics or no obvious signs at all. Persons who study Tourette's now believe it is much commoner than was first thought (originally diagnosed at two to five persons per ten thousand), with many mild cases never reaching clinical diagnosis.

Any tic or obsessive compulsion should be investigated whenever there is reason for concern. The child or adult should be evaluated by a physician familiar with Tourette's. Not all tics are caused by Tourette's; certain other disorders and some stimuli can mock the syndrome. Stimuli that pep up the person's general activity level can increase the frequency and severity of tics, both Tourette's and others.

There's a rub. Early on, when a child is small, ADD and certain forms of Tourette's may look alike. The rub comes because children who have Tourette's to any degree at all must avoid stimulant drugs such as Ritalin, even in mild cases. In fact, the child with Tourette's will develop noticeable tics when taking stimulants. ADD children without Tourette's will not.

Anxiety

Whittaker, Andrew's classmate, was suffering severe anxiety. His family, his whole universe, was breaking up. He knew no other world. Any anxiety in that situation would be justifiable. Whittaker's anxiety expressed itself in ADD-like signs. Full-blown ADD can also generate strong anxiety symptoms.

Anxiety may reveal itself with an intense fearfulness about past events, the future, or the present situation. The child may show a strong fear of being separated from significant people in his or her life. The child's anxieties may be fixed, like phobias, or obsessive-compulsive, or characterized by intrusive, unpleasant thoughts that just won't go away. All this may be accompanied by compulsions seemingly designed to decrease anxiety.

Does growing up in a traditional family prevent problems? Hardly. Remember that the foundation of ADD is neurological, not cultural. However, the longitudinal studies beginning to emerge (that is, studies that follow the subjects through a span of time) indicate that, no matter how you try to interpret the flat data or put a political twist to it one way or another, the traditional situation seems to produce the best chance for kids to grow up well and launch themselves into the world successfully.

In our culture with so many single-parent families, anxiety is a common result; and that anxiety can produce ADD-like behavior in the children. These kids may or may not be ADD; their parent(s) may or may not be ADD. How much mind control through medication is appropriate here, if any, and why? A multitude of questions plague our new culture, and they haven't begun to be addressed yet. At the bottom of it are the children like Andrew, helpless to shape themselves, being shaped from outside by forces and theories that have never been tested.

Add to it all the cultural pressures on families these days, and particularly on ADD children. Surely we're all aware of the intense jitters and dangerous aggressiveness in today's society, the worship of fast motion, and the tidy endings at the close of all one-hour television episodes. The real world demands far different behavior, and real stories don't often see a satisfactory conclusion. No wonder children are anxious; no wonder ADD kids feel the weight so much.

Depression

Depression and anxiety often dance together cheek to cheek.

A majority of ADD children experience depression at some time during childhood, and for a large number of them, low-grade, long-term depression is a significant problem. Symptoms include abrupt changes in mood, withdrawal, crying spells, irritability, acting out, changes in sleep patterns, changes in appetite, a decrease in concentration and school performance, self-deprecation, talking about death, and making comments such as, "I'd be better off dead" and "I'm gonna kill myself."

Pile that kind of behavior on top of the problems ADD itself causes and you can see a child in heavy trouble indeed. Anxiety and depression are not the only specters waiting behind the door. There are other complications as well, imbalances such as hyperthyroidism, and behavioral disorders.

Other Problems

Hyperthyroidism isn't common. But where it occurs it causes the same kinds of symptoms as does classic ADD—excessive activity, nervousness and restlessness, and an inability to concentrate.

Manic-depressive disorder, we now realize, does not wait until adulthood to manifest itself. Frequently, children with problems such as this one seem confused, agitated, hyperactive, and impulsive. Behaviorists spot it and separate it from classic ADD by its relatively recent onset of symptoms, a family history of bipolar illness, and the failure of the child to respond to the usual ADD medications. Unfortunately, manic-depressive disorder and ADD are not mutually exclusive.

Overlapping all these are behavioral disorders that arise along with ADD and at least in part because of it.

Oppositional Defiant Disorder

"I know what that is just from hearing the name," Gunther Steinfelder would claim. He would see it as a persistence of negative, argumentative, defiant, even hostile behavior in William toward others, but especially toward parents and other authority figures. Research shows that perhaps 60 percent of kids diagnosed with ADD sooner or later develop significant behavioral kinks to warrant being placed in this category.

The problem is seen most commonly at home and in preschool, eventually to spill over into other situations where adults are in charge—school, scouts, Sunday school. Physical aggressiveness is not the hallmark here. The major indications include argument for the sake of argument, defiance, limit-testing, antisocial behavior, and the blatant breaking of rules.

Other Conduct Disorders

Beth Mulroney was running scared, terrified of the day the police officer would knock at her door. Gunther was surprised the cops hadn't come yet. To an extent, both parents were justified. Their kids, Beth's Andrew especially, were vulnerable.

Violence and just plain meanness may not be a hallmark of oppositional defiant disorder, but in 20 to 30 percent of ADD kids, violence and other strongly antisocial behaviors will eventually rear their ugly heads. Called conduct disorders, these behaviors are just plain old lawbreaking, the stuff you get arrested for.

The blanket description of these problems is a persistent pattern of behavior in which the basic rights of others as well as societal norms are violated. That's cold, impersonal phrasing for what is in fact heartbreaking, emotionally devastating tragedy.

The kid identified with a conduct disorder has probably stolen on more than one occasion, has probably run away from home overnight, often lies, may have set fires intentionally, is often truant, possibly has broken into someone else's house or car, or has deliberately destroyed others' property.

Although arson, theft, and vandalism are part of the picture, physical aggression and destruction are much more common. This kid has probably been excessively cruel toward animals and possibly also toward people, has used weapons, has raped, and often initiates physical fights.

"That's not a misguided ADD kid," Gunther would fume. "That's a thug!"

Gunther's right. A high proportion of prison inmates are global thinkers in general and ADD in particular. That doesn't mean, of course, that an ADD child or a kinesthetic learner is unerringly headed for the slammer. But it does send the signal: "These kids are at risk." With good training, affirmation and learning methods, they are brilliant, gifted people with much to contribute to society. On the positive side, the tactile/kinesthetic learning style preference also provides us with an exceptional number of nurses, police officers, hairdressers, and mechanics. The secret lies in affirming and teaching according to their bent.

Kids may exhibit conduct disorders and oppositional disorder without the presence of ADD, and they may have ADD without significant antisocial behavior. But the three seem to occur together with hideous regularity, with one disorder or another developing as the child grows. It's not surprising that they cluster. All three are problems of regulatory functions and difficulty processing interpersonal experience. And all three can rip a family apart in nothing flat.

All three contribute greatly to poor school performance, and poor school performance can lay unacceptable stress on a family just by itself. Desperate parents can hardly be faulted for grasping at any answer— any answer at all—that they think might work.

Possible Answers

Beth Mulroney sat at a red light in stop-and-go traffic on her way to pick up Andrew from soccer practice. Her mind drifted, as it often did, to thoughts of Andrew and what she could do next to improve his situation. She had not yet been able to come up with any real answers for Andrew's difficulties, but Beth could not stop trying to think of something—*anything* that might help. Just as she was about to formulate yet another plan of action, Beth was jolted out of her thoughts by the honk of an angry driver behind her. Sure enough, the light had changed to green and Beth had been too absorbed in her thoughts to notice. As she hit the accelerator Beth thought how her life had become like a constant chase. Her mind was continually racing for answers, and she was always running to avert or escape some disaster with Andrew. It seemed that as long as she kept running she could keep things together but the moment she gave up the chase everything would fall apart. But she was tired—exhausted!

We are pretending for the time being, remember, that Miss Pruitt had refused to consider any changes whatsoever in her teaching method, that she despised Andrew, and was making school virtually intolerable for him. Sadly, that's exactly what happens to ADD kids so very, very frequently. We're pretending that as a result of his deteriorating situation at school, Andrew was failing, depressed, and growing increasingly restive and antisocial.

A new mother had recently joined the parents' support group Beth attended, and the woman said she home-schooled her ADD daughter. "It's the only way to make sure your child is learning," she insisted. "Report cards just don't tell the story. Control is the key. It's all a matter of control."

Control. The word had a wonderful ring to it.

Perhaps Beth ought to consider home-schooling Andrew.

Is Home-Schooling an Answer?

Jody Capehart waxes philosophical on the subject. "Home-schooling is something of a calling. If God has called you to it, realize that it is God's calling for your child *for this season of your life*. It may not be the plan for next year and perhaps not for all the kids in the household. However God has called you, please realize it's your calling and no one else's.

"The tendency of too many home-schoolers is that if it works for me it will work for all my friends. In essence we try to become the Holy Spirit for all our friends, trying to force the divine calling or make it a barometer of spirituality, charging, 'If you *really* cared about your child, you'd take him out of that godless situation!'

"If I come on like gangbusters with my 'Let's all home-school!' sermon, I pose a serious problem for all my brow-beaten friends. Not only am I applying pressure they don't need if it's not right for them or no longer right for them, but how do they slip out of it gracefully?"

It may, for example, be wise to home-school an ADD child in the first grade, teaching him or her the skills for public school. Give the child's maturity a little more room to grow. It may then be wise to mainstream the child beginning in second grade and on through the system. Or perhaps the child starts school just fine but flunks third grade, or nearly so. It may then be smart in what would be the child's fourth year to home-school him or her, find out where he or she got off the track. Then the child could repeat third grade and complete fourth grade during the next year at home (yes, you certainly can pull it off!), and go back into fifth grade on schedule. You just have to take it year by year, listening to the still small voice.

Advantages and Disadvantages of Home-Schooling

Were Beth to consider home-schooling, she would find the advantages and disadvantages intertwined so tightly that they cannot be separated out here as subheads. Each advantage has its dark side, each disadvantage its silver lining.

Home-schooling parents usually fall into one of three categories:

First, there's the strongly legalistic parent, left-brained and rigid, who imposes his or her structure upon the child. The advantage is that the ADD child needs structure. But . . . there is an educator who claims that ADD is nothing more than the foolishness decried in the book of Proverbs and recommends beating it out of the child. People who deal with ADD kids daily know whether that approach would work. In any case, the legalistic parent is going to see trouble blossom as the polarity between parent and child increases. Moreover, if the parent tries to teach the child with the same left-brain, sequential methods most schools do—workbooks, pages of problems, acres of reading—the parent will fail as miserably as he or she thinks the school did.

The second type of home-school parent, who is most likely ADD as well, probably remembers how crippling and painful school was and sees that it's painful for the child. The parent pulls the child out—an advantage if the child is struggling that hard—but unfortunately the parent lacks the teaching skills to make home-school work. The child loses academic ground, and the experiment becomes a disaster.

The third type of home-school parent is one who feels called by God to do this for the child. This parent prepares by reading up on research and techniques, attends conferences, sees that this will probably benefit the struggling child, and is willing to try some creative teaching. These are the ones who win, big time. These are the parents who want their kids to win, and that is the only real question a parent ought ask: *Am I called to this for my child's sake?*

This parent will also find powerful disadvantages and major challenges in this calling. One is that the child is just plain irritating. The parent who lacks a solid background of training in technique can go nuts trying to handle this obstreperous, perhaps antisocial kid. School provided a spacer, a break in which the parent didn't have to deal with the child. Suddenly the parent has the child twenty-four hours a day. With ADD kids, that doesn't always succeed.

Home-school, then, can ease family stress—or greatly increase it.

Establishing Ground Rules

Were Beth to seriously consider home-schooling, she'd have to check out three factors: her own availability and whether she could work it into her schedule, her state's laws regarding home-schools, and her own learning style.

Schedule? Home-schoolers claim they are done with academics before noon. In truth, schools spend a lot of time not in instruction and learning but in peripheral things, many of them mandated by state laws. Beth would need three to four hours a day, and then she would also have to arrange for Andrew to be overseen for the remainder of the day. But she had to arrange after-school child care anyway.

Laws? The woman who already home-schooled was the logical first place to ask for names of other people involved in home-schooling. But Beth ought not to take any home-schooler's word about what laws do or don't say. Few home-schoolers are legal professionals or education pros. Check with people who know; the library can provide the names of school-board people, state and district legislators, and others who can help.

Learning style? By knowing how she herself learned best, Beth would know what her own tendencies were as she taught Andrew according to *his* learning style. Forewarned is forearmed.

The beauty of home-school in Beth's case—in most cases—would be her ability to create the specific learning environment Andrew needed. She could also provide firm, one-on-one control, which Andrew also needed.

The disadvantage that Beth and anyone else involved with home-school must guard against is the desire to make the child "think like I think." If the parent believes his or her opinions are the only right opinions, the child is expected to share those opinions. The real goal, of course, is to teach the child to think for himself or herself, but that is downright frightening for a parent. What if the child thinks "wrong" things, makes "wrong" decisions? The parent who truly and earnestly wants to give the ADD child wings has to fight hard to get past that mind-set. And ADD kids give their parents the distinct impression that they can't think at all.

A possible alternative to home-schooling might be other schooling with special training added.

Is Special Training an Answer?

Yes! We waffled on the home-school question because God's calling and kids' needs vary so widely across several spectra. But we can unequivocally say training of some sort is absolutely necessary . . . for the parents!

You know by now that usually, ADD kids do not think and feel in the same way their parents do. Yet the parents automatically believe the child approaches life from the same perspective they do or did at that age. The parents then tragically misread their child's behavior.

Training, either formal parenting classes for parents of ADD kids or a self-help tool such as this book, can help parents work past that blind spot and manage the child more effectively, to the child's benefit.

Training can make the difference between a family that raises an ADD child to be a responsible member of society or that breaks up and destroys everyone within it. Family deterioration follows a fairly uniform sequence.

The Path of Family Deterioration

Of course, many families of ADD children remain intact and provide strong and loving support for all members of the family. However, it's very common for the opposite to happen: The family disintegrates. Here's a typical scenario for how that sad state comes about.

1. *The young child's impulsivity and distractibility cause what parents see as willful misbehavior.* Believing that the child is merely trying to garner attention, the parents at first attempt to ignore the misbehavior, assuming it will go away if it's not encouraged.

2. *The behavior, being neurologically governed, of course does not go away.* It gets worse as the child grows. Ignoring it does nothing toward altering it, so the parents, already losing patience, give more and more commands and punishments. That doesn't work either. The child still does not remember or obey. He or she disregards the simplest tasks, the easiest commands.

3. *The parents' tactics escalate to threats in order to get the kid to listen and obey.* Anger has replaced any desire to understand or nurture. The child returns the anger in kind.

4. *Now the parents start actually carrying out the threats.* They find themselves constantly disciplining, constantly meting out punishment. They have gone from nagging to threatening to punishing, all to no effect. They now have a sullen, defiant, nasty kid who still fails to obey and who "conveniently forgets."

It is common for parents by this stage to be suffering some serious marital difficulties. The problems may be rooted in any of a full range of reasons, but whatever the source, they will be projected onto management of the child.

Mother will complain that she has tried everything, nothing worked, and she's exhausted. The father swoops in, tries a couple of parenting methods he's certain ought to work, lays down some ultimata, and gets angry and irritated. No matter what the realities, the parents will be at each other, disagreeing loudly about how to manage the child and blaming each other for the problems: "If you were just more strict . . ." "If you would just be a little more forgiving . . ."

5. *The parents give up.* The child's age at which this happens will depend upon the severity of the symptoms; it may occur anywhere from age five or six to ten or eleven.

By now the child is deeply insecure, defiant, and hostile as a defense against the insecurity. Worst of all, he or she is totally without resources. The parents feel helpless. Their marriage may be in a shambles, perhaps irreparably so.

6. *Sometimes the child will turn the corner and realize or be convinced by someone respected that there is worth here; that he or she has value.* Sometimes the child's antisocial behavior comes strongly close to the point of sociopathy. But even if the child takes his or her place in the world, a powerful undercurrent of anger and frustration will dog the person for a lifetime.

Deterioration is not a certainty though. And it's not inevitable. The family can be turned down other roads.

An Alternative Path

Training parents consists primarily of helping them realize how their child thinks and how the child processes the surrounding world. Once the parents realize the child is not seeing life from the parents' perspective and once they can adjust to meet the child's needs, family friction can be greatly reduced.

Parents of ADD kids, you see, are not dealing with a known quantity. The ADD child is so fundamentally different that the parenting methods they learned in their own youth don't work. Training, either formal or through a resource such as this book, helps parents control themselves better. Training helps them learn how to teach their kids to monitor and maintain their own behavior. And that, as much as anything else, will keep the family structure solid, the relationships healthy.

Keeping the Family Healthy

Let us offer some guidelines for preventing the family friction and the family disintegration described above. The points we've already made about the options of medication and similar interventions, of discipline techniques in school and out, and of learning styles all fit into a family perspective. But there is more.

Know Thy Kid

Most children tend to respond better to a man than to a woman and ADD kids especially so. In the presence of a male, the kids tend to be more structured, tend to hear better. Dr. Warren sees this all the time. The mother says, "The child is impossible!" and Dr. Warren gets along just great (it helps that the tall, hefty doctor cuts quite a large, imposing figure while at the same time presenting a very gentle, non-threatening demeanor).

The ADD child's sharp dichotomy of response to male and female can create serious friction in the marriage.

Says she: "I cannot control the child! She won't do a thing I ask."

Says he: "Well, then, you're not trying or you're doing something wrong, because she behaves all right for me."

From there the exchange usually degenerates into the "If you would just . . ." argument.

The phenomenon is not Mom's fault, of course. It isn't anyone's fault. But unless parents are aware of ADD kids' natural response to males, friction mounts.

That response is exactly why we encourage fathers to take a prominent day-to-day role in their ADD child's life, helping the child get up and get off to school each morning, reading a story and putting the child to bed, managing this problem or that. Dad's involvement also helps another source of friction, enmeshment between the child and mother.

Enmeshment is a fancy word we professionals use to indicate that the relationship between two people is so tight and intense that one or both of them cannot grow. An ADD child's enmeshment generally occurs with Mom because she usually invests the most energy in child care. She is the one who provides the child structure, which is to say she has to hound the kid constantly to do what must be done. She disciplines. She cajoles. She bribes and baits and yells.

As time goes on and the child wants to provide his or her own structure, enmeshment gets worse because the child's efforts fall short and the kid projects blame for that onto the closest person around, Mom. By the time the child enters adolescence, a lot of anger and a lot of conflict are sparking in the air.

A solution? Again, Dad has to take a larger role, giving Mom a break and giving the child a strong male perspective.

Throughout this book we have been explaining how the ADD child's mind-set differs from most folks'. But we have not yet emphasized the intensity of anger in the ADD child's life. Anger is as much a factor in the child's life as the impulsivity, short-term memory glitches, and attention problems. The child is steeped in it. Second-grader Andrew burned with it. Midteen William seethed. Even ditzy preteen Amy Eglund carried a heavy load of anger, which would probably emerge eventually as extreme dissatisfaction, bitterness, and criticism of life.

Where does the anger come from?

Frustration can generate kilowatts of anger quickly. The child wants to conform, to achieve, to learn—and he or she cannot. The neurons simply do not connect up. The gap between what the child wants to achieve and what the child can actually accomplish becomes frustratingly wide.

Also, all children develop a powerful sense of what's fair by about the age of four. Their concept of what's fair may be warped or immature, but it generates instant fury when it's violated. "It's not fair! He got three and I only got two!" "She gets to stay up but I have to go to bed!" "You paddled me but not her!" *It's not fair!*

ADD kids most of all see the world treating them worse than others, unfairly. That's one source of anger, and reason won't touch it. Possibly the other person received three because he or she *earned* three. That fact escapes attention. Perhaps the other person can stay up because he or she is four years older. Perhaps the child got paddled and the other child did not because the other child was not involved in the infraction. None of that matters to an indignant child who thinks the fairness scale has been tipped against him or her. (Tipping the fairness scale toward the child goes unnoticed.) The parent cannot avoid that anger or force it to abate. You'll have to deal with it as it is.

Also, ADD kids love to be in conflict. It's hard for parents to grasp that fact. Winning the conflict is not the primary aim; being in it is. The child will create conflict wherever the chance arises. Arguments and power struggles are the most common chances.

Anger and conflict are the two aspects of the ADD child's youth that really tear the family fabric. Parents know that anger begets anger. Gunther certainly knew. That's how he and William ended up in that altercation. Deep inside, the ADD child knows it, too, although he or she probably doesn't recognize it at a conscious level.

Parents can offset much anger and conflict by adopting a corrective attitude to counter the child's. For one thing, parents can simply remember that the child's anger is there, inextinguishable, ready to flare up at any moment, and be ready for it. It should never come as a surprise to the parents. For another, parents can model nonanger, something few parents of ADD kids do. Modeling is by far the best way to teach a child to cope. How do you do that? By keeping control.

If the child makes you angry who is in control? The child! He or she manipulated you. In anger you're likely to act irrationally, and the kid has gotcha again.

"Sorry, kid. I'm not going to let you make me angry." The parent who can say that with honesty is well down the road toward preventing the escalation of most situations. When the parent controls himself or herself, the first prerequisite to success is in place.

"We have set up the rules [that is, the structure in black and white], and the objectives and goals are clear. Follow them or experience the clearly defined consequences." The parent is not going to make that announcement in those particular words, but if the meaning is there and it's clear, the parent has taken the big step toward avoiding power struggles.

Let's summarize:

1. Set the expectation. "Time to clean the room, do homework," etc.
2. Set clear consequences, both positive and negative.
3. No argument, no debate. "These are your choices. They are your only choices."
4. Follow through with consequences as specified.
5. Say yes whenever you possibly can. Many ADD kids are extremely negative to start with; bumping into a harsh string of negativity doesn't help discipline in the least.

The child, nobody's fool, will try to switch the parent's focus from clarifying or repeating the expectation to arguing, an attempt to convince the kid he or she should do it. Only the parent can head that one off by being aware of the ploy and sticking to the original plan. No argument. Act according to the consequences you prefer.

Parents must sort out their own feelings and habits just as much as they analyze the child's.

Know Thyself

You know that ADD is genetically predisposed, not caused. Race is caused genetically. "Predisposed" means the tendency is there, not the surety. Thus, one child may be ADD while the siblings are not. One of the ADD child's parents may be ADD also, but maybe not.

Both parents, however, should carefully examine their childhoods and their present skills and shortcomings to identify ADD-like signs and symptoms if they are there. Look at the signs, not formal diagnoses. ADD tendencies in either parent are going to strain family relations whether or not there is a child. Awareness of those strains in itself can help allay the stresses. The spouses can both make allowances for each other's differences, averting a lot of friction.

As we have seen, an ADD parent must deal emotionally with an ADD child's lot in life, and that isn't always easy. An ADD adult may find the child's struggle too painful to deal with and skip out on the family, as Andrew's father did, or the parent may deny the problem, causing woes for the child. Face the prospect head-on if you want to avert family friction from this source.

Knowing your preferred learning style can also help you avoid friction between yourself and the children and even between each other. If, for instance, Dad is an auditory learner who remembers best if he repeats the instructions, the grocery list, the laundry methods, or whatever, Mom would do well to cater to that. Understanding each other and adjusting to that understanding improves any marriage.

In fact, we'd like to recommend Rick and Jeri Fowler's book, *"Honey, Are You Listening?"* (Nashville: Thomas Nelson, 1994). In the book, Rick, an ADD adult, and his wife, Jeri, explore ways to make an ADD/non-ADD marriage work well.

Most of all, work on the marriage union. Therein is the key, the linchpin upon which all the relationships swing.

Build the Marriage First

Almost nothing in an ADD child's life is stable; the parents' union must be. So little in the child's life is dependable; the home must be. In a sense, the child needs the marriage even more than the parents do. Adults can survive the tragedy of divorce, pick up the pieces, and struggle on. But the child is shattered—so shattered, statistics suggest, that he or she is often beyond repair.

It is tempting, indeed it is pressing, to invest every spare bit of energy into the ADD child. Like a sponge, an ADD child can quickly sop up the greater part of family resources and energy. Resist that pressing temptation. We do not suggest that nurturing the spouse at the expense of the child become the habit, but sometimes, on occasion, it must happen. The marriage serves the child and must never ever be sacrificed.

Many excellent books can help you understand the dynamics of marriage and improve your union. We urge you to spend at least some time and energy specifically on that very thing. Get away on occasion. Date. Spell each other with the kids. You've heard all that before. Enlarge upon it. Get creative.

Speaking of creativity, who is probably the most creative thinker in the family? The ADD child. Ask the child for suggestions on how to strengthen your marriage bond. You will be surprised and perhaps shocked by some of the answers; these kids can be wickedly observant and bright, and they have an enormous vested interest in a strong, safe home.

The best and safest marital unions place God at their center. To maintain the bond of faith within the bond of matrimony, the family must join together in the body of believers. And that, short and quick, means taking the kids to church. All the kids, including the ADD child. We know what you're thinking. That's not always a pleasant prospect.

The old saw is now a running joke—except when parents try to strengthen the family with regular and frequent church attendance, an excellent and necessary strengthener. ADD kids in church just don't cut it. They grow quickly to hate it, and most churches aren't any better pleased with them.

What's a parent to do? Let's see . . .

THE
ADD CHILD
IN CHURCH

*B*ETH MULRONEY TRIED. Oh yes, she tried. The only Sunday she took Andrew to church he got kicked out of Sunday school for interrupting and refusing to sit still.

During the worship service, he repeatedly kicked the pew in front of them, wiggled their own pew—the whole pew—by rocking back and forth, crackled candy wrappers, noisily turned pages in the hymnal, belched during prayer—twice—and persisted in whispering loud enough to catch the attention of the organist, who sat catty-corner across the sanctuary from them.

Beth didn't try again.

Gunther felt embarrassed every time he dragged his teenaged William to church. The kid refused to pay attention, doodled on the bulletin, loudly cleared his throat whether or not it needed clearing, and picked his nose. William had long since lost interest in Sunday school, and his instructor had made it clear that he had lost interest in William.

Gunther kept trying, but it was a humiliating battle with no winner.

Peter and Viveca Eglund never failed to attend Sunday services. They let Amy be the nursery sitter. Out in the sanctuary she was worth piddly, always trying to talk to her friends, waving across the room, actually tossing notes, never paying attention to the service. At least in the nursery she was still able to hear the choir and the pastor's message over the speaker system, and she was isolated. She needed caging more than the tots did.

The Eglunds had given up trying. Now they were coping.

The Church Atmosphere

Thanks to the hypersensory acuity we mentioned previously that causes most ADD kids to have so much sensory information coming in their minds flit like popcorn popping, church is the worst place in the world for them. Look around your own sanctuary. Do you see ornamentation and stained glass, banners and flags? Think what the ADD child sees. Most of us relegate the surroundings to the background and concentrate on worship itself. Bombarded sensorily, distracted by random sounds, sights, and motion, the ADD child cannot sift sensations, cannot decide what to tune out and what to allow in. Even if your sanctuary consists of nothing but cement-block walls and a lectern, the surroundings are as distracting as the action.

And then there's the action, or lack of it. Children in high church are able to stand, kneel, get up, sit down. That helps. Many services, though, leave people sitting and sitting and sitting. ADD kids don't sit well.

And what about the message? The pastor's three-point sermon, to be followed sequentially, cannot be followed by the ADD child for whom sequence and progression are beyond understanding. (Let's face it; unless the speaker's good, the adults don't follow it either. Can you repeat last Sunday's sermon?)

Some services feature a five-minute children's message in which the kids come trooping forward to sit at the speaker's feet. No wallflower, the ADD child will come tumbling down the aisle to take part—interrupting, blurting, squirming, and otherwise drawing attention to himself, to the parents' chagrin.

But to the child, church is two separate worlds, the worship service and the Sunday school. They differ radically. Sunday school is like school, with answers to make and blanks to fill in. Somehow, you're not expected to learn in worship.

The Learning Atmosphere

In Sunday school the child comes up against the same brick walls that plague him or her in weekday school. Moreover, the instructor is rarely trained to handle any but the most lethargic left-brain learner, if that. ADD kids who use medication during the week to improve attention in school are probably off it on the weekend. The instructor, lucky person, sees the child with the total range of ADD characters in full cry. That can be downright unsettling for the nonprofessional volunteer teacher in a Sunday school classroom.

People not trained in alternative learning methods and ADD management invariably assume that if the child is better disciplined, problems will shrink. The instructor comes on hard and heavy, clamping a lid on the ADD child, and the behavior worsens. Catch-22. So what do we do?

The church worker must adopt a set of teaching parameters the outside world does not always need. Primarily, the church worker must remember the eternal goal.

Keep the Eye on the Prize

The academic school's goals are to train the child to function in the adult world and to absorb something of society's heritage, historical and cultural, that the child might feel a sense of belonging—kid stuff, compared to the church's goals.

The church's mandate is to reach every child for the kingdom. We're talking about eternal life and values, and that lifts church participation to a new level of importance and urgency. It is critical that parents bring their child to church and lead that child to Christ. Every person needs the power of God working in his or her life, but ADD kids need it even more than most of us. And that's just the temporal importance, which pales to nothingness in the glare of eternity.

The prize, then, becomes the reason for being. It is therefore imperative that the beleaguered Sunday school instructor remember the goal. Human nature, particularly for an instructor poorly trained in ADD management, makes survival the goal: "God, get me through this next hour." Instead, how about whispering, "What I am about to do counts for eternity" as a better goal? In that light, the instructor's perspective changes completely regarding how he or she views the instructional hour and also views the ADD child.

Understand this at a spiritual level, ye who are called to teach Sunday school: This rambunctious ADD child was created by God for His purpose. Therefore ask God to provide you a window to see the child as He designed him or her. You already pray for wisdom and strength. Expand your prayer to beg the specialized wisdom and strength required to teach an ADD child.

This is not to say there are no immediate and temporal benefits the Sunday school instructor can bestow. When the child's home life is all ashambles and his or her school life weighs heavily, an enlightened Sunday school may be the only psychologically rewarding hour of the week. Do you realize how important that can be for an ADD child?

The caustic humor so typical of ADD kids is their response to feeling alienated and out of the loop. Feeling put upon. Older kids especially would rather get negative attention than no attention. Those habits cannot be easily put aside for one hour a week and will probably come through regardless what the child actually thinks and feels. The kid can't help it. But even the child who responds with acid and anti-social jabs hungers for acceptance and nurturing. The instructor who can step past the antisocial surface and love and respond to the hurting kid inside will work temporal miracles to eternal benefit, whether those miracles happen to show at the time or not. Count on it.

ADD kids who reach William's age need a whole other dimension of love and acceptance. They are at the time of life when the final stage of separation from family is beginning. They need someone outside the family, someone safe, to look up to. That someone will bridge the gap between dependence upon family and total independence. That someone very often is an understanding Sunday school or youth group leader.

The child who is made to believe that he or she is a pain and therefore unwanted will get out of that situation at the first opportunity. This is especially true around William's age, and it's hard to lure in a kid Amy's age. What a tragic waste for the kingdom! The child you affirm and love today in the church sanctuary and classroom may well be the dynamic leader for the kingdom tomorrow.

Make no mistake; ADD kids can do great things with their lives, marvelous things for the kingdom of God. The wise church worker views this incredible energy as a force vitally needed in the kingdom of God, for so it truly is. That person then can, Lord willing, become more patient and willing to work with this child. Assuming that ADD is a normal part of God's creation, helping that child blossom requires a different approach.

With that awareness, the instructor has the motivation to shift from survival plans to a real, working teaching plan that reflects the way modern life is.

Adjust to the Reality

Survival is a will-o'-the-wisp anyway. You, the Sunday school instructor who has an ADD child in your class or group, pray that you won't have any next year. Guaranteed, you'll have two or three next year. Not only is our modern society producing a more aggressive, hyper kid, the games, culture, and fast pace make it more difficult for the traditional Sunday school instructor to hold any child's interest. Traditional instruction methods don't hold the distractible, impulsive ADD child at all.

Obviously, working with kids in today's church presents challenges yesterday's workers didn't have to face. Fortunately, it's easier to accept challenges when you understand them. Besides, as teachers improve their understanding of today's kids and ADD kids in particular, it's easier to find practical ways to deal with them. The job ceases to appear so scary and onerous.

It becomes even less burdensome as the worker develops some practical ways of helping different kids.

Adopt Some Practical Habits

The church worker dealing with ADD kids, and this includes not only instructors and youth leaders but the pastor and the parents too, can adopt some habits to minimize disruption and maximize the benefits the child will receive.

Let's say Beth decides she's going to return to active church participation. She'd been slipping away during the months after the divorce. She needs the spiritual nurturing. She's hungry. She's coming back because it's too important a thing to neglect, and Andrew is just going to have to fit in somehow.

The same general guidelines that we suggested for school success apply to both Sunday school and worship service. Foremost is the need to build a team. Beth can't just dump Andrew into the appropriate Sunday school class and skip out to the coffee urn. She, the instructor, and/or youth pastor, and Andrew need to work together.

For starters, we suggest that each adult write the child's name on a three-by-five card and put it on the desk, kitchen counter, car dash, or bathroom mirror as a reminder to pray for that child.

Then every time you see that card . . . *Andrew Mulroney* . . . remember that God is the only One who can provide the wisdom to reach Andrew Mulroney. Human understanding hardly suffices. This kid too often violates adults' comfort zones, their need for order and control. The adults will try nearly any measure to get him under control. Those measures will work, at best, sporadically. Prayer is the key to unlocking Andrew Mulroney, to understanding this troubled child of God at a spiritual level.

Beth can sit down with the instructor or worker ahead of time, explain what ADD is all about, and describe what works and doesn't work. She's becoming quite an expert on ADD in general and Andrew in particular. Whatever expertise she can pass on at the outset will help the other team member avoid reinventing wheels.

She might sit in on the class the first few weeks to help out while Andrew is adjusting. She might also indicate her continuing availability. For many teachers, simply knowing that the parents are supportive is all they need. If it turns out that Andrew is having an especially hard morning, it's a real comfort to know Beth is available to come help or, in the worst-case scenario, take Andrew out.

Presumably, she will not identify Andrew as damaged. She may perhaps point out that were a blind child to come in, the instructor would do what is necessary to compensate for the child's disability. ADD doesn't look like an obvious disability; it looks like plain, old, obstinate misbehavior, and there may be some of that mixed in by age seven or eight, when most ADD kids have started to play the game for which they have the name. But it is a disability primarily, and compensatory techniques help immensely.

That certainly does not mean that church workers, or Beth either, ought to dismiss misbehavior. One of the chief jobs of the parent and the church worker is to ingrain in the child godly qualities and ways to deal with life. To discipline kids is to help them be all they can be for Jesus.

With that goal, the worker or instructor can help Andrew immensely by keeping him close, using hands and eyes to guide him rather than harsh words. Realizing that Andrew can't sit still long, the worker will provide opportunities to move, to touch, to do.

Of course, the usual environmental guidelines pertain; for instance, the worker won't want to sit Andrew under a bright fluorescent light. He or she will not want to plop Andrew down next to a similarly hyperactive, kinesthetic child who will set him off. Kids of that kind feed off each other, and the clowning reaches uncontrollable levels immediately.

She or he will want to give Andrew structured transition times. The minutes before class gets going, the time between Sunday school and church, getting-out time when Beth wants to stand around a while talking, greeting, and renewing friendships—they're all hard for him. Thanks to that impulsivity, his body moves faster than his brain and repeatedly gets him into trouble.

As the kids are lining up to go somewhere else, the instructor might give Andrew a task—just one at a time, remember—that will garner him some praise. How about pushing all the chairs in neatly? Erasing the blackboard? Putting away the flannelgraph figures? Sweeping? The instructor might even have a vacuum cleaner lurking in the corner for Andrew to use (vacuum cleaners are great because they make plenty of noise for whatever actually happens). Of course it's the custodian's job to vacuum. But Andrew needs the work more than the custodian does, and he needs it now.

The instructor can just about guarantee failure by asking Andrew to stand in line and wait. By reducing the opportunities to fail and increasing the opportunities to succeed, the instructor gives Andrew a profound gift. With a couple of dozen kids to keep in line, Andrew's academic schoolteacher cannot always provide active alternatives to waiting, which gives the church instructor with a smaller class a particularly good opportunity to build up Andrew.

Teach in Practical Ways

All the guidelines offered parents and teachers in previous chapters apply equally to the Sunday school instructor and group leader. Avoid being totally cognitive in your approach to learning. This ADD child may not be able to sit through the whole Bible story, may not be able to memorize as easily as most. The ADD child isn't going to respond well to those traditional Sunday school lessons with fill-in-the-blanks.

For some kinesthetic variety, try throwing a beanbag back and forth to memorize, sing verses to music, incorporate lots of action. The left-brainers will still learn well, and the right-brainers will learn no other way. Rick Fowler's son Chip had trouble focusing, so he learned sign language. It was a brilliant ploy! His hands fruitfully employed, his brain did much better.

Obviously, to achieve good results, the instructor has to commit to far more than just showing up. He or she must know the pupils. That's a universally good thing. All children value relationships above all else, and ADD kids are even heavier into relationships than are most because they have so few rewarding ones. The instructor might do very well to develop a one-on-one relationship. Andrew's teacher might leave the class in the care of an aide during storytime or something and take Andrew for a walk. Get to know him. At the very least, the instructor will discover Andrew's delightful side. Yes, he has one. Beth is well aware of it. And in a situation such as together-time, it shows up.

Andrew will be interested primarily in the relationships between God and man, between him and Jesus. To reach him—indeed, to reach every child—the instructor will emphasize the relational aspect of the love of God, and that is also a good thing. So many times adults shortchange that most important and overreaching truth. God loves us.

God loves us.

God loves us.

We urge you: Never lose sight of the weighty task you have. These are the kids Jesus loved most.

So tell them so.

When either of us is involved in a church teaching situation—and that happens every now and then—we show kids the features they share in common with the people to whom Jesus ministered. He didn't come to sell the Pharisees in His kingdom. Left-brained rule-lovers, they were full of their own wisdom and therefore on their own. But look at what happened when the children came running (impulsively!) to Jesus. The disciples tried to chase them off, but Jesus summoned them and gathered them in.

Many are the people of Scripture who acted impulsively. For instance David, the apple of God's eye, was always going off half-cocked. Had Abigail not interceded and bribed some common sense into him, he would have destroyed Nabal, to his own eternal grief. Peter walked on the water. Zacchaeus climbed a tree. Moses' impulsivity cost him the Promised Land. All these people shared the qualities that make the ADD child so special. He or she should know that.

Most of all, what he or she needs to know is love: 1 Corinthians 13. Love is affirmation.

Praise, Praise, Praise

"What did you learn in Sunday school today?"

"Sit down. Sit down. Be still."

How sad. It happens constantly.

When kids so often feel that they are victims in a world where no one likes them, understands them, or wants them, what more wonderful place could there be to feel affirmed than in the church! This could be the first step in a child choosing to follow Jesus. The church worker must never, ever forget that.

Sure, affirmation builds good old self-esteem. Sure, affirmation makes the child more cooperative. Sure, affirmation is what the "spiritual" worker is called to do. Think what it does for God!

What are some affirmations the instructor or worker might employ?

"You drew a great picture today during the lesson."

"I noticed how still you sat during storytime. That's great, Andrew!"

"God gave you a body that likes to move. I appreciate that."

"You had some very good ideas there when we were discussing how to help smaller children. Thanks for your input."

"I really like your hair today. Is French braiding hard to do?"

Ever and always, the ultimate motivation is to bring kids to the kingdom.

We've been talking about what adults can do to help ADD children be accepted in a Sunday school class or a kids' group. There remains that daunting antithesis of saintly ADD behavior, the worship service. Let's assume there is no concurrent children's worship service. What is Beth to do?

God's Child in the Sanctuary

Andrew will be highly responsive to the mood of the church service. If the service is relaxed, he will be relaxed too—at least somewhat. Very stern, formal, traditional services tend to be more difficult for an ADD child. Be aware that within a single church, services may vary. For example, an early service, 7 or 8 A.M. perhaps, is usually more informal (and frequently shorter) than the 11 A.M. one. Beth might consider shopping around to find a casual service that's satisfactory for both her and Andrew. In this shopping around she must place her needs above Andrew's. She needs the feeding. She needs the companionship. She needs the Light.

She or the church or both might provide things of interest for Andrew to do. As they hand out bulletins, church greeters and ushers often pass out kids' sheets with a picture on one side to color and a maze, puzzle, or quiz on the other. Coloring sheets or a Bible coloring book should keep him occupied awhile.

Beth might also reserve a bag of quiet things Andrew could use only during the worship service, not at home or elsewhere. It could contain some Bible lessons with small felt characters, such as those produced by Betty Luken. The child can use the characters to build his or her own story. A notebook of plain paper to draw in and various drawing supplies allow creativity. We suggest having the things in the "quiet-play" materials relate to the Bible, perhaps even the readings or the message of the day, rather than merely providing busy work. Your local Christian supply house or bookstore has lots of interesting things to do and ideas to exploit. (Betty Luken's felts are also available through Scripture Press, 1-800-828-1825.)

Andrew happens to be one of those kids who has to swim in noise every waking minute. Beth can minimize his noisemaking during the service by providing cassettes and a player with earphones. True, he won't hear the sermon. But he doesn't listen anyway. Beth would limit its use to certain parts of the worship service that are of minimal interest to a seven-year-old, the sermon being one part, and forbid its use during prayer and singing. The content of the tapes would be appropriate for worship, needless to say.

Meanwhile, up at the lectern, the pastor or presider should keep in mind that not all the congregation are left-brained visual or auditory learners. The message should be reaching everyone.

Says a mutual friend of ours, "You know, if I could just bring my knitting to church, I would retain so much more!"

And it's true. The gifted pastor and writer Stephen Bly claims he gets the solutions to his problem and his best ideas for books and sermons when he's out jogging.

The congregation cannot get out and jog in rhythm to the pastor's message, but the pastor ought to consider ways to allow kinesthetic learning now and then. Not only would it help Andrew immensely (and even more the older kids like Amy and William), it would improve these listeners' perception and appreciation of church as a place to learn and feel good.

In the church the position of the parents, the pastor, the workers, and the instructors is always and ever, "We care about you. We want you in church for your sake. We'll help you stay and help you learn. Let's work together."

Jody Capehart summarizes how this attitude helped her family achieve its goal for Damon.

"Getting these children through high school and getting them saved is absolutely critical. Our son will say it was because of the structure in our family and because of the church that he made it. And you can believe we were worried awhile. Damon is an excellent musician like his father. However, because of his ADD and resulting low self-esteem, we were concerned that he might get into the "wrong" kind of music.

"But he came through wonderfully. Praise God!"

Mrs. Capehart rightly identifies adolescence as a make-or-break time. Techniques that work very well on Andrew might work poorly or not at all on the older, more mature, more savvy and cynical teen. As important as a good start is, in some ways, Gunther's William and Peter's Amy needed a higher level of understanding and nurturing than would Andrew. In the next chapter we'll look briefly at the special challenges of adolescence.

THE ADD CHILD AS A TEENAGER

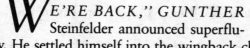

WE'RE BACK," GUNTHER Steinfelder announced superfluously. He settled himself into the wingback chair next to Dr. Warren's. On the opposite side of the office, William flopped into the other wingback. Blind Freddie could see that it was not William's idea to be here.

"Another fight?" Dr. Warren did not notice any bandages or bruises, but that doesn't mean a lot.

"In a sense. Certainly not fisticuffs. I have developed much better control of myself," said Gunther with just a trace of a smile.

"And how is William's control doing?" Dr. Warren looked at the teenager.

William sulked.

Gunther was sulking, too, sort of. "He's nowhere near perfect."

"Neither are you or I. How is he doing compared to six months ago when we last talked? Behavior, schoolwork, self-control?"

It almost appeared that dentistry without novocaine would appeal to Gunther better than would praising his son. "His schoolwork? His mother is extremely well pleased with the improvement in his grades. He's taken to dribbling a tennis ball while he memorizes dates for an upcoming test. Bup, bup, bup. You hear it all over the house."

"So the boy who was dismissed from all those schools is considering college?" Dr. Warren directed his question to William.

The kid shrugged dramatically. "Teacher's college."

"What field?"

"Dual major, industrial arts and fine arts."

"A unique mix."

William grinned impishly. "Couple of months ago I made a sculpture out of welding rods and entered it at the fine arts fair. They gave it a special award because it didn't fit in any of the regular categories." He held one hand above the other. "It's maybe this high and weighs twelve pounds."

"If you don't mind lugging twelve pounds around, I'd love to see it."

Another of those melodramatic shrugs flung his thin, bony shoulders upward again. "Sure." He popped to his feet, strolled to the window, and perched on the windowsill.

Dr. Warren returned his attention to Gunther. "What is the occasion of this visit?"

"The driver's license. You thought we had that all taken care of, right? So did I. The agreement was, he works on a car for two years and gets his license at eighteen. Fine. I got him a Pontiac Firebird, and I have to admit, he's doing an excellent job on it. But lately he's been making my life a misery, insisting on getting his license now. He's abrogated our agreement."

"So you took the car away from him."

Gunther stopped in midbreath. "How did you know?"

"Just a guess, a shot in the dark. You've forbidden him to mention the license, but he forgets and starts the argument all over again—frequently."

"Yes! That's it exactly!"

Dr. Warren looked at William. "I don't doubt you have reasons for asking to renegotiate the agreement."

"That's it!" William gloated. "That's the word I was looking for. *Renegotiate.*" His arms windmilled with enthusiasm. "I kind of got my act together. I've got lists and stuff to keep me organized, and I even clean up my room sometimes. My grades are a lot better. I haven't forgotten my homework for months. I figure I've proven myself and shown I've grown up, and I deserve to get my license earlier than eighteen."

"And besides . . . ?" Dr. Warren let the word hang like a question.

The windmilling ceased. "And besides, every other kid in my class has a driver's license except me. Every one."

"That's not true," Gunther chided.

"Okay, everybody except Betty Lou. She skipped eighth grade and she's still too young. That doesn't count. She's getting her permit in a month though. Everybody who's old enough has one."

Gunther pressed his case. "My position is that keeping lists is not the same thing as maintaining attention in busy traffic. Just because he is improving in one area of his life does not mean he is capable of mature action in some other unrelated area."

"This is a matter to be worked out between the two of you. Why have you enlisted me?" Dr. Warren looked from face to face.

"We are at loggerheads. Tension is building, perhaps to unacceptable levels. Ellen suggested an arbiter we both respect." Gunther seemed mildly embarrassed. "Besides, she wanted you to know how much improvement William has made."

"And please tell her I am delighted to hear it. Delighted. So you two consider this a situation of binding arbitration? Is that correct?"

Gunther nodded.

William said, "Huh?"

"I am not a Solomon, to sit in judgment."

"But perhaps," Gunther replied, "you can offer some suggestions, a way to break the deadlock of wills."

"What's binding arbitration?" asked William.

"Arbitration is a legal term." Dr. Warren explained. "You agree that you are bound to go along with whatever I say."

"Oh." William licked his lips.

And the uncomfortable look on Gunther's face suggested that he thought his Ellen was getting altogether too many ideas of late. "We are here for two reasons, I assume. One is to hear any suggestions you might have for reducing the friction because of this insufferable driver's license row. The other is to receive any other advice you may have for William's continued improvement."

"Suggestions and advice." Dr. Warren sat back. "I believe I can offer some of each."

William blurted, "Whoa! I'm not so sure I like this blinding aberration."

The New ADD Child

William was a whole different kid from what he had been six months before, and both he and his father recognized that. In some ways he was coming to grips much better with the demands life made upon him. But the changes that were occurring ran far deeper than that.

As children enter their teens they undergo a number of stressful changes whether or not they are ADD. As always, the ADD kids appear to go to extremes; their changes seem particularly wild and hairy, the differences especially marked.

The Changes Inside and Out

As ADD kids enter their teens, they frequently appear less impulsive and less distractible externally. An outside observer might say these children are growing past their disorder and seem now to be closer to, forgive the expression, "normal." That is not necessarily the case. Often the impulsivity and distractibility are still there, but they are more internalized. The child may no longer be excessively distracted by things going on the outside, but he or she is still excessively distracted by things on the inside—mental pictures, random thoughts, ideas, and memories. The observer will notice it as a marked increase in daydreaming and inattention.

Perhaps because the external signs are often somewhat reduced, high schools tend to think that learning disabilities and problems like ADD have magically disappeared. The prevailing attitude of too many high school educators seems to be, "You've had years to come to grips with it. It's time to grow up and learn the way everyone else does. ADD at this age is a lazy person's excuse." This attitude is what accounts for the notable lack of special education resources in junior and senior high schools. It's wrongly assumed that ADD kids and others don't need them anymore. In an atmosphere like that, ADD kids have a hard time surviving academically.

Over and over, we hear that community colleges offer far better services for these kids than do the high schools, with modification available for alternative learning styles. Kids often tell us they wish they'd had the support and understanding in high school that they do in college. Even so, academics are usually still very difficult.

The raging hormones of this age don't help a bit.

All by itself, the male hormone testosterone tends to make a young man more moody, intense, aggressive, and impulsive. Just what the ADD kid needs. Girls' hormonal surges make them still more histrionic and moody. In short, hormones plus ADD is a really awkward combination.

The hormonal changes, inflicted on top of the other physiological shifts of this age, greatly increase storms, and ADD kids are caught in too many storms anyway. Family stress, already tight, increases. Torn by these additional forces, ADD teens end up at very high risk for drug use and trafficking, alcohol use, and other self-destructive behavior. What the drugs and alcohol are is self-medication. These kids will try anything to ease the chaos in their lives.

Certainly not all changes are so grim. Most are harmless.

Amy Eglund, the twelve-year-old who flustered her father Peter so, was already auditory to the max, but she became even more so for a while. She needed music *all* the time, talked on the phone *all* the time, tried to fill every family dinner conversation with her own voice. Peter the silence-lover survived the temporary escalation of noise only barely.

A left-brained ADD girl in Dr. Warren's counsel suddenly turned right-brained at the age of sixteen. She changed the lighting in her room to provide dark corners and borrowed her little brother's boom box. The shift lasted about two years, then she returned to her left-brain preferences. The anomaly phased out, you might say, as her adolescence phased out. That phenomenon occurs every now and then. And no, there is no explanation for that sort of thing.

There are important—we should say, *crucial*—changes going on at a social level during this time also, including problems with sexual drives and separation.

Sexual Problems

We cannot write a chapter on ADD in adolescents without leaning heavily on sexual matters because these things lean so very, very heavily upon the kids. You, the reader, are quite well aware that as puberty progresses, males and females differ in their responses to the opposite sex.

Boys find themselves fantasizing upon sex itself. Their fantasies can be G-rated and harmless or sexually explicit. Frequently, even in virgin boys, they are both. This preoccupation through the midteens is a common denominator in males. Their thoughts can be controlled to an extent, especially in the later teen years when they develop greater maturity, but they cannot be mastered.

Girls go off on a different track. They become dramatic and romantic. Romance is the soft, formless ecstasy of being desired, pampered, cosseted, cherished, admired, adored. Sex, particularly for virgin girls, is secondary and need not even be a part of the romance scene at all.

Now picture the situation as it affects ADD kids. Because of the random nature of their thought patterns, ADD kids seem to be subject to a higher degree of fantasizing than are most. Boys find themselves engaging in a rich sexual fantasy life they did not actually invite. They may have the best intentions about avoiding "dirty" thoughts, but their brain waves slosh about on a sea of hormones anyway.

And the girls? Feminists lambaste the *Sleeping Beauty* and *Cinderella* scenarios in which the gallant hero rides up to save the smitten maid and sweep her off her feet. Only an airhead female undeserving of the epithet "woman," they claim, would buy the white knight story in this day and age.

Oh yeah? The feminists miss the whole point. This is *romance* of the first order. ADD girls such as Amy are often identified as airheads anyway, which doesn't help their case, but they could not avoid the fantasy if they wanted to. More than most emergent women, they hunger for that white knight, for the man who lays his life before them.

Against her parents' wishes, Amy developed an intense appetite for romance novels.

"Trash!" Peter fumed. "I forbid it. For her whole life she had so little interest in reading, and suddenly now she reads trash. Why not the classics? *Little Women* or something?"

They're not romantic enough; that's why. For the benefit of Peter and other addled parents, let us take a moment to talk about romance novels since so many girls become enamored of them at this age.

"Romance novel" and "sex trash" are not synonymous. A good many excellent romances upholding strong values are available. At a well-stocked Christian bookstore, go through their publishers' catalogues. Few bookstores actually stock many romances, but they can get them for you. Try Barbour, Bethany House, Moody, Thomas Nelson, Word, Harvest, and the *Guideposts* reprints of the Zondervan "Serenade-Saga" series.

In the secular marketplace, romance publishers provide several different lines across a spectrum from "traditional," or "sweet," in which no sex is portrayed, up to the steamy, explicit stuff. Regency romances usually do not contain sex. Talk to a knowledgeable bookseller.

Why let impressionable girls like Amy read "that stuff" at all? Their greatly heightened hunger for romance, produced not by auto-suggestion or lascivious dreaming but by their very God-given nature, will be satisfied one way or another until it subsides and can be brought under control. The right books, especially those from Christian publishers, are safe, and they impart wholesome messages.

By their midteens, with the shift from girl to woman nearly complete, these ADD kids fall victim to moods and emotions that swing wider than Tarzan on a hundred-foot-long vine. Maniacal laughter. Giggling *ad nauseam*. Tears by the wheelbarrow. Shrieks and moans. Oh, the drama of it all!

The girls fall in love with just about any old representation of a male and make utter fools of themselves. They fall out just as quickly. In their fantasy life they picture "that boy" as being madly in love with them. The romance crashes—probably it was never launched to start with—and their self-image crashes with it.

Guys suffer the same slings and arrows of outrageous fantasy. However, they invest all of their identity in their sexual appeal. The girls of their dreams ignore them and slobber all over pictures of the current hunks of series television, sending the flesh-and-blood guys' self-images into the ditch as well. Reject the man's sexual appeal, and you reject the whole man. Thanks to the basic nature of ADD kids during puberty, the ditches are plumb full.

Runaway fantasizing is only the tip of the iceberg, though. These kids also have impulsivity to deal with, and that's far more dangerous than fantasy. Acting on fantasy hurts your feelings. Acting on impulse can get you into a compromising situation (or worse) in a big fat hurry. And then there's that innate difficulty with regulation. The ADD kids are tempted in all things just as other kids are, but so much more intensely.

Sexual Solutions

It sounds as if ADD kids are helpless victims of their basest instincts. Hardly. ADD kids can weave through this perilous maze safely, but they need help that works.

When the apostle Paul nurtured Thessalonica, he wrote, he imparted not just the gospel but also his very self. It is the secret to being an effective adult in the lives of ADD kids. The adult who would mentor the child must impart himself or herself. Sex education and guidance, then, begins not at the onset of puberty but at the child's birth.

The boy and girl see male and female modeled as they grow. They see male and female interact on a nonsexual basis. Male and female invest themselves in the child at a variety of levels, each level a lesson in the nature of man and woman. All this is sex education, and it must precede any talk of sex itself. It plows the field, for better or worse. Now comes the seed, planted by the mentor, one on one.

Reluctant to talk about sex, are you? Too bad, because you're going to have to find a way. In Deuteronomy 6:6–9, adults are told to impress God's commands upon their children. That's kinesthetic learning. Not other people's children, either. You can't get off the hook that easily. Tossing the ADD kid a book on sex ed isn't going to cut it.

What do they have to know, and when do they have to know it? Unfortunately, in today's society—and you know this—the truth must begin to be imparted at a tragically tender age—during the early to middle grades for fielding the first questions, answering only what is asked. When the juices start flowing, and that is the onset of puberty as physical build begins to change, these impulsive, unregulated, often overactive kids have to be given the straight stuff whether or not they ask. In this day and age, that's nothing less than self-defense.

It gets worse, friend. If your child is a tactile or kinesthetic learner, you may have to dream up some *modest* way to explain the facts other than a tidy little one-on-one speech about the birds and bees.

But the raw facts are the lesser part of the lesson. We recommend explaining to ADD kids, especially guys, that because of their unique mind-set they should pre-decide the issues most people don't think about: "What will be my stand regarding sex?" Decide now, then stay out of situations that are adverse to your decision.

This pre-deciding is certainly not limited to sexual matters. It is also needed in other situations such as, "Am I going to try pot?" Decide now, and then stick to it. "Hang around with so-and-so?" If hanging around with so-and-so is likely to get the kid into trouble, now is the time to decide to avoid this person. So-and-so is probably a pretty persuasive bozo who can appeal to your teenager's impulsivity.

And we repeat: The adult who is gently guiding this process is not going to get out of the dugout, let alone to first base, if a heavily vested relationship is not in place.

That adult, however, may or may not be a parent. Certainly parents are the ones to discuss the facts of life, and they are the ones to guide the children's maturation. However, they can't do it all. Just at this time when kids most need the wise leadership of parents, they are wrenching themselves away, fledging from the nest by slow and painful degrees.

This separation in itself is traumatic.

The Separation Problem

Somewhere around the age of twelve or thirteen, kids adopt a common costume, language, and behavior artfully designed to make all the kids look exactly alike and also drive all the parents right out of their collective tree. This is what psychologists who do not themselves have kids in this age group euphemistically call "normal separation and individuation behavior."

"Normal in a pig's eye!" Gunther would scream.

The kids are not quite bold enough to step from the sheltered status of Family Child out into the cold, cruel world of Independent Adult. They aren't really equipped for it yet, either; they still have to learn a lot about how other human beings interact. In emotionally distancing the family, they temporarily take refuge in their peer group before emerging as adults beyond the group into the world at large.

During this period of a few years in which they carbon copy each other, they use their group for support as they test the standards and claims of the adult world in which they will soon take part. The challenges and experimentation answer their unspoken questions, and the kids, to quote parents, "finally straighten up."

That's the "normal" thing, the comparatively easy way.

ADD kids can't do anything the easy way. ADD is a tremendous boondoggle to separation and individuation. All the problems that have plagued these kids since age four now keep them from growing past the external structure imposed by parents. The children need independence from parents but cannot yet afford it. But that's not all by any means.

For one thing, their self-image is zip because they've been yelled at and blamed for everything their whole lives. Kids' self-images take a beating even in normal circumstances; ADD kids' can't take much more pummeling. For another thing, they are probably coming from behind scholastically. Schoolwork, already marginal, generally takes a dip. Theirs takes two.

Worst of all, too often, they have not been fully accepted into the group. Remember that their social skills are very slow to bloom, making them appear nerdy or obnoxious or insensitive. The peer group doesn't put up with much of that. You have to be like everyone else. ADD kids aren't. Their developmental schedule forces them to distance themselves from the family, but they have no safe intermediate haven.

This is a reason why ADD kids fight so desperately to look like their peer group in every way. In a social milieu that values appearance above all else, these kids increasingly resist accepting any modifications whatsoever that might set them apart.

That includes taking medicine when no one else does. The early teen or teen wanna-be on Ritalin or another drug quite often will campaign to get off it. Besides, the drug regimen was bestowed from on high—from Adultland—and the kids are beginning to resist and challenge everything that has come down from Adultland.

We mentioned in the chapter on the various drug therapies that although the parents oversee their use, we like to keep the actual discussion and contact regarding drugs between the doctor and the child. Leaving the parent out of that loop, at least from the child's point of view, eases parent-child friction, removes one of the darts from the quiverful these kids are always throwing at parental authority, and provides an emotionally distant mentor with whom the child can talk about such things.

For example, Dr. Warren, as a nonfamily member, comes across as a neutral soul upon whom the child can vent feelings. Not surprising; that's what he is. A conversation might go like this:

The child: "I hate this drug business. I want off it."

Dr. Warren: "What do you hate about it?"

The child: "Oh, you know, everything. Like I hafta pop this pill every noon. But in our school you're not allowed to. You have to leave your supply in the office and you go there and the secretary watches you pop it out of the bottle. Then she writes something down. It makes me look like a freak."

Dr. Warren: "You know, I get that a lot from people your age. You're not alone, and your point about looking out of place or different is valid. However, here is why I feel continuing your medication can help you." He discusses the reasons. "You're going to have to make the decision. I can't. Your parents can't. The ball is in your court."

"Wait!" a person like Gunther or Peter would shout. "You're expecting *this* kid to make a decision? The kid can't find a grand piano in a one-room house and you want [him or her] to make an intelligent choice that's going to affect school and home life and everything! That's nuts!"

Not really.

Simply having veto power may be all the kid needs in the way of reassurance. Or feeling that he or she has some choice. Most of the time, the child elects to continue for a while, understanding that it's voluntary. Dr. Warren makes it clear neither he nor the parents are involving themselves in a struggle for compliance, and he will certainly not stop seeing or supporting the child.

Frequently he gets this comment. "Okay, I think it helps too. I want to take it, but I don't want Mom to know. I don't want her to think I'm taking it just to please her. I don't want her to think the medication controls me. That's what she thinks, you know. That's wrong. It helps me control myself better. See the difference?"

Dr. Warren ends with this assurance. "If you have concerns or problems, talk to me. It's okay to get mad at me."

Let us say that the child elects to quit medication. Again, he or she gets no fight from Dr. Warren. For example, one of his significantly ADD young charges who ended Ritalin therapy at thirteen seemed to get along pretty well. She didn't ping off the walls the way she had done as a grade-schooler. Her external distractibility was fairly low. But she could not sit through a lecture without her mind wandering. When she got into tenth grade and faced a 1.5 grade point average for the year, she changed her mind.

Dr. Warren summarizes the situation. "Kids walk through a narrow gorge at this time of life. We want them to act responsibly, to make responsible decisions. But they have very little experience in that regard, far less than most kids their age. The only way they can learn to do that is by making decisions and seeing the consequences. They will decide, 'This is what's best for me.' Sometimes it is and sometimes it isn't, looking at it from an objective viewpoint. But it is always best in that they are learning to make important decisions. Any decision that's reversible, such as whether to continue medication, is a safe decision."

Kids have a few alternatives to fitting in closely with peers. For example, there came a point in his midteens when Jody Capehart's Damon decided to concentrate on his eccentricities, enlarging and capitalizing upon them. This is exactly the means by which comedians develop a unique persona to separate themselves from each other. He wasn't clicking into a peer group, but he was achieving what he needed; he had separated himself from the adults. Harmlessly, too. It wasn't a bad ploy.

Kids who yearn for maturity are not yet well enough developed and schooled to handle it. It's hard.

The Essence of Maturity

What is maturity?

Almost-a-teen Amy would say, "Having your own phone and credit cards and things. You know."

Almost-an-adult William? "That's simple: driving."

Second-grader Andrew: "When I'm grown up I'll do math and it won't scare me."

Jody Capehart and Dr. Warren: "The real essence of emotional maturity is not independence from the parents but rather coming to grips with your own strengths and weaknesses. You know what you can do well and what you cannot do well, and you know what you're going to do about it."

In most cultures, specific rites usher the child into adulthood. That's the easy way to grow up and, curiously, it works. The boy or girl who was a child yesterday and thought in childish ways goes through a prescribed ritual and the next morning begins thinking in mature ways. Strong cultural expectations help the child take that giant step.

The closest thing to a rite of passage Americans offer emergent adults is the driver's license. The ticket to freedom. The privilege of operating a motor vehicle on the public right-of-way as granted by that bit of laminated cardboard (but if you're as sick as you look in the license photo, you shouldn't be on the highway at all).

And now we're right back to William and his obsession.

No rite of passage bestows instant adulthood. It is a culmination. A declaration. The real preparation begins years before. This is true of the driver's license as well. Gunther did or did not prepare William years in advance, not by teaching driving skills but by teaching William how to come to grips with what was going on within him.

William wouldn't like to admit it, but he realized how distractible he still was. He knew drivers as distractible as he is have a higher accident rate and tend to be more reckless and impulsive in their driving. He did not appreciate, though, the stress this brings to Mom and Dad as their kid approaches sixteen.

"It's like giving a two-year-old a loaded gun," Gunther grumbled.

And yet, because the driver's license in our culture is such a rite of passage, holding the kid back until he or she is eighteen makes a significant negative impact on his or her maturation. Damon Capehart was much more in tune with his strengths and weaknesses than are most ADD kids at sixteen. He elected voluntarily to wait until eighteen, aware that he didn't have the attention control to drive safely. That kind of savvy is a blessing, though it doesn't often happen.

The opposite of the negative effect occurs also. Just as the rite in other cultures bestows with the title of adulthood the ability to assume adult thoughts and responsibilities, allowing the license makes a positive impact on maturation.

"Yes, but . . ." And Gunther sank back in his chair, aware that he was about to enter a lose-lose situation: Hold William back, and he caused the boy damage. Let William go, and he caused the boy damage. The emergency room doctors, who already knew William well, would start making plans for that vacation on Rarotonga.

And then Dr. Warren quietly stated the obvious that Gunther had never considered. "Growing up and getting your license is not at all the same thing as being allowed to drive any time you want to."

William completed driver's ed.

He got his license.

He continued restoring his Firebird.

It's still in the garage, still in need of a few things that William can buy as soon as he gets a little ahead at the auto repair shop where he works part-time. He hasn't driven it yet; he has to save up for the insurance.

Amy? She isn't particularly interested in driving. She wants to be driven. Peter and Viveca do so gladly, hoping that it never occurs to her that she should get along without a chauffeur.

And when you analyze it, Miss Pruitt did a little maturing herself.

Ira Chapin stopped by her room the week before spring break. Three months ago she would have been mortified that he would walk in on this chaos. Two children sprawled on the floor reading, and a couple sat at their desks. Half a dozen kids were gathered at each of the tables by the windows. At one table, a castle was rising. Amid a welter of open books, charts, encyclopedias, and other references, the kids were building all the various parts of a medieval castle, from dungeon to drawbridge. At another, the kids were assembling a jigsaw puzzle of endangered species. Maps lay at their feet. At the third table . . .

Chapin frowned. "Three tables? I thought you had two."

"We managed to squeeze in one more. Here. I want to show you the essay Whittaker wrote." She marched to her desk and picked up a neatly rendered computer printout. "Actually, he didn't write it as such. He dictated it orally and Cathy Bursall typed it in for him."

"Cathy. The spina bifida?"

"Her legs are useless but you should see her fingers fly. She is absolutely amazing! Almost eighty words a minute in second grade! Can you imagine what she's going to be when she grows up? I would never have guessed she had latent talent of that magnitude if we hadn't put a computer on the floor for Andrew. She prefers stretching out on her tummy, just as he does."

"Speaking of which, where is the problem child?"

"He finished his subtraction nicely, so I sent him with the custodian to fix that broken chair-desk." She paused. "I assume you stopped by for a reason."

"I have your retirement papers here. Look over them at your convenience and we'll go through them."

"Retirement?! Ira, I'm nowhere near ready to retire!"

The door slammed open. With a cascade of rattles and clunks, a scrawny, tow-headed kid dragged the repaired chair-desk through the doorway, scuffed a long scratch in the carpet, spilled Martha's books and papers out of her desk trying to reposition the mended one, and yelled, "It's fixed!"

Andrew was back.

Being Different

Andrew was different.

Amy was different. William and Gunther were different.

Dr. Warren is different. He readily admits he's a superior-grade klutz. "Growing up, I wasn't good at athletics or mechanical things. I was good academically. In medical school, I saved countless lives by discovering immediately that surgery wasn't going to be my thing. I came to grips with that. It's okay. I found what I'm good at."

It is exactly the same thing with ADD. ADD kids' klutziness is in performing the way others, people totally unlike them, want them to perform. Dr. Warren didn't have to deal with his ineptitudes every day all day when he was going to school. ADD kids do. People who would never presume to expect and demand that a med student get into surgery demand that ADD kids conform to some strangers' expectations.

Ah, but once these kids find what they're good at, it makes all the difference. Just as an academically gifted man turned his back on surgery because he can't section an orange neatly, so can ADD kids find their niche, given the opportunity.

Jody Capehart talks about that opportunity. "For twenty-five years I've been suggesting that multisensory teaching is the way to go. Few agreed. But traditional methods are no longer working the way they used to; we have more at-risk kids, and teachers are looking to alternatives. Now when I teach at, for example, a home-school or a teachers' conference, I'm finding people are much more responsive to this way of teaching. At last people are awakening to the limitless possibilities of saving children out of the academic ghetto and giving them the skills they need.

"We *have* to use multisensory techniques for raising kids these days. We *have* to be sensitive to the needs of ADD children and all the others. There are so many kids out there who are learning to a different drummer, and the numbers are growing."

The Bottom Line

There is a trend in today's society to make everyone a super-performer. Pop a Prozac, whether it is clinically indicated or not, and *achieve*. A woman like Beth Mulroney, forced into the workplace, is still expected to be not just Mom but the perfect mother, free of any parenting flaws (flaws that may be already identified or to be announced in the future) that might damage her child. "Be all that you can be," but for heaven's sake don't stop there.

Disturbing as it is all by itself, that trend also has some ugly ramifications. There's a book that's been out awhile now that tells people to use the right side of their brain, as if this were a fantastic new idea. And yet, the ADD kids who do are told they are broken. They are expected to become all that other people think they should be. They may march to their own drummer only if the drummer leads them to the college, the boardroom, the research lab. The "successful" venues.

It's not a consensus by any means. There are a number of independent souls out there who resist the trend. They have perceived that we are a land of big organizations. Big organizations are governed by the bottom line and it pays them by and large to homogenize everybody, make everyone fit into a few tidy, low-maintenance, easily managed pigeonholes. The independent people, however, know that garden-grown green beans are tastier than are canned. They therefore see the treatment and management of ADD as a thin facade hiding that national desire to control everything and make everyone alike, and they resist.

Treatment and management of ADD, however, transcends the trends of both independent thinkers and corporate giants. This is for the child. It's not to fit the child into anyone's cookie cutter. It is to reduce the anger quotient, to improve those skills the child wants and needs, to avoid antisocial acts that lead to misery and tragedy, to allow the child to build and enjoy the kind of close relationships that make life rich.

That is the bottom line.

Appendix A: Resources

The *Diagnostic and Statistical Review Manual-Fourth Edition (DSM-IV)* lists and quantifies the symptoms and other criteria for every mental and behavioral disorder recognized by psychiatrists. Then it assigns a code number to the disorder, based upon the criteria listed. Persons who wish to examine the formal criteria for ADD should consult page 63 and following of *DSM-IV*.

The code numbers are:
314.01: Attention-Deficit/Hyperactivity Disorder, Combined Type (both inattention and compulsive hyperactivity are present).

314.00: Attention-Deficit/Hyperactivity Disorder, Predominantly Inattentive Type.

314.01: Attention-Deficit/Hyperactivity Disorder, Predominantly Hyperactive-Impulsive Type.

A few children whose criteria are an odd mix of types may fall into:

314.9: Attention-Deficit/Hyperactivity Disorder Not Otherwise Specified.

For more information on ADD contact:

Children and Adults with Attention
    Deficit Disorder (CHADD)
499 Northwest 70th Avenue, #101
Plantation, Florida 33317
305-587-3700

The National Attention Deficit Disorder
    Association/Support Network
800-487-2282

Appendix B

Praying for Your Child

Know Christ as personal Savior
Be a prayer warrior
Love the Word
Desire to tell others about the Lord Jesus
Christ-like character
A worshipful heart
Disciplined with time and money
Honor God in his/her work
Future mate to be a godly believer
Commit to a life of service to God
Protection: physical, emotional, mental, spiritual, sexual
Your child's future children to know Christ

© 1993 Jody Capehart

Lettered by Sue Bohlin

Bibliography

Ames, Louise Bates. *Is Your Child in the Wrong Grade?* Lumberville, PA: Modern Learning Press, 1978.

Ames, Louise Bates, Sidney Baker, and Frances L. Ilg. *Child Behavior.* New York: Barnes and Noble Books, 1981.

Ames, et al. *Don't Push Your Preschooler.* New York: Harper and Row, 1981.

———. *Stop School Failure.* Lumberville, PA: Modern Learning Press, 1978.

Armstrong, Thomas. *In Their Own Way.* New York: St. Martin's Press, 1987. Dr. Armstrong was a learning disabilities specialist who took the writings of Dr. Howard Gardner and put them into a "reader friendly" form to help us better understand that children learn in their own way.

———. *7 Kinds of Smart.* New York: Penguin Books, 1993. Dr. Armstrong delineates the different levels of intelligence and presents ways to identify and teach them.

———. *Multiple Intelligences in the Classroom.* Alexandria, VA: Association for Supervision and Curriculum Development, 1994. This book is a must for teachers, home-schoolers, and parents committed to helping their children learn through their own "multiple intelligence areas."

Barbe, Walter B. *Growing Up Learning.* Washington, DC: Acropolis Books, 1985. Take a trip to the library for this book as it is out of print. Barbe, the former editor of *Highlights Magazine,* offers practical information to help your child learn through different modalities.

Barbe, Walter B. and Raymond Swassing. *Teaching Through Modality Strengths: Concepts and Practices.* Columbus, OH: Zaner-Bloser, 1979.

Bell, Helen Davis. *Individualizing Instruction.* Chicago: Science Research Associates, 1972.

Bloom, Benjamin S. *Human Characteristics and School Learning.* New York: McGraw-Hill, 1976.

Breyfogle, Ethel, Sue Nelson, Carol Pitts, and Pamela Santich. *Creating a Learning Environment.* Santa Monica, CA: Goodyear Publishing, 1976.

Brophy, Jere E., and Carolyn M. Everston. *Learning from Teaching: A Developmental Perspective.* Boston: Allyn and Bacon, 1976.

Brown, B. Frank. *The Reform of Secondary Education: A Report of the National Commission on the Reform of Secondary Education.* New York: McGraw-Hill, 1973.

Bruno, Angela and Karen Jessie. *Hands-On Approach to Grammar, Spelling, and Handwriting.* Dubuque, IA: Kendall/Hunt, 1976.

Butler, Kathleen. *It's All in Your Mind: A Student's Guide to Learning Style.* Columbia, CT: The Learner's Dimension, 1988. A practical workbook to help teenagers identify their best learning styles.

———. *Learning and Teaching Style: In Theory and Practice,* 2nd ed. Columbia, CT: The Learner's Dimension, 1988.

———. *A Teacher's Guide to It's All in Your Mind.* Columbia, CT: The Learner's Dimension, 1988. Each lesson plan is stylistically designed so teachers can teach their students about style *using* style.

Button, Christine Bennett. "Teaching for Individual and Cultural Differences: A Necessary Interaction." *Educational Leadership* 34 (March 1977): 435–38.

Capehart, Jody. *Cherishing and Challenging Your Children.* Wheaton, IL: Victor Books, 1991. A practical guide for parents to better understand how personalities, modalities, and learning styles impact the home scene. Topics include discipline, communication, self-esteem, spiritual development, and more.

———. *Becoming a Treasured Teacher.* Wheaton, IL: Victor Books, 1992. This book synthesizes various learning models and provides a simple model for lesson planning, teaching with centers, discipline, and more.

_____. *Families Under Fire* (manual and video). Fort Worth, TX: Resources for Ministry, 1993.

_____. *Once Upon a Time*. Wheaton, IL: Victor Books, 1994.

Carbo, Marie, Rita Dunn, and Kenneth Dunn. *Teaching Students to Read Through Their Individual Learning Styles*. Englewood Cliffs, NJ: Prentice-Hall, 1987. Based on extensive research, this book provides practical helps for teaching the "at risk" student to read.

Chess, Stella and Alexander Thoma. *Know Your Child*. New York: Basic Books, 1987. Provides information and longitudinal research studies to show how children have their own unique temperaments from birth.

Christie, Les. *How to Work with Rude, Obnoxious, and Apathetic Kids*. Wheaton, IL: Victor Books, 1994. This book looks at issues that drive adults "up the wall" in dealing with today's kids (including ADD kids), and provides practical helps to dealing with tough issues.

Corcoran, John with Carole C. Carlson. *The Teacher Who Couldn't Read*. Colorado Springs, CO: Focus on the Family, 1994. This is the heart-warming true story of one man's battle to find victory over illiteracy. It shows the courage of one man to learn to read with dyslexia.

Costa, A. L., ed. *Developing Minds: A Resource Book for Teaching Thinking*. Alexandria, VA: Association for Supervision and Curriculum Development, 1985.

Dobson, James C. *Parenting Isn't for Cowards*. Dallas: Word, 1987. Practical advice for helping parents better understand their children's personality and temperament.

Dunn, Rita. *Practical Approaches to Individualizing Instruction: Contracts and Other Effective Teaching Strategies*. West Nyack, NY: Parker Publishing, 1972.

_____. *Educator's Self-Teaching Guide to Individualizing Instructional Programs*. West Nyack, NY: Parker Publishing, 1975.

_____. *Teaching Students Through Their Individual Learning Styles*. Reston, VA: Reston Publishing, 1978. Based on extensive research at St. John's University, this book launched the learning styles revolution based upon modalities and environmental preferences in learning.

Dunn, Rita and Shirley Griggs. *Learning Styles: Quiet Revolution in American Secondary Schools*. Reston, VA: National Association of Secondary School Principals, 1988.

Dunn, Rita, Kenneth Dunn and Gary E. Price. "Learning as a Matter of Style." *The Journal* (New York: School Administrators' Association of NY) 6 (Fall 1976): 11–12.

_____. "Diagnosing Learning Styles: A Prescription for Avoiding Malpractice Suits Against School Systems." *Kappan*, January 1977, 418–20.

_____. *Identifying Individual Learning Styles and the Instructional Methods and/or Resources to Which They Respond*. Paper presented at the Annual Meeting of the American Educational Research Association, New York, NY, March 1977.

Dunn, Rita and Alonzo H. Shockley, *That a Child May Reach: Expanded Education in Freeport, New York*. Freeport Public Schools, pursuant to a U.S. Office of Health, Education, and Welfare grant, under the supervision of the New York State Education Department, 1971.

Elkind, David. *Miseducation: Preschoolers at Risk*. Alfred A. Knopf, 1987.

Fisk, Lori and Henry Clay Lindgren. *Learning Centers*. Glen Ridge, NJ: Exceptional Press, 1974.

Gardner, Howard. *Frames of Mind: The Theory of Multiple Intelligence*. New York: Basic Books, 1983. Harvard University's Dr. Gardner develops a model of seven intelligences that shows how people learn differently.

Gardner, Howard. *The Unschooled Mind: How Children Think and How Schools Should Teach*. New York: Basic Books, 1991. Dr. Gardner merges science with education to show how ill-suited our minds and natural patterns of learning are to current educational practices, and makes an eloquent case for restructuring our schools.

Gesell, Arnold, et al. *The Child from Five to Ten,* New York: Harper and Row, 1977.

Gilbert, Anne Green. *Teaching the Three Rs Through Movement Experiences*. New York: MacMillan Publishing Co., 1977.

Golstein, Sam. *Why Won't My Child Pay Attention?* (video) Salt Lake City: Neurology, Learning and Behavior Center, 1990. This video is an excellent tool to help parents understand and deal with ADD kids.

Gregorc, Anthony. *An Adult's Guide to Style*. Columbia, CT: Gregorc Associates, 1982. For serious students, this book explains the Gregorc model of learning styles.

_____. *Inside Styles: Beyond the Basics*. Columbia, CT: Gregorc Associates, 1985.

Gregorc, Anthony F., and Helen B. Ward. "A New Definition for Individual." *NASSP Bulletin* 61 (February 1977): 20–26.

Hudes, Sonie Antoinette Saladino, and Donna Siegler Meibach. "Learning Style Sub-Scales and Self-Concept among Third Graders." *The Journal* (New York: School Administrators' Association of New York State) 6 (January 1977): 27–28.

Keirsey, David and Marilyn Bates. *Please Understand Me: Character and Temperament Types.* Del Mar, CA: Prometheus Nemesis, 1978. Provides a fascinating look at personality types and temperament, and how the two affect our lives.

Kolb, David A. *Experiential Learning.* Englewood Cliffs, NJ: Prentice-Hall, 1984.

Kroeger, Otto and Janet M. Theusen. *Type Talk.* New York: Delacorte Press, 1988. This fun, easy-to-read book about the Myers-Briggs' version of Carol Jung's personality types is loaded with anecdotal stories to help you understand this more detailed personality model.

Lawrence, Gordon. *People Types and Tiger Stripes.* Gainesville, FL: Center for Applications of Psychological Type, 1982.

Levinson, Harold N., M.D. *Total Concentration: How to Understand Attention Deficit Disorder, Maximize Your Mental Energy, and Reach Your Full Potential.* New York: M. Evans and Co., 1990.

Marcus, Lee. "A Comparison of Selected 9th Grade Male and Female Students' Learning Styles." *The Journal* (New York: School Administrators' Association of New York State) 6 (January 1977): 27–28.

_____. "How Teachers View Student Learning Styles." *NASSP Bulletin* (National Association of Secondary School Principals) 61 (April 1977): 112–14.

Martin, Grant. *The Hyperactive Child.* Wheaton, IL: Victor Books, 1992.

Montessori, Maria. *The Absorbent Mind.* New York: Dell Publishing, 1980.

_____. *Childhood Education.* New York: Meridian, 1955.

_____. *The Montessori Method.* New York: Schocken Books, 1964.

Moss, Robert A. and Helen Huff Dunlap. *Why Johnny Can't Concentrate.* New York: Bantam Books, 1990.

Pratt, David. *Curriculum Design and Development.* New York: Harcourt Brace Jovanovich, 1980.

Price, Gary E., Rita Dunn, and Kenneth Dunn. *Summary of Research on Learning Style Inventory.* Paper presented at the Annual Conference of the American Educational Research Association, New York, NY, March 1977.

Raywid, Mary Anne. "Models of the Teaching-Learning Situation." *Kappan,* April 1977, 631–35.

Reinert, Harry. "One Picture Is Worth a Thousand Words? Not Necessarily!" *The Modern Language Journal* 60 (April 1976): 160–68.

The Rise Report, Report of the California Commission for Reform of Intermediate and Secondary Education. Sacramento: California State Department of Education, 1975.

Rusch, Shari Lyn. *Stumbling Blocks to Stepping Stones.* Seattle: Arc Press, 1991. This is a true story of a girl with multiple learning disabilities who "made it" through a school that provided little support.

Scribner, Harvey B. *Make Your Schools Work.* New York: Simon and Schuster, 1975.

Stephens, Lilian S. *The Teacher's Guide to Open Education.* New York: Holt, Rinehart, and Winston, 1974.

Swindoll, Charles R. *You and Your Child: A Biblical Guide for Nurturing Confident Children from Infancy to Independence.* Nashville, TN: Thomas Nelson, 1990. An eye-opening book for parents who want to instill lasting moral and spiritual values in their children.

Taylor, John F. *Answers to A.D.D.* (video) Salem, OR: Sun Media, 1992.

Thomas, John L. *Learning Centers: Opening Up the Classroom.* Boston: Holbrook Press, 1975.

Tobias, Cynthia. *The Way They Learn: How to Discover and Teach to Your Child's Strengths.* Colorado Springs, CO: Focus on the Family, 1994. This books examines various learning models to help parents and teachers better understand how children learn.

Wender, Paul H. *The Hyperactive Child, Adolescent, and Adult.* New York: Oxford Univ. Press, 1987.

Williams, Linda VerLee. *Teaching for the Two-Sided Mind.* New York: Simon and Schuster, 1983.

Wlodkowski, Raymond and Judith Jaynes. *Eager to Learn: Helping Children Become Motivated and Love Learning.* San Francisco: Jossey Bass, 1990. Provides a wealth of ways to help students become more motivated and successful in the learning process.

About the Authors

Paul Warren, M.D., is a behavioral pediatrician and adolescent medicine specialist. He serves as medical director of the Child and Adolescent Division at the Minirth Meier New Life Clinics in Richardson, Texas, and also has an active outpatient practice. In addition, he is a professional associate with the Center for Marriage and Family Intimacy in Austin.

Dr. Warren received his M.D. degree from the University of Oklahoma Medical School, and completed his internship and residency at Children's Medical Center in Dallas, Texas where he served as chief resident. An expert in child and adolescent issues, Dr. Warren is a popular seminar speaker and a regular guest on the Minirth Meier New Life Clinics radio program. His other books include *Kids Who Carry Our Pain, The Father Book, Things That Go Bump in the Night,* and *The Stepping-Stone-Series: My Infant, My Toddler,* and *My Preschooler.*

Dr. Warren and his wife, Vicky, have a son, Matthew.

Jody Capehart is an educator with more than twenty-five years of experience in public and private schools. She is founder of Grace Academy, where she served as principal for fifteen years. Currently she serves as principal of Covenant Christian Family School and director of children's ministries at Grace Bible Church in Dallas, Texas.

Capehart is a much-in-demand speaker for school, church, women's, and home-school conferences throughout the country. She is the author of seven books, including *A Gift of Time, Becoming a Treasured Teacher, Cherishing and Challenging Your Children, Discipline to the Design of the Child, Zillions of Hands-On Teaching Techniques, Once Upon a Time,* and *Families Under Fire.*

Jody and her husband, Paul, have three children and live in Dallas, Texas.